Disability and Dissensus: Strategies of Disability Representation and Inclusion in Contemporary Culture

International Comparative Social Studies

VOLUME 47

The titles published in this series are listed at *brill.com/icss*

Disability and Dissensus: Strategies of Disability Representation and Inclusion in Contemporary Culture

Edited by

Katarzyna Ojrzyńska
Maciej Wieczorek

BRILL

LEIDEN | BOSTON

Originally published in hardback in 2020.

Chapter 4, "Disability Cinema: Charting Alternative Ethical Maps of Living on Film", was originally published as as "Global In(ter)dependent Disability Cinema: Targeting Ephemeral Domains of Belief and Cultivating Aficionados of the Body" in *Cultures of Representation: Disability in World Cinema Contexts* by Benjamin Fraser, ed. Copyright © 2016 Columbia University Press. Reprinted with permission of Columbia University Press.

Cover illustration: The cover illustration presents a two-part mural created in the Polish city of Łódź as part of the action "Mural. Zamalowujemy stereotypy" ("Mural. Painting Over Stereotypes"). Photo by Katarzyna Ojrzyńska

The Library of Congress Cataloging-in-Publication Data is available online at http://catalog.loc.gov
LC record available at http://lccn.loc.gov/2020019185

Typeface for the Latin, Greek, and Cyrillic scripts: "Brill". See and download: brill.com/brill-typeface.

ISSN 1568-4474
ISBN 978-90-04-47143-6 (paperback, 2021)
ISBN 978-90-04-40598-1 (hardback)
ISBN 978-90-04-42467-8 (e-book)

This book is printed on acid-free paper and produced in a sustainable manner.

Contents

Acknowledgements

We would like to express our gratitude to a number of people without whom this volume would not be possible. Most importantly, we would like to thank our contributors for their hard work, patience, and support.

The idea for the book first came to our minds in the aftermath of an event that took place at the University of Łódź in 2015. That year, we organized one of the first international cultural disability studies conferences in Poland. The event was attended by a large number of scholars from all around the world. Our intention was to provide a space for creative exchange and debate, a space that would be open to crip culture and crip theory. We wanted to crip the local academia and to crip Łódź, which is known as the city of four cultures, a place of intercultural exchange and understanding. Thus, we invited both experienced and young academics, disability activists, and artists who work in diverse areas yet share a critical outlook on disability. The conference offered us a unique opportunity to network and exchange ideas in a truly interdisciplinary manner, paving the way for many fruitful collaborations and eventually giving rise to this book. Therefore, we would like to extend our gratitude to everyone who helped us organize this event: the former head of the Department of English Studies in Drama, Theatre, and Film (the former Department of Studies in Drama and Pre-1800 English Literature) Literature Jadwiga Uchman; our sponsor, the PGE Group; our patrons: Jarosław Duda, the former Secretary of State in the Ministry of Labour and Social Policy of the Republic of Poland and the Government Plenipotentiary for Disabled People; PFRON (Polish State Fund for the Rehabilitation of Disabled Persons), Hanna Zdanowska, the Mayor of the City of Łódź, and Radio Żak.

Putting this volume together was a long process that cost a lot of collaborative effort, but it gave us a sense that what we were creating was not only an academic artefact, but also a collectivity of people who have their share in creating dissensual space for disability not only in the academia, but also in contemporary culture and society. Of course, we do not wish to deflate the importance of the volume in any way. To the contrary, the long process of manuscript preparation gave us plenty of time to rethink and refine our arguments. With this in mind, we are very grateful to the reviewers for their insightful comments and valuable suggestions. Also, we would like to thank the series editors for being supportive and willing to take on such an interdisciplinary book project whose aim is to promote Cultural Disability Studies in various disciplines of the humanities. Last but not least, we would like to give our special thanks to Charlie Ivamy, our colleague from the Department of English Studies in Drama, Theatre, and Film for his help with proofreading the manuscript, as well as to our partners, families, and friends for their emotional support.

Finally, Katarzyna would like to give her special thanks to Rosemarie Garland-Thomson who introduced her to Critical Disability Studies in the humanities and showed her the "alternative maps" of the academic world, to use David T. Mitchell and Sharon L. Snyder's phrase.

Katarzyna Ojrzyńska and Maciej Wieczorek

Illustrations

Abbreviations

CDS	Critical Disability Studies
CIL	Centre for Independent Living
CP	cerebral palsy
CPee	a person with cerebral palsy
FAR	Fundacja Aktywnej Rehabilitacji (Polish Foundation for Active Rehabilitation)
ID	intellectual disability
MS	multiple sclerosis
PAC	Professionals Allied to the Community
PAM	Professionals Allied to Medicine
PFRON	Państwowy Fundusz Rehabilitacji Osób Niepełnosprawnych (Polish State Fund for the Rehabilitation of Disabled Persons)
RON	Rodzice Osób Niepełnosprawnych (Parents of Disabled People)
SDS	Society for Disability Studies
T21	Theatre 21 (a Warsaw-based professional theatre company of people with intellectual disability)
UPIAS	The Union of the Physically Impaired Against Segregation

Contributors

James Casey
has taught courses on film, media and literature, and critical/cultural disability studies. He has worked as an equality awareness consultant, an editor, and as a reviewer for several international journals. He holds a BA in English and Philosophy, an MA in Film Studies, and a PhD from the National University of Ireland, Galway. His research focuses on how films represent and construct disability and impairments and how these function in the adaptation process. A disabled activist, he is currently working with Independent Living Movement Ireland, the only rights-based Disabled People's Organization in the Republic of Ireland.

Len Collin
is a screenwriter, director, and academic with a strong interest in disability advocacy and disability studies. As director of the film *Sanctuary*, Collin has travelled the world and picked up a number of film awards including a Best Director award at the prestigious Newport Beach International Film Festival. His television credits as a screenwriter are extensive and include: *Ultimate Force*, *London's Burning*, *Eastenders*, and *The Bill*. Currently he is a senior Lecturer on the Film and Television Production course at Northumbria University in Newcastle where he teaches screenwriting.

Rosemarie Garland-Thomson
is a disability justice and culture thought leader, bioethicist, teacher, and humanities scholar. Her 2016 editorial, "Becoming Disabled," was the inaugural article in the ongoing weekly series in the *New York Times* about disability by people living with disabilities. She is a professor of English and bioethics at Emory University, where she teaches disability studies, bioethics, American literature and culture, and feminist theory. Her work develops the field of Critical Disability Studies in the health humanities to bring forward disability access, inclusion, and identity to a broad range of institutions and communities. She is co-editor of *About Us: Essays from the New York Times about Disability by People with Disabilities* (2019) and the author of *Staring: How We Look* (2009) and several other books. Her current project is *Embracing Our Humanity: A Bioethics of Disability and Health.*

Dan Goodley
is Professor of Disability Studies and Education at the University of Sheffield, UK, and co-director the interdisciplinary research centre iHuman. He has

written a number of publications in the field of Critical Disability Studies including *Dis/ability Studies* (Routledge, 2014) and *Disability Studies* (second edition, Sage, 2016). He is a proud father to young women, a Sleaford Mods fan, and a long suffering supporter of Nottingham Forest Football Club (who were the best team in Europe forty years ago).

Agnieszka Izdebska
is Associate Professor at the Department of Literary Theory in the Institute of Contemporary Culture, University of Łódź, Poland. She is the author of *Forma, ciało i brzemię imperium. O prozie Władysława L. Terleckiego* [*The Form, Body and Burden of the Empire. Władysław L. Terlecki's Prose*] (2010). Her research interests include: the theory of novel (e.g. historical novel), gender studies, the evolution of the gothic convention, the relations between photography and narrative/language, and popular literature (especially crime fiction).

Edyta Lorek-Jezińska
is Assistant Professor in the Department of English at Nicolaus Copernicus University in Toruń (Poland). Her research interests include alternative theatre, drama by women, theories of trauma and hauntology, as well as disability drama. She is the author of *Hauntology and Intertextuality in Contemporary British Drama by Women Playwrights* (2013), and co-editor of themed issues of *Theoria et Historia Scientiarum* (Spectrality and Cognition: Haunted Cultures, Ghostly Communications) (2017) and *AVANT. Trends in Interdisciplinary Studies* (Haunted Cultures/Haunting Cultures, 2017). She is the Editor-in-Chief of the doctoral students' academic journal *Currents: A Journal of Young English Philology Thought and Review.*

Dorota Krzemińska
is Assistant Professor at the Department of Special Education, University of Gdańsk, Poland. Her academic interests oscillate around diverse experiences of disability and, in particular, intellectual disability. In her research, Dorota explores the subjective perceptions of the world of people with ID and examines crucial aspects of their individual and collective lives. She has written a number of articles and three books in Polish: *Język i dyskurs codzienny osób z niepełnosprawnością intelektualną* [*Everyday Language and Discourse of People with Intellectual Disability*] (2012), *Być parą z niepełnosprawnością intelektualną. Studium mikroetnograficzne w kontekście teorii postkolonialnej Homiego K. Bhabhy* [*Being a Couple with Intellectual Disability. A Microetnographic Study in the Context of Homi K. Bhabha's Postcolonial Theory*] (2019), and, co-authored

by Iwona Lindyberg, *Wokół dorosłości z niepełnosprawnością intelektualną. Teksty rozproszone* [*Adulthood of People with Intellectual Disability. Miscellaneuous Texts*] (2012).

Marek Mackiewicz-Ziccardi
is a disabled man who holds a BA in English Philology (State School of Higher Education in Biała Podlaska, Poland) and an MA in Psychology and Education from the University of Sheffield, UK. Before deserting academia, he used to work on a funded PhD project on the cultural representations of disabled people's sexuality. He is happily married to Caterina – a fellow disabled person – and lives with her and several cats in Lincoln, UK, while looking for employment that would be less likely to feed his raging perfectionism.

David T. Mitchell
is a scholar, editor, history and film exhibition curator, and filmmaker in the field of disability studies. His books include the monographs: *Narrative Prosthesis: Discourses of Disability* (2000); *Cultural Locations of Disability* (2005); *The Biopolitics of Disability: Neoliberalism, Ablenationalism, and Peripheral Embodiment* (2015); and the collections *The Body and Physical Difference: Discourses of Disability* (1997); *A History of Disability in Primary Sources*, volume 5 of *The Encyclopedia of Disability*; *The Matter of Disability* (2019). He curated *The Chicago Disability History Exhibit* (Vietnam Veterans Memorial Museum, 2006) and assembled the programmes for the Screening Disability Film Festival (Chicago, 2006) as well as the DisArt Independent Film Festival (Grand Rapids, MI, 2015). His four award-winning films include *Vital Signs: Crip Culture Talks Back* (1995), *A World without Bodies* (2002), *Self Preservation: The Art of Riva Lehrer* (1995), and *Disability Takes on the Arts* (1996). He is currently working on a new book and feature-length documentary film on disability and the Holocaust tentatively titled *Disposable Humanity*.

Katarzyna Ojrzyńska
is Assistant Professor at the Department of English Studies in Drama, Theatre, and Film, University of Łódź, Poland. Her research interests focus on cultural disability studies, performance studies, and Irish studies. She is the author of *"Dancing as if language no longer existed": Dance in Contemporary Irish Drama* (Reimagining Ireland 61, Peter Lang, 2015). Katarzyna has been promoting cultural disability studies in Poland in collaboration with the Theatre 21 Foundation and the Downtown Centre of Inclusive Art. She has translated Rosemarie Garland-Thomson's book on staring into Polish (2020).

Christian O'Reilly
is an award-winning playwright and screenwriter based in Galway, Ireland. Christian's plays include: *It Just Came Out* (Druid Debut Series, 2001), *The Good Father* (Druid, 2002), *Is It about Sex?* (Rough Magic, 2007), *Here We Are Again Still* (Decadent, 2009), *Sanctuary* (Blue Teapot, 2012), and *Chapatti* (Northlight/Galway International Arts Festival, 2014). His screen credits include *Inside I'm Dancing*, a feature film based on his original story (2004). Christian's screen adaptation of his play *Sanctuary* won the award for Best First Irish Feature at the 2016 Galway Film Fleadh. Its ensemble cast of actors with intellectual disabilities from Blue Teapot Theatre Company was awarded the Michael Dwyer Discovery Award by the Dublin Critics Circle at the 2017 Dublin Audi International Film Festival.

Jolanta Rzeźnicka-Krupa
is Assistant Professor at the Faculty of Social Sciences, University of Gdańsk, Poland. Her research interests cover: subjectivity and identity in the contemporary world, the social construction of disability and its cultural and post-scientific contexts, the human body in the contemporary humanities, as well as art and (dis)ability. She has published extensively in the fields of the ethnography of communication and disability studies. Her academic output includes three books in Polish: *Komunikacja, edukacja, społeczeństwo. O dyskursie dzieci z niepełnosprawnością intelektualną* [*Communication, Education, and Society. The Discourse of Children with Intellectual Disability*] (2007), *Niepełnosprawność i świat społeczny. Szkice Metodologiczne* [*Disability and the Social World. Methodological Sketches*] (2009), *Społeczne ontologie niepełnosprawności* [*Social Ontologies of Disability*] (2019), and several dozen articles on educational, social, cultural, and philosophical aspects of disability.

Murray K. Simpson
is a Reader in the School of Education and Social Work, University of Dundee (UK). Murray has written extensively on the history of the concept of intellectual disability, including a monograph, *Modernity and the Appearance of Idiocy* (2014). His current work includes a book in preparation on cinema and corporeal variance, disability, and ageing, and a Hegelian analysis of the governance of social work. He is co-editor, with Dr Alison Wilde, of the book series on *Disability, Media, Culture* with Peter Lang.

Wiktoria Siedlecka-Dorosz
specializes in theatre studies and art therapy. She graduated from the Zbigniew Raszewski Theatre Institute in Warsaw and the Maria Grzegorzewska University

in Warsaw. She worked at the Department of Pedagogy of the Zbigniew Raszewski Theatre Institute and as the director of the Korczak Montessori School in Warsaw. Wiktoria Siedlecka-Dorosz has ran numerous workshops at schools and therapy and care centres. She teaches art therapy courses at the Academy of Special Education in Warsaw and has for many years been collaborating with Warsaw's Theatre 21.

Sharon L. Snyder's
career includes a range of work as an author, artist, activist, and filmmaker. Her books include *Narrative Prosthesis: Disability and the Dependencies of Discourse* (2000); *Cultural Locations of Disability* (2006); and *The Biopolitics of Disability: Neoliberalism, Ablenationalism, and Peripheral Embodiment* (2015). She has also edited 3 collections *The Body and Physical Difference: Discourses of Disability* (1997); *A History of Disability in Primary Sources*, volume 5 of *The Encyclopedia of Disability*; *The Matter of Disability* (2019) as well as authored more than thirty-five journal articles and chapters. She has curated a museum exhibit on disability history at the National Vietnam Veterans Memorial Museum, curated disability film and arts programming for festivals and conferences, and created four award-winning documentary films: *Vital Signs: Crip Culture Talks Back* (1995), *A World without Bodies* (2002), *Self Preservation: The Art of Riva Lehrer* (2005), and *Disability Takes on the Arts* (2006).

Małgorzata Sugiera
is Full Professor at the Jagiellonian University in Kraków, Poland, and the Head of Department of Performativity Studies. She has published twelve single-authored books in Polish, the most recent of which are: *Nieludzie. Donosy ze sztucznych natur* [*Non-humans. Reports from Non-natural Natures*] (2015), *W pułapce przeciwieństw. Ideologie tożsamości* [*In the Trap of Opposites. Ideologies of Identity*] (co-authored by Mateusz Borowski, 2012), and *Sztuczne natury. Performanse technonauki i sztuki* [*Artificial Natures: Performances of Technoscience and Arts*] (2017). She co-edited volumes in English and German, and lectured and ran seminars at universities in Germany, France, Switzerland, and Brazil. Her main research fields are theories of performativity, and cultural and decolonial studies. She has translated a number of academic books and theatre plays into Polish.

Maria Tsakiri
is a Lecturer at the European University Cyprus with fifteen years of experience in teaching and supporting disabled students and children in primary, further and higher education. She lectures on the theoretical perspectives and

implications of Disability Studies and Inclusive Education at undergraduate and postgraduate levels. Her current research interests lie in inclusive education, body politics and the politics of disability, crip activism, as well as cultural representations of disability and intersectionality. She is an active member of the Disability Research Edinburgh network which is coordinated by the University of Edinburgh. Her current involvement with disability activism and her expertise in critical disability studies has led to new collaborations with Schools of Education and Inclusive Education, Disability Research Fora and autonomous feminist research centres in the UK and Greece.

Maciej Wieczorek
is a doctoral candidate at the Department of English Studies in Drama, Theatre, and Film, University of Łódź, Poland, where he is currently working on a dissertation devoted to British left-wing political drama in the new millennium. His academic interests include theatre theory, political drama, and identity politics. He has published a number of articles on political theatre, and has recently translated "The Fundamental Principles of Disability," a transcript of the seminal debate between the Union of the Physically Impaired Against Segregation and the Disability Alliance into Polish.

Disability and Dissensus

Katarzyna Ojrzyńska and Maciej Wieczorek

The image on this book's cover represents a two-part mural which can be found in the city of Łódź – one of the major urban areas in Poland. As the inscriptions indicate, the artwork celebrates the UN Convention on the Rights of Persons with Disabilities, which was ratified by Poland in 2012, and promotes both FAR (Fundacja Aktywnej Rehabilitacji, or the Foundation for Active Rehabilitation), a Polish non-government organization supporting wheelchair users with permanent spinal cord injuries, and PFRON (Państwowy Fundusz Rehabilitacji Osób Niepełnosprawnych, or the State Fund for the Rehabilitation of Disabled Persons). Most importantly, though, the mural was made as part of the action "Mural. Zamalowujemy stereotypy" ("Mural. Painting Over Stereotypes") that was initiated in Gdynia in 2012. Like other similar works created by artists, people with disabilities, disability activists, and all those who chose to participate in this project, the mural seeks to challenge certain preconceptions which still determine the ways in which many Polish people conceptualize disability and their predominantly negative perception of individuals who do not meet the normative physical standards as defective, asexual, and generally dissatisfied with their lives.

On the left hand side of the mural we see a good-looking young man in a dark vest and trousers, casually strolling the city streets. His body position indicates that he has paused midstep in order to take a look back over his shoulder at a person whom he has just passed by and whom he finds alluring. On the right hand side, we see the object of his attraction: an attractive, long-haired blonde wearing a tight white vest, who confidently moves in the opposite direction in her wheelchair. The young woman reciprocates the stare and looks back at the man. The two figures are juxtaposed with each other in kinetic terms. Unlike the man, the young woman does not stop, but rolls on dynamically, which is evident in the fact that her hair is flowing in the air, presumably set in motion by her energetic movement. The man's more static posture suggests that his stare is prolonged, while the woman gives him only a short yet coquettish glance, the flirtatious nature of which is further highlighted by the fact that her eyes are closed and her lips slightly parted.

Every day hundreds of people pass the mural, adopting the perspective of the young man – the male voyeur – and asking themselves: What is it that attracts my attention? Or, to use some of the key questions which Rosemarie Garland-Thomson addresses in her seminal book on staring, "Why do we stare?

 | DOI:10.1163/9789004424678_002

... What do we stare at? Why can't we stop staring? ... Should we stare?" (3). Garland-Thomson explains this phenomenon in the following way: "Staring is an ocular response to what we don't expect to see. Novelty arouses our eyes" (3). This explanation brings us to another crucial question: what makes the young woman depicted in the mural so stareable? Is it the incongruity between social expectations and her representation as sexually attractive, active, and confident? Perhaps to some extent. Yet, we would argue that the viewer's stare mainly focuses on the woman's attractive appearance rather than on her wheelchair or physical difference. Indeed, a sense of physical otherness seems to be absent from this representation, since both bodies depicted in the mural almost perfectly fit the contemporary standards of beauty. Even the wheelchair does not seem to disturb the woman's perfect proportions – it rather serves as an accessory of secondary importance.

With all this in mind, one may ask to what extent this representation of motor impairment is successful in challenging ableist preconceptions about this form of impairment, as well as disability in general. On the one hand, the mural undoubtedly shows the wheelchair user as a sexually attractive woman who actively engages in a casual flirtatious ocular interaction. Furthermore, much like the hotly debated performance of Lady Gaga as a mermaid in a wheelchair, it destigmatizes the wheelchair which no longer epitomizes the 'tragedy' of being 'wheelchair-bound,' but rather serves as an enabling and liberating device: both functional and aesthetically pleasing. On the other hand, however, one may also argue that to a certain extent the mural reinforces the major premises upon which ableist, normative standards are built. It communicates the message that a disabled person can still be considered 'sexy' as long as his or her body meets the generally accepted standards of beauty.

One could also ask about the real political potential of the mural: does it actively advance and promote the principles of the convention that it overtly invokes? Is there any way in which it can contribute to a gradual change towards the full inclusion and participation of individuals with disabilities in society? One possible answer to these questions is to be found in the works of Jacques Rancière which discuss the relationship between politics and aesthetics at length. To understand how the two intersect, one must briefly recount his arguments related to the political sphere. Rancière distinguishes between real politics and what he calls the police. The latter is defined as "a distribution of the sensible (*partage du sensible*) whose principle is the absence of void and of supplement" ("Ten Theses on Politics" 44). In other words, it is a system of rules that both assigns the roles and functions that people have in a society and determines what can be said and seen. The police is complicit with the workings of contemporary post-democratic states in which the politics of consensus provides grounds for the claim that public opinion adequately represents the needs, aspirations, and desires of each and every individual. This leads to a situation in which people

> are always both totally present and totally absent at once. They are entirely caught in a structure of the visible where everything is on show and where there is thus no longer any place for appearance,
>
> RANCIÈRE, *Disagreement* 103

in this way preventing any forms of subjectification. The police logic is completely at odds with real politics which is, by contrast, "an intervention in the visible and the sayable" (Rancière, "Ten Theses on Politics" 45). Its essence is dissensus – the act of putting the existing distribution of the sensible at a distance and reconfiguring it. It makes it possible for those who were neither heard nor seen to be validated, to be recognized as speaking beings who have the right to fully partake in the life of the community, and allows for the emergence of "a part of those who have no part," to use Rancière's turn of phrase. Unlike the ubiquitous police logic which works to uphold the exclusionary status quo, real politics is rare, disruptive, and egalitarian.

Art can be a vehicle for such dissensus. As Rancière puts it in *The Politics of Aesthetics*,

> [p]olitical statements and literary locutions produce effects in reality.... They draft maps of the visible, trajectories between the visible and the sayable, relationships between modes of being, modes of saying, and modes of doing and making.
>
> RANCIÈRE 35

In short, like real politics, aesthetic practices have the power to put a given distribution of the sensible at a distance, to reframe and reconfigure it, in order to disrupt the consensus. This is especially true of the works created under what Rancière labels "the aesthetic regime of the arts," which differs from other regimes in that it is undoes the relationship between form and subject matter, liberating itself from the constraints imposed by artistic conventions and by the societal demand that a given topic be appropriate. This means that no subjects are unfit for art, that no mode of representation should be considered superior, and that the means of expression selected by the artist should in no way be determined by their topic of choice. The aesthetic regime, however, is not only egalitarian in its approach to the problem of representation, but also in terms of its modes of production and reception: everyone is capable of producing and appreciating a work of art. By redirecting the focus from the lives of kings and nobility to the lives of ordinary people, the aesthetic revolution has also made it possible to create artworks that locate "symptoms of an epoch, a society, or a civilization in the minute details of ordinary life" (Rancière, *The Politics of Aesthetics* 29). In this respect, Rancière's theory resonates well with New Historicism, as one of the main tenets of the latter is that art is inseparable from history, culture, and social life in general (Veeser xi; Gallagher and Greenblatt 7). Artistic works not only produce social relations, but are also produced by social relations in that they are created in accordance with one's beliefs, biases, customs, etc. In short, they are deeply embedded in specific cultural and ideological constructs. Liberated from the constraints imposed by conventions, the artworks subsumed under the Rancierian aesthetic regime also have the potential to focus on a whole array of subjects that have heretofore been ignored. This gives them the means to challenge a given distribution of the sensible by either producing what New Historicism calls counter histories, providing accounts focusing on and/or created by those excluded from the social order, thus laying bare its exclusionary logic and giving voice to the ones that have not been heard, or by anticipating alternative forms and configurations of the sensible.

In one of his articles, the late Tobin Siebers argues that there are no adequate means for representing disabled bodies because representations are informed by misconceptions and because the bodies themselves affect the process of representation (180). On the one hand, then, the way in which non-standard embodiments are represented is affected by the social stigma attached to them, and by "compulsory able-bodiedness" (McRuer 2) or "the hegemony of normalcy" (Davis 45–49, 170).[1] On the other hand, though, the body "is as capable of influencing and transforming social languages as [social languages] are capable of influencing and transforming [the body]" (Siebers 180). For Siebers, then, the political struggle of people with disabilities demands a realistic approach to the body, one that refuses to view it as "an extraordinary power or an alternative

1 The concept is greatly indebted to Antonio Gramsci's idea of hegemony, understood as a discreet imposition of the worldview of the ruling group in order to preserve the existing social hierarchies. For Gramsci, hegemony corresponds to the "private" sphere of the "civil society," and its aim is to generate "consent given by the great masses of the population to the direction imposed on social life by the dominant fundamental group" as a result of their prestige and "position in the world of production" (12). Obviously, this gives rise to a particular division of labour and, consequently, social hierarchy (Gramsci 13). Hegemony thus relies on cultural and intellectual persuasion, rather than physical coercion which could be exercised by the state. The concept of hegemony has often been used in relation to the class struggle, but disability scholars have appropriated it to reflect society's bias towards able-bodiedness and the myriad social relations that it produces.

image of ability," but accepts it for what it is (180). Once this fact is recognized, one can begin to tackle issues such as accessibility or social exclusion. While people with disabilities are increasingly present in the public sphere, a large number of them are still deprived of the chance to fully participate in all aspects of the life of the community. They may speak out and stand up for their rights yet their voices often remain unheard. As Petra Kuppers puts it, people with disabilities are invisible as members of the public sphere and hypervisible as individuals who face immediate categorization (25). The real point is to turn this around – to make them hypervisible as members of the community and invisible as individual people who are currently often viewed solely through the prism of their impairments. In other words, the distribution of the sensible should be rearranged in such a way as to provide people with disabilities with full access to the public sphere on equal terms and to oppose the stereotypes that stigmatize them and construct their otherness.[2]

It is our belief that art can facilitate this change. The mural that we discussed earlier exemplifies the egalitarian principles of Rancière's dissensus by challenging ableist preconceptions and portraying the wheelchair user as active and sexually attractive. Although foregrounded by the presence of the wheelchair, the woman's disability is neither a source of power nor something that subjects her to the ableist gaze. It is destigmatized and no longer evokes a sense of physical otherness. While it would be nearly impossible for a single work to achieve the goal of reconfiguring the distribution of the sensible, it should be stressed that FAR has painted similar murals in many other Polish cities, both in metropolitan areas (e.g. Poznań, Wrocław, or Warsaw) and in smaller towns (e.g. Iława, Kutno, or Namysłów). Furthermore, we are now witnessing a proliferation not only of works which feature or focus on disability, but also of those created by disabled people themselves. Such works frequently offer an alternative to the stereotypical portrayals of disability perpetuated and fossilized within the mainstream since they rely on self-representation. Thus, a work created by a disabled person can challenge ableist narratives of overcoming impairment and sensitize people to the problems and obstacles that people with disabilities face on a daily basis. By doing so, it puts the

2 As Janice Allan points out, otherness "is best thought of as a site or location upon which we project all the qualities that we – as individual subjects, social groups or even nations – most fear, or dislike, about ourselves" (164). It is an artificial construct produced by ideologies and biases, but, like hegemony, it nevertheless leads to the creation of hierarchies between social groups in which the (male, European, non-disabled, etc.) self is seen as superior to the (female, Oriental, disabled, etc.) Other. Obviously, this hierarchization also affects the power relations between individual groups.

existing distribution of the sensible at a distance, allowing us to approach it critically, and paving the way for the full subjectification of people with disabilities in the public sphere, for their emergence as "a part of those who have no part."

The aim of the present collection is not just to look for interpretations of works about or by people with disabilities, but also to see what dissensual potential they have and how they fulfil it. The authors of the articles gathered in this volume investigate a number of twentieth and twenty-first century representations of disability, understood as a broad, culturally constructed category encompassing a wide range of impairments and non-standard embodiments which carry varying degrees of social stigma. They examine the nuances of various art forms and cultural media, such as film, drama, and theatre, as well as the relational value of artistic events connected to disability art, e.g. independent film festivals. These festivals, like a number of other disability arts events, may be seen as examples of what Nicholas Bourriaud terms relational art whose role is "no longer to form imaginary and utopian realities, but to actually be ways of living and models of action within the existing real" (13), thus exerting a lasting influence on contemporary societies and helping them develop appreciation for alternative ways of being in the world.

Since cultural disability studies is an essentially interdisciplinary academic field, the collection includes articles written by specialists in different areas of the humanities (literature, film, performance, drama and theatre, sociology and bioethics) as well as practitioners working in the field of disability art. These texts show the diversity of approaches represented by established and emerging disability scholars working in various cultural contexts which include countries where cultural disability studies already have a strong position in academia (the US and the UK) and those where they have recently been evolving (Ireland, Greece, and Poland). What all these articles also have in common is that they critically approach the status quo – the Rancierian distribution of the sensible – by deconstructing the stereotypes and prejudices informing ableist perceptions of disability. In addition, by so doing, they often delineate the problems and challenges facing not only disability studies specialists but also societies in general. Many of the articles in the collection, including the texts authored by practitioners, focus on disability cultures and works created by members of the disabled community. They offer novel perspectives on the past, as well as contemporary social, cultural, and political realities. Responding to the recent development of disability cultures in various countries, they also demonstrate the ways in which recent theoretical approaches to disability inform new artistic endeavours and help revise canonical cultural texts. By the same token, the use of different methodological approaches allows for the emergence of productive tensions between disability studies, and other dissensual critical trends, such as feminist or gender studies. By uncovering these intersections, the authors also demonstrate the way in which the battle-tested ideas from these fields may be used to challenge a form of hegemonic oppression that is both different from and similar to patriarchy or compulsory heterosexuality – the hegemony of normalcy.

The book opens with a selection of articles offering a comprehensive introduction to cultural disability studies and useful contexts for further analyses. Written by scholars who have their backgrounds in the humanities and social sciences, the section reflects the ways in which Critical Disability Studies has recently been going from strength to strength as a distinct research field and as a discipline which has been permeating and intersecting with other areas of study. Illustrated with numerous examples from diverse cultural backgrounds, the first text by Rosemarie Garland-Thomson and Katarzyna Ojrzyńska explains the basic tenets of Critical Disability Studies in the humanities. Underscoring the social constructionism of disability, the chapter defines it as a representational system which shapes the environment we live in, as well as our identities and interpersonal relations. Delineating the major areas of interest which Critical Disability Studies explores, the comprehensive introduction to this research area also includes a thorough diachronic overview of the major models of perceiving and representing disability, and various examples of the ways in which contemporary artists and writers challenge and revise these models in their works.

The second chapter in this section of the book offers further insight into the theory of Critical Disability Studies. Underscoring the key concepts in this field of study, such as the notions of criticality and intersectionality, it presents the major trends and directions in CDS. In terms of form, Dan Goodley and Marek Mackiewicz-Ziccardi's article reflects the dialogic character of this volume. The chapter is closely based on the conversations between an accomplished disability scholar and a young academic and activist with cerebral palsy, both of whom research disability studies, but who come from two essentially different backgrounds: British and Polish. The inclusion of these two distinct perspectives in the article allows its authors to present a full and complex image of the major approaches to and trends in Critical Disability Studies, as well as to highlight the downsides of the social model of disability and the potential of crip theory and activism to shake the foundations of the fossilized social and cultural status quo.

Małgorzata Sugiera's chapter contributes to the revisionist aims of this volume by laying bare the ways of constituting and sustaining normative categories in the arts and sciences. The article analyses the mutual relationships between these two disciplines by examining a selection of works of art, ranging from Rembrandt's *The Anatomy Lesson of Dr. Nicolaes Tulp* (1632) to Jill Scott's multimedia installation *Somabook* (2012). Sugiera highlights the fact that science does not give direct, objective access to nature. By accentuating historical and cultural mediation in the processes of body analysis and representation in the arts and sciences, it provides a valuable cultural and historical framework for questioning the idea of 'the norm' in Critical Disability Studies and exposing its subjectivity and constructedness. Thus, written from the perspective of cultural studies, the chapter offers an inspiring starting point for further study at the crossroads of sciences, cultural studies, and disability studies, and an invitation to closely examine the factors involved in various inevitably mediated cultural, artistic, and scientific representations of both 'normal' and 'abnormal' forms of human embodiment. It thus paves the way for productive forms of exchange and collaboration between Critical Disability Studies and other fields of academic research.

The next section of the book is devoted to disability film festivals and their potential to counter and change ableist perceptions of disability. David T. Mitchell and Sharon L. Snyder's chapter focuses on a number of independent disability films, especially those screened within international disability film festivals. They discuss motion pictures such as *O Lubvi* (2003), *Sang Froid* (2002), and *I'm in Away from Here* (2007) and argue that they offer alternative perspectives on interdependent living. By complicating conventional assumptions about disability, exposing viewers to bodily variation, and forcing them to adopt non-normative perspectives, these films challenge the stigma attached to disability, presenting it as "a productive social identity in its own right" (69). Maria Tsakiri's chapter builds on a similar premise – namely that the representations of disability in films have the power to transform our assumptions and enhance our understanding of non-normative lives. She claims that this is especially true of the representations of "crip killjoys" and further argues that disability film festivals are a privileged site of political subjectification since they bring crip killjoys together and open up a space in which they can take action. Tsakiri focuses on Emotion Pictures – Documentary & Disability International Festival which was first held in Athens in 2007. She illustrates her claims by analyzing Stefanos Mondelos' *Masterpiece – Part 1* (2007) and Dan Habib's *Including Samuel* (2009) which were screened during the event's 2007 and 2009 editions respectively, and by discussing the political activism of the two collectives of people with disabilities that were founded in the festival's aftermath.

The chapters on disability film festivals are followed by a section that also focuses on films, albeit outside of the festival context. It examines the tensions between 'the reel' and 'the real' – between filmic representations of disability and the real world, both in terms of the effects these films produce in everyday life and in terms of the tensions that the source material inevitably introduces into the fictional narratives. The section opens with a chapter by Murray K. Simpson who analyzes the portrayal of three characters with disabilities in two of Russ Meyer's films – *Mudhoney* (1965) and *Faster Pussycat! Kill! Kill!* (1966) – with a view to discussing the relationship between the body and the semiotic concept of signification – the process of creating signs, in other words arbitrary bonds between what Ferdinand de Saussure called "the signifier" (the sound-image) and "the signified" (the concept) (67). While, historically, critics tended to focus on the connection between impairment and morality as well as on the 'inspirational' narratives of overcoming, disability is now often seen as infinitely more complex than previous approaches would suggest. This complexity also calls for a refining of the critical apparatus. In this case, Simpson suggests, the concept of 'signification' should be preferred over the term 'representation' which allows for the confusion of the signifier and the signified. The text draws heavily on semiotics and shows that it is often reductive to claim that specific bodily variations represent disability per se and that while impairments can signify moral qualities, the logic cannot be reversed, i.e. moral qualities cannot signify impairments. Simpson also argues that while it is possible for a body to be signified, the process of signification cannot be assumed to exist in every single case and it has to be approached individually. The second text included in the section is an analysis of Jessica Hausner's critically acclaimed *Lourdes* (2009). In it, James Casey discusses how the film exposes the hypocrisy of ideological myths of impairment and argues that it offers a satirical look at the shaky foundations that the ideologies of (dis)ability or gender are built upon. For Casey, the identities presented in the film are flexible, rather than fixed. He supports his claim with an analysis of the depiction of its protagonist, Christine (Sylvie Testud), and her interactions with other characters. By showing disability to be an incredibly complex and flexible category, the film unsettles certain popular assumptions and heightens our understanding of human variation. Finally, the chapter also points to how sexuality and gender affect the representation of disability.

The fourth section of the book is devoted to the question of representing and experiencing non-standard physiques. One of its primary goals is to examine the way in which the established discourses about disability affect the process of representation and to see how the bodies themselves influence that process. Written by Agnieszka Izdebska, the first text discusses the evolution of the representations of people of short stature in twentieth-century Western literature. Izdebska's main contention is that while non-normative bodies have traditionally functioned as metaphors, they are now increasingly often depicted just as bodies which define us as human beings. She supports her claim by discussing several works written in different historical and cultural contexts from Pär Lagerkvist's *The Dwarf* (1944), through Władysław L. Terlecki's *Drabina Jakubowa albo Podróż* (*Jacob's Ladder or the Journey*, 1988), to George R.R. Martin's series of fantasy novels – *A Song of Ice and Fire* (1996–2011) to mention but three examples. While the chapter offers a comprehensive introduction to the topic, Izdebska's intimate familiarity not only with literary conventions, but also with Western history and culture, add greater depth to her text.

The next article, written by Edyta Lorek-Jezińska, focuses on what the author identifies as "conflicting discourses of disability" in Susan Nussbaum's *No One as Nasty*. Like the other plays collected in *Beyond Victims and Villains: Contemporary Plays by Disabled Playwrights* (2006), Nussbaum's drama rejects the conventional ways of representing disability signalled by the title of the anthology and, instead, negotiates a more realistic space for disability. Lorek-Jezińska's main goal, then, is to show the way in which theatre and drama recycle the established discourses of disability in order to bring them into crisis. Her analysis mainly centres on the play's protagonist who fluctuates between complete denial of disability and attempts at mapping it against other forms of social and cultural exclusion. In addition, the chapter also touches upon the aesthetic consequences and dissensual potential of introducing a disabled perspective on the theatrical stage.

The last two sections examine the works of Polish and Irish theatre companies of people with intellectual disability. Since intellectual disability and, more generally, neurodiversity often tend to be associated with particularly strong social stigma, the subversive and innovative work of these companies is an excellent example of what we wish to call Dis(sensual)Art or the art of dissensus, in the Rancierian sense. We define it as any form of art that allows for the emergence of the egalitarian principle, giving voice to those who have traditionally been deprived of it and placing their problems in the spotlight, thus leading to the subjectification of people with disabilities. The first chapter in the penultimate section, written by Jolanta Rzeźnicka-Krupa and Dorota Krzemińska, focuses on the work of Polish theatre companies that are members of an informal association: IM+. The article examines selected fragments of interviews conducted with the disabled actors as well as non-disabled therapists and theatre practitioners who collaborate with these ensembles. Placing their analysis in the context of Homi Bhabha's third space and Mikhail Bakhtin's borderline, Rzeźnicka-Krupa and Krzemińska illustrate how the members of IM+ venture beyond the narrow medical context of occupational therapy, which is symptomatic of a slow but persistent change that has been taking place in Polish disability culture over the last few decades. The second chapter in this section sheds more light on these transformations by examining the work of the first professional Polish theatre company of people with intellectual disability – the Warsaw-based Theatre 21 (T21). Unlike most similar Polish ensembles of learning disabled actors, T21 is not run by a therapist but rather by a theatre pedagogue, Justyna Sobczyk, who has recently earned great critical acclaim for the groundbreaking work she has been doing with T21 over the course of more than ten years. Wiktoria Siedlecka-Dorosz's article describes the company's path to success, professionalism, and recognition on both national and international levels.

The last section of this volume presents a similar narrative, telling the story of the success and achievement of the Irish play and film *Sanctuary*. This work boldly exposes the legal obstacles that Irish people with intellectual disabilities encountered when they sought emotional and sexual fulfilment, addressing such issues as their infantilization and lack of privacy, their limited opportunities for independent living, and their reproductive rights. Both the play and the film feature actors from Blue Teapot, a professional Irish theatre company of people with intellectual disability, and have met with great acclaim in Ireland and beyond. The first chapter in this section is written by Len Collin who directed the film adaptation of the play, lauded by the Irish film scholar Seán Crosson as "one of the most ambitious, innovative and deeply moving Irish films of recent times." In his article, Collin presents *Sanctuary* in the context of other representations of disability in contemporary cinema. Furthermore, by offering a detailed insight into his collaboration with the actors from Blue Teapot, Collin's chapter contributes to the ongoing discussion on the place and status of learning disabled actors in the film industry. The section concludes with a transcript of a talk given by Christian O'Reilly, the author of the play *Sanctuary* that he wrote for, and in close collaboration with, the actors of Blue Teapot. The text not only offers an insight into their fruitful collaboration, but also describes the rise of Irish disability activism, which O'Reilly closely witnessed in the 1990s.

Although they all express it in different terms, the authors who contributed to this volume share the conviction that art can help change reality. Humankind is believed to be an "imagined community," to appropriate Benedict Anderson's term, and cultural texts have the power to define who belongs to it and who does not.[3] These texts help to create the Rancierian distribution of the

3 When discussing the concept of the nation, Benedict Anderson describes it as an "imagined community" because of the fact that "the members of even the smallest nation will never know most of their fellow-members, meet them, or even hear of them, yet in the minds of

sensible, assigning social roles and determining which voices are recognized and which go unheard. On the one hand, then, art can be used to reinforce the existing, consensual status quo which is supposedly inclusionary and embraces diversity but nevertheless continues to stigmatize people with disabilities. On the other hand, though, as all the texts collected in the present book suggest, art can carry a disruptive, subversive potential. Film festivals, novels, theatrical works, murals, performances, literary texts, paintings, multimedia installations, and sculptures can all be vehicles for dissent and challenge the ideological import of the more conventional works created within the mainstream. They can offer counter histories, recontextualize disability alongside other identities and areas of study, anticipate new social arrangements, or directly lead to political subjectification. In short, texts of culture have the power to take us out of our comfort zones, to build critical distance, and to put our conventional assumptions to the test. Importantly, all the works discussed in this volume do not try to erase human variation. Rather, they all demonstrate that disability is an extremely productive identity that has no need to be normalized or accounted for through the narratives of super crips overcoming their impairments and passing as non-disabled. By bringing this to light, criticism promotes equality and inclusion and facilitates the political subjectification of people with disabilities. In this sense, we believe that the present book is our intervention in the visible and sayable. It, too, constitutes a collective act of dissent, no matter how small.

Works Cited

Allan, Janice. "Other, the." *The Routledge Dictionary of Literary Terms*. Ed. Peter Childs and Roger Fowler. London: Taylor & Francis e-Library, 2006. 164–65. E-book.

Anderson, Benedict. *Imagined Communities: Reflections on the Origin and Spread of Nationalism*. Rev. ed. London: Verso, 1991. Print.

Bourriaud, Nicholas. *Relational Aesthetics*. Trans. Simon Pleasance, Fronza Woods, and Mathieu Copeland. Dijon: Les presses du réel, 2002. Print.

each lives the image of their communion" (6). Instead, people's sense of belonging to a given community is produced by engaging in certain socially and culturally prescribed activities, such as reading newspapers or novels, as they create a sense of simultaneity and make people aware of the fact that there are others who lead similar lives (Anderson 22–36). Artworks also have the power to define who belongs to the imagined community and who does not. Analogous tendencies can be observed in the global context, as our sense of belonging to the world populace also relies on similar processes. In this case, however, it is not being part of the nation that is at stake, but being perceived as a full-fledged human being.

Crosson, Seán. "Review of Irish Film at Galway Film Fleadh: *Sanctuary*." *Film Ireland* 5 Sept. 2016, https://web.archive.org/web/20191204233230/http://filmireland.net/2016/09/05/review-of-irish-film-at-galway-film-fleadh-sanctuary/. Accessed: 27 Apr. 2019.

Davis, Lennard J. *Enforcing Normalcy: Disability, Deafness, and the Body*. London: Verso, 1995. Print.

Gallagher, Christine, and Stephen Greenblatt. *Practicing New Historicism*. Chicago, IL: The University of Chicago Press, 2000. Print.

Garland-Thomson, Rosemarie. *Staring: How We Look*. Oxford: Oxford University Press, 2009. Print.

Gramsci, Antonio. *Selections from the Prison Notebooks*. Ed. and trans. Quintin Hoare and Geoffrey Nowell Smith. 11th ed. New York, NY: International Publishers, 1992. Print.

Kuppers, Petra. "Deconstructing Images: Performing Disability." *Contemporary Theatre Review* 11.3–4 (2001): 25–40. https://www.tandfonline.com/doi/abs/10.1080/10486800108568636. Accessed 10 Jun. 2019.

McRuer, Robert. *Crip Theory: Cultural Sign of Queerness and Disability*. New York, NY: New York University Press, 2006. Print.

Rancière, Jacques. *Disagreement: Politics and Philosophy*. Trans. Julie Rose. Minneapolis, MN: University of Minnesota Press, 1999. Print.

Rancière, Jacques. *The Politics of Aesthetics*. Ed. and trans. Gabriel Rockhill. London: Bloomsbury Academic, 2013. Print.

Rancière, Jacques. "Ten Theses on Politics." *Dissensus: On Politics and Aesthetics*. Trans. Steven Corcoran. London: Bloomsbury Academic, 2015. 35–52. Print.

Saussure, Ferdinand de. *Course in General Linguistics*. Trans. Wade Baskin. New York, NY: Columbia University Press, 2011. Print.

Siebers, Tobin. "Disability in Theory: From Social Constructionism to the New Realism of the Body." *The Disability Studies Reader*. Ed. Lennard J. Davis. 2nd ed. New York, NY: Routledge, 2006. 173–83. Print.

Veeser, H. Aram. "Introduction." *The New Historicism*. Ed. H. Aram Veeser. London: Routledge, 1989. ix–xvi. Print.

PART 1

(Re)Defining Models of Disability and Normalcy: Theories and Contexts

∴

CHAPTER 1

Critical Disability Studies in the Humanities

Rosemarie Garland-Thomson and Katarzyna Ojrzyńska

Just as the academic world imagined what we now think of as the social construction of race and gender as being something invisible, narrow, or marginal prior to the 1970s, it also, until recently, viewed disability as a medical issue or specialized training area peripheral to consideration in the humanities. The grass-roots scholarly movement called Critical Disability Studies (CDS) in the humanities seeks, however, to change this by implementing a new model of disability that earlier gained recognition in social sciences to literature, history, art, and philosophy. In this way, it broadens the scope of critical and analytical reflection on disability and opens new perspectives on a question that is central to the humanities – the question of what makes us human. Alluding to Virginia Woolf's seminal essay "A Room of One's Own" which describes the life of Shakespeare's imaginary sister, one of us created the fictional character of Franklin Delano Roosevelt's sister Judith, a person with cerebral palsy who becomes a pioneer in CDS in the humanities (Garland-Thomson, "Roosevelt's Sister"). Numerous disability scholars have in many respects shared Judith's story, striving to establish CDS in the humanities as an independent interdisciplinary research field or to incorporate its tenets into the already existing areas of academic inquiry. As a result of their sustained efforts, this field of study has earned a firm position at a number of universities in the US, such as the University of California, Berkeley, Emory University, The Ohio State University, and the University at Buffalo. It is strongly present in various humanities departments, such the Department of English at The George Washington University, where it has been developing thanks to the lasting contribution of such scholars as Robert McRuer, David T. Mitchell, and Sharon L. Snyder. In the United Kingdom, CDS in the humanities is most firmly established at Liverpool Hope University, thanks to the groundbreaking work done by David Bolt, the founding editor-in-chief of *Journal of Literary and Cultural Disability Studies*. CDS has found its way into gender studies in Nordic countries (among others, thanks to Margrit Schildrick, Linkoping University, Sweden) and the Czech Republic (Kateřina Kolářová, Charles University), literary studies (e.g. Marion Rana, University of Bremen, Germany), history (e.g. Jane Buckingham, University of Canterbury, New Zealand; Esme Cleall, University of Sheffield, the UK),

 | DOI:10.1163/9789004424678_003

drama and performance studies (e.g. Bree Hadley, The Queensland University of Technology, Australia), theatre and film studies (e.g. Janice Hladki, McMaster University, Canada) and many more fields of study within the humanities.

The scholarly perspective that CDS offers expands a medicalized understanding of disability by introducing a social model of disability. This scholarly perspective defines "disability" not as a physical defect inherent in bodies (just as gender is not simply a matter of genitals, nor race a matter of skin pigmentation), but rather as a way of interpreting human variation. The parallels between disability and gender as well as between CDS and gender studies seem particularly relevant and well-grounded since

> [d]isability – like gender – is a concept that pervades all aspects of culture: its structuring institutions, social identities, cultural practices, political positions, historical communities, and the shared human experience of embodiment.
>
> GARLAND-THOMSON, "Integrating Disability" 4

Both can be seen as naturalized categories which are in fact social and cultural constructs that serve to preserve certain established social hierarchies. In fact, over the years CDS has been exploring various problem areas which were earlier identified by gender studies. These are, for instance: basic civil rights and social participation (first-wave feminism), the political dimensions of such aspects of the private lives of disabled people as sexuality, family, reproductive rights, etc. (second-wave feminism), positive identity politics (second-wave feminism) and resistance to normalization (body-positive feminism), the intersectional character of various stigmatizing and discriminating categories which often overlap with disability (third-wave feminism), the dissolution of the disabled non-disabled dichotomy in favour of the spectral model of human diversity or even replacing a minoritizing view with a universalizing disability discourse based on the model in which disability constitutes an integral aspect of human life (the non-binary thinking typical of postfeminism).

Within such a critical frame, disability becomes a representational system more than a medical problem, a social construction rather than a personal misfortune or a bodily flaw, and a subject appropriate for wide-ranging intellectual inquiry that augments the medical, rehabilitation, or social work approach to disability. Extending the constructivist analysis that informs gender and race studies, this New Disability Studies insists, at the same time, on the materiality of the body – its embeddedness in the world – by focusing on issues such as equal access for all, integration of institutions, and the historical exclusion of people with disabilities from the public sphere. It values alternative ways of being in the world, and privileges human diversity over homogeneity and uniformity.

Critical Disability Studies explores disability as a historical system of thought, belief, and knowledge that represents some bodies as inferior and in need of being somehow changed so as to conform to what the cultural imagination considers to be a standard body. Critical Disability Studies looks, for example, at such issues as: changes in the way disability has been interpreted over time and within varying cultural contexts; the development of the disabled as a community and a social identity; the political and material circumstances resulting from the system of assigning value to bodies; the history of how disability influences and is influenced by the distribution of resources, power, and status, and how it affects artistic production.

The term Critical Disability Studies follows the premises set forth by critical theory which, according to Max Horkheimer's definition, "is an essential element in the historical effort to create a world which satisfies the needs and powers of men" (246). As he further explains, critical theory "never aims simply at an increase of knowledge as such. Its goal is man's emancipation from slavery" (Horkheimer 246). In this respect, one could argue, the tenets of critical theory overlap the fundamental principles of humanism which Edward Said defines as the critique of the status quo, which promotes and enables what he calls "participatory citizenship" (*Humanism* 22). As he then points out, humanism opposes "withdrawal and exclusion" through revising, improving, or overturning "human misreadings or misinterpretations of the collective past and present" (*Humanism* 22), which brings us back to the central area of interest in Critical Disability Studies – the question of the interpretation and representation of human variety. The above-mentioned revisionist and liberatory agenda is reflected in the fact that CDS derives from, and has a strong connection with disability activism. It has its roots in the British and American disability rights movements of the 1970s, promoting the autonomy and self-advocacy of people with disabilities, in line with the slogan 'Nothing about us without us,' which continues to be an internationally recognized guiding principle of contemporary disability rights organizations.

Critical Disability Studies is an essentially interdisciplinary research field which shares its constructivist foundations with gender, queer, and race studies. In some respects, the area of research delineated by CDS also intersects with issues of interest to postcolonial scholars, since it examines the discriminatory representations of those perceived as 'the Other.' In their book on imagology, in other words the study of national stereotypes (mental images of nations) encoded in literary discourse, Manfred Beller and Joseph Theodoor Leerssen offer an insight into the "selective perception" and "selective evaluation" (Beller 5) that lead to stereotyping and prejudice. This synecdochic process results from restricted perception and ignorance which facilitates oversimplification, "turning a single attribute into the essence of the entire nation" (Beller 9) or, one could argue, any other predefined group. This observation also seems strongly relevant to the common social attitudes to people with disabilities, who are frequently perceived solely through the prism of their impairment often seen as a source of misery and pain. Bill Shannon, an American dancer who was born with a degenerative hip condition and therefore in his innovative choreographies uses crutches and, occasionally, a skateboard, calls this process "condition arriving." As he explains,

> People make assumptions based on strictly visual consumption of my condition – without verbal communication with me. I call that 'condition arriving' – the condition arrived but I didn't. I have this ghost-like presence that people see. I think it's something a lot people with physical disabilities experience.
>
> qtd. in MATTINGLY

Such simplified interpretations often give rise to stereotyped and prejudiced images which serve as false simulacra, preventing us from recognizing those whom we label as the Other as complex and diverse individuals. As Zygmunt Bauman argues, the dichotomous binary perception of 'us' and 'them,' 'the self' and 'the Other' "creates an illusion of symmetry," but, in fact, "conceals the asymmetry of power" (14). Thus, as the philosopher argues,

> abnormality is the other of the norm, deviation the other of law-abiding, illness the other of health, barbarity the other of civilisation, animal the other of the human, woman the other of man, stranger the other of the native, enemy the other of friend, "them" the other of "us," insanity the other of reason, foreigner the other of the state subject, but the dependence is not symmetrical. The second side depends on the first for its contrived and enforced isolation. The first depends on the second for its self-assertion.
>
> BAUMAN 14

Consequently, the concept of the Other has played a key role in women's studies (e.g. Simone de Beauvoir's *The Second Sex*), postcolonialism (e.g. Edward Said's concepts of the Orient and the Occident which he explores in *Orientalism*) and in CDS which explores the ways in which the disabled Other has been defining what one of us has termed "the normate" – "the veiled subject position of cultural self, the figure outlined by the array of deviant others whose marked bodies shore up the normate's boundaries" (Garland-Thomson, *Extraordinary Bodies* 8).

The notion of 'the Other' also brings Critical Disability Studies close to many other disciplines which have their roots in the humanities. It shares a number of common goals with ecocriticism, or even with posthumanist and transhumanist studies, as it investigates the changing definitions of a human being, and the approaches to the augmentation of human capacities by such means as prosthetic devices whose function is no longer solely limited to meeting the given normative standards, but may also involve enhancing the aesthetic and functional aspects of a human body – an idea which has long been explored in popular culture, for instance, through the characters of Robocop and Iron Man, and, more recently, the character created by Viktoria Modesta in her music video "Prototype." Investigating how CDS prompts us to rethink the category of human, Dan Goodley et al. examine, for instance, "the ways in which disability epitomizes a posthuman enhancement of the self while, simultaneously, demanding recognition of the self in the humanist register" ("Posthuman Disability" 342). They put forward the concept of dishumanism which challenges the "shrinking" human category whose defining features are self-sufficiency and independence (Goodley et al., "A DisHuman Manifesto" 161)[1] and seeks to re-evaluate and appreciate the dishuman notions of (inter)dependence, mutuality, and connectedness with both human and non-human world.

In short, Critical Disability Studies rests on strong interdisciplinary foundations and its role is to change the perceptions of disability, laying bare the single-dimensional, often prejudiced definitions of alternative human embodiments. The two major models against which CDS defines itself and which for centuries strongly dominated, yet did not monopolize, the ways of thinking about disability are: the moral/religious and the medical models. As regards the former, older model, it explains disability as a form of divine punishment for the sins of a given person or his/her ancestors. This paradigm is also sometimes referred to as the symbolic model, since it interprets impairment beyond its material reality as a sign endowed with symbolic meanings. A 'flawed' body is seen as indicative of a moral flaw and uncleanness, which needs to be atoned for by, for instance, assuming a stoic stance when enduring the suffering which this model envisages as a fundamental aspect of experiencing disability. The religious model is, for instance, prevalent in the Old Testament, its most obvious example being the much-quoted excerpt from Leviticus, in which God instructs Moses to:

1 See also their former project website in the Internet Archive: https://web.archive.org/web/20181124125625/https://dishuman.com/.

> [s]ay to Aaron: For the generations to come none of your descendants who has a defect may come near to offer the food of his God. No man who has any defect may come near: no man who is blind or lame, disfigured or deformed; no man with a crippled foot or hand, or who is a hunchback or a dwarf, or who has any eye defect, or who has festering or running sores or damaged testicles.
>
> Lev. 21.17–20

Some faint echoes of these ecclesiastical rules can still can still be heard today, as shown by the example of the late Father Jan Kaczkowski – a Polish Catholic priest and the founder and director of the Father Pio Hospice in Puck. In the late 1990s, Kaczkowski was not admitted to a Jesuit seminar because of his visual impairment. In an interview given in 2014, two years before his death from cancer, he recalls this situation, not without a hint of resentment:

> I read books in a non-standard way, because I have to keep them close to my eyes. Some found this shocking. They publically tested me in reading. But I think that my bad sight was just an excuse. I think they feared that if my condition deteriorates, they will need to provide for me and I'll be useless.

Reminding one of the remnants of the religious model that can still be found even in contemporary secularized societies, Kaczkowski's story is above all an example of the contemporary capitalist logic of disposability,[2] based on an individual's usefulness and productivity and closely connected with the medical model which defines disability, like illness, as a form of deviance which needs to be healed so that the previously ill individual will be able to return to society as its fully functional member.

Another curious offshoot of the religious model can be found in Irish fairy lore, specifically in the figure of a changeling (who in Gaelic is called *síofra*, *iarlais*, *fágálach*, or *malartán*) – equivalents of which are the Polish *odmieniec*, the German *Wechselbalg*, or the Swedish *bortbyting*, in addition to those found in a number of other cultures. According to local beliefs, newborn babies were in need of special protection against fairies, who might abduct them to their world whilst leaving behind one of their own, or an object resembling a human being – an enchanted piece of wood called a stock. Susan Schoon Eberly

2 The concept of disposability has been investigated by numerous contemporary thinkers, such as Slavoj Žižek, Zygmunt Bauman, and Cynthia Enloe, in a series of lectures published online under the title *Disposable Lives*, available at http://historiesofviolence.com/special-series/disposable-life/full-lectures/.

provides convincing evidence that many of the descriptions of changelings correspond to specific congenital bodily variations and metabolic conditions, which "evoked a … response of mingled awe and fear" (59). Thus, the concept of a changeling can be seen as an attempt to come to terms with the birth of a disabled child in times when medicine could not provide a sufficient, rational explanation for such phenomena. The supernatural provenance of disability, in this particular case, can be perceived as an instance of relegating disability outside the boundaries of humanity into the liminal fairy domain, underscoring the mismatch between the child and the environment into which it was born. Frequently, there was also a dark side to these Irish folk stories about changelings, since fairy lore was sometimes used to justify any violence targeted at impaired offspring. According to Irish folk beliefs, the best way to force fairies to return a human child to his or her parents was to threaten the changeling or to exert actual violence on it. As mentioned above, such approaches to congenital disorders were not, however, exclusively limited to Ireland. Instead, they are indicative of a wider tendency. Writing about the early modern period in Europe, Josef Warkany argues that

> [w]hen a deformed child showed any sign which resembled the imaginary features of the devil, the demonic origin was suggested. Hairy nevi, ichthyosis, club feet, shortening of the upper extremities, long and deformed ears, syndactylism, and similar anomalies could be interpreted as signs of satanic origin.
>
> WARKANY 12

Numerous stories similar to those found in Irish folklore in which non-standard embodiment is attributed to demonic intervention can also be found in other parts of the world.

Yet, the moral model also fostered perceptions of disability from the other end of the spectrum, since impairment could be a more positive sign of divine election too. The archetypal figure of a blind seer serves as an excellent example of this tendency. Some scholars, such as Owsei Temkin, also draw a possible connection between epilepsy and prophetic trance, suggesting that "the Sybil, the Delphic Pythia, and other divinely inspired persons of ancient legend and institutional life fell into this category" (155). The concept of illness and impairment as a sign of divine election also resonates in the Bible, in the stories of the virtuous sufferer Job whose disabling condition is nothing but a divine trial through which he perfects himself. Once again, one cannot help but notice remnants of such beliefs in today's world, for instance, in the case of Indian "god babies" who may be born with the additional limbs of underdeveloped conjoined twins, and are worshipped as incarnations of a Hindu deity.

Another paradigm of disability which Critical Disability Studies seeks to challenge is the medical model. It became prevalent with the birth of the clinic and the Industrial Revolution which introduced new work standards required from those labourers involved in the process of manufacturing goods. Yet, certain social phenomena, anticipating the transition towards the medical model, can be found at least as early as in the first half of the nineteenth century, in popular freak shows which frequently merged the focus on the unique, extraordinary physique of the performer, who would often be given some exotic provenance, and the medical gaze which was directed at the 'anomaly' rather than at a person as a whole. As Michel Foucault argues, "If one wishes to know the illness from which he is suffering, one must subtract the individual, with his particular qualities" (14). Among numerous individuals who gained recognition by performing in freak shows, one may, for instance, consider the famous Salvadoran siblings with microcephaly – Maximo and Bartola. In the mid-nineteenth century, they were widely known by their stage name "the Aztec children." In his book *Freak Show: Presenting Human Oddities for Amusement and Profit*, Robert Bogdan presents the details of the legend fabricated and published by their manager, in 1860, in the form of a booklet. According to the story, Maximo and Bartola were discovered

> in the temple in the ancient Aztec kingdom.... The children were said to have been found squatting on an altar as idols. They were, it was claimed, members of a sacred race worshipped by the city's inhabitants.
>
> BOGDAN 129

The allegedly divine origin of Maximo and Bartola is an obvious allusion to the religious model of disability, which fuelled the audience's curiosity and imagination.

The costumes in which the siblings performed were, unsurprisingly, modelled on Aztec clothing. However, some of the photos, preserved until contemporary times, present them without their conventional costumes – stripped naked and against a blank background, which is strongly suggestive of a clinical setting. Similar depictions of medical curiosity can be found in the photos of the twins Millie and Christine McKoy, in which they reveal their conjoined backs, having their fronts covered with only two pieces of dark cloth. Stripped of their theatrical costuming, they are reduced to naked, medical specimens who, when presented against a plain background, again remind the viewer of a clinical setting.

Yet, one may argue that the gaze of the representatives of the medical world was directed at those who did not fit the normative standards required even earlier than in the nineteenth century. The story of the eighteenth-century

"Irish Giant" Charles Byrne serves as a case in point. The poem entitled "The Skeleton of the Great Irish Giant" by Northern Irish poet Moyra Donaldson includes fragments of archival texts about Byrne presented in verse, and forming a narrative story. The Irish Giant was reportedly so afraid that his body would be dissected after his death that while still being alive, he employed fishermen to drown his corpse subsequent to his demise. Yet, the men proved unreliable. They were bribed by John Hunter, whom Donaldson describes as "a true scientist," and the foremost of the surgeons who "gathered around the house where he [Byrne] lay like harpooners round a whale" (19). As a consequence, Byrne's body became a medical specimen in Hunter's collection. The first part of the poem also offers a detailed description of how the skeleton was obtained from the corpse, and concludes with a statement that it is still exhibited at the Hunterian in London. In the second part of the poem, Donaldson places the skeleton among other medical exhibits – "sliced" and "hacked" remains of non-standard bodies – displayed inside the museum: fragments of a face, a penis, and a bladder, a skull, a cancerous breast, a foetus, a vagina, etc., which remain "constantly on show" (21). The poem ends with a question posed from the perspective of the specimens: "Expendable, all of us, voiceless in death as in life, we serve to illustrate. What?" (Donaldson 22). One possible answer is that the exhibition lays bare the workings of both the medical gaze and the fascinated stare of the viewers who are still attracted to that which does not meet the normative standards of bodily appearance.

This medical model, which dominated the twentieth century, and is still prevalent in various parts of the world, pictures disability in terms of defect, deficit, and malfunction which need to be compensated for or healed. It seeks to produce an 'objective,' scientific image of disability that is demystified and deprived of the symbolic and moral dimensions characteristic of the earlier model. At the same time, the medical model blurs the boundary between disability and illness and forces a person with an atypical body to accept what Talcott Parsons called a "sick role," in order to be restored to the fixed functional and aesthetic standards. The role involves a passive "withdrawal into a dependent relation" with representatives of the medical profession (Parsons 193), and the acceptance of a degree of alienation, so that one can undergo a process of healing which will enable one to return to society as a useful member.

Since the medical model defines disability in purely negative terms, it largely overlaps with what is sometimes referred to as the individual model which conceptualizes disability as a personal tragedy. A person with disability is thus portrayed as an object of pity. Such an image is still often used by some charities in order to gain financial support from potential, non-disabled donors.

This concept has been subjected to critique and mockery by a number of contemporary artists, both those who identify themselves as members of the disabled community, and those who usually work outside the disability context. One representative of the latter group is the Young British Artist Damien Hirst. He is the author of a seven-meter high bronze sculpture entitled *Charity* (2002–2003), which was originally displayed in the cityscape, in one of London's parks. The sculpture alludes to the charity dolls of the British Spastics Society that represented a sad disabled blonde girl with a teddy bear and a collection box in her hands. Such life-sized collection boxes were commonly exhibited outside local chemists in the 1960s and 1970s, until some years later they were found to be inappropriate and offensive, and were removed from the public space by the Spastic Society, which, in 1994, also decided to change its name to Scope on the grounds that "'the word 'spastic' had become a term of abuse" (Siddique). Hirst's sculpture uses the image of the doll to comment upon the more contemporary concept of charity. Its very size suggests that such emotive images are still at the core of popular perceptions of disability. Yet, apart from being enlarged to grotesque proportions, the collection doll has not been left intact. Hirst presents the failure of the charity model, which the image represents, by opening the doll's back and placing a crowbar at its feet together with a few coins which the robber has left behind.

A similar concept was explored by the late Katherine Araniello, a London-based video and performance artist who creates subversive and satirical works which, as she explains in her "Artist's Statement," were inspired by

> society's ignorance towards disability and negative representation that undermines disabled people's lives and creates an imbalance between those people who sit outside of what is considered normal.

Araniello channels her ideas through an artistic persona which she calls Sick Bitch Crip (SBC). In her manifesto, she explains the ways in which this triad mocks certain prevalent ableist preconceptions about disability, many of which are deeply rooted in the medical model. As she elaborates,

> [SBC] holds the world record for being the sickest cripple ever.... Everyone adores her and she is a Sick celebrity lapping up all the sympathy and pity she can muster. [She] is fantastic at playing the Crip card and has a natural gift for pulling at the heartstrings and making people weep.
>
> ARANIELLO, "Artist Statement""

A similar form of mockery targeted at the idea of evoking compassion through framing disability in terms of personal tragedy is strongly present in Araniello's performance entitled *Pity*, which was given at the Lock-up Performance Art Fête in London in June 2013. Inspired by Hirst's work, Araniello transformed herself into a charity doll, by donning stiff yellow headgear to imitate the statue's blond hair, and a light-blue cape. With excessive pink make-up, she sits still in her wheelchair throughout the performance, holding a white and pink collection box with the inscription: "PLEASE HELP SickBitchCrips." She is accompanied by a tiny dog which sits under her arm, and a woman with a small rattle-like collection box adorned with the photo of an impaired dog similar to Araniello's pet. Wearing dark glasses, the woman sits on the artist's right hand side and plays the role of a supporting beggar and busker. She is holding a wooden walking stick in one hand and keeps rattling the collection box with the other. She uses it as a musical instrument, reminding the passers-by about their moral duty. Araniello's performance was filmed and turned into a short video clip with a soundtrack which, as the author explains, "plays on the theme of pity that is prevalent in the economics of charities to this day" ("Pity"). This message is most evident in the line "Pity does not grow on trees," alluding to an English idiom about money. In this way, in her performance and film, Araniello deconstructs the contemporary notions of charity which are deeply rooted in the individual and medical models of disability.

As Pierre Bourdieu notes, language plays a crucial role in shaping our social realities. He also underscores the importance of "the act of naming" in "establish[ing] the structure of this world" – a privilege which we all desire to exercise (105). Like a number of other marginalized groups, people who have been grouped under the label of disability are no exception to this rule. Thus, Critical Disability Studies in the humanities is also concerned with the role that language plays in disability identity politics, as well as in challenging the fixed social hierarchies. This form of empowerment is conspicuous in its departure from earlier derogatory terms, such as handicapped, crippled, or invalid, since it replaces them with more positive forms. The term that has been predominantly used in the United States – 'a person with disability' – is representative of the 'people-first approach,' which underscores our shared humanity, envisages disability as a secondary attribute of a person, and undermines the binary able-bodied/disabled dichotomy. It has, however, been criticized by some scholars and activists who find the term 'a disabled person' more appropriate. On the one hand, the latter term highlights the fact that disability, as a social construct, has a disabling effect on people's lives. On the other, the term underscores the person's social identity and sense of belonging to the disabled community.

Similarly, some members of the disabled community have reclaimed the term 'cripple' by endowing it with a positive and, at the same time, deeply subversive meaning. Such a celebration of disability as a value to be promoted rather than feared is, for instance, visible in the concept of crip pride, as well as in Robert McRuer's crip theory, or in the collection of essays edited by Caitlin Wood and entitled *Criptiques*, which responds to recent developments in crip culture. Wood opens her introductory essay with a definition of 'crip,' which accurately conveys the rebellious nature of the concept, and thus deserves to be quoted in its entirety:

> Crip is my favorite four-letter word. Succinct and blunt, profane to some, crip packs a punch. Crip is unapologetic. Audacious. Noncompliant. Crip takes pleasure in its boldness and utter disinterest in appearing "respectable" to the status quo. It's a powerful self-descriptor, a cultural signifier, and a challenge to anyone attempting to conceal disability off in the shadows. Crip is anti-assimilationist and proud of it. Crip is outspoken with no patience for nonsense. Crip is my culture and it's where I want to be.
> WOOD 1–2

Mention should be made of the term that has recently been strongly promoted in Critical Disability Studies – TAB (temporarily able bodied), which emphasizes the fact that most people will experience some, even if brief, form of disability at some point of their lives.[3] While the term 'people with disabilities' highlights our shared humanity, TAB underscores the shared experience of disability and thus promotes a majoritarian rather than minoritarian approach to disability.

The attitude to disability perceived as a lack, defect, or dysfunction to be cured or compensated for and a source of individual tragedy has left a lasting mark on our language. Developing an impairment is usually described in terms of losing rather than gaining something valuable. As the visually impaired disability scholar Georgina Kleege notes, "People speak of losing sight, never of gaining blindness." We have often heard the phrase 'confined to a wheelchair,' which conceptualizes an essentially enabling device as a prison, or 'people suffering from Down syndrome,' which ignores the fact that the vast majority of individuals with an additional copy of chromosome 21 lead happy and fulfilling lives (Skotko, Levine, and Goldstein). Thus, CDS seeks to change the public discourse of disability by promoting neutral terms, such as: a wheelchair-user or a person with Down syndrome. Another term it proposes, 'neurodiversity,' indicates that various neurological conditions are a form of human variety rather than an abnormality or dysfunction, while the adjective 'non-disabled' skilfully reverses the traditional perspective, defining able-bodiedness in terms

3 See, for instance, Dan Goodley's commentary on "The Global of Disability" (1–2).

of lack and deficiency, being unacquainted with alternative ways of living that people with disabilities know very well.

Last but not least, Critical Disability Studies also investigates the discourse of disability from a diachronic perspective. It probes the historical formation and social identity of the key term 'disabled,' presenting it as a way of organizing physical, mental, and emotional variations into a large and diverse group of people who may have no more in common than the stigmatized designation of abnormality. In other words, we study the historical and cultural consequences of how this interpretive system creates what Benedict Anderson calls an "imagined community" of the disabled, a social group that all people will join if they live long enough.

Critical Disability Studies is strongly indebted to the social model but, at the same time, by highlighting the limiting, exclusionary nature of the moral and medical models, it opens up disability studies to a plurality of perspectives which envisage disability as a complex, multidimensional phenomenon. In this context, it is worth mentioning some other models of disability, which have emerged in recent decades and which offer complementary outlooks on alternative embodiment. The civil and human rights model, for instance, is deeply rooted in the disability rights movement's struggle to provide disabled citizens with equal treatment and the same opportunities as non-disabled members of society. It aims to grant independence and a political voice to people with disabilities. The affirmative model presents disability as an asset to be celebrated and protected rather than a burdensome liability. The relational model, mostly associated with the Nordic context, underscores "*a mismatch between the person's capabilities and the functional demands of the environment*" (qtd. in Tøssebro 4).[4] Last but not least, Tom Shakespeare puts forward an interactional model which "balance[s] the medical and social aspects" (59). It is based on the assumption that "people are disabled by society *and* by their bodies" (Shakespeare 2) and it examines individual factors, societal factors and factors related to the system of support which produce and define disabled people's experience (Shakespeare 59).

Bringing together a number of complementary outlooks on disability, Critical Disability Studies is burgeoning in the humanities, reflecting major paradigm shifts in recent critical thought and practice. Here are some examples: first, recovering the history of disabled people is part of the shift in the practice of social history from studying the powerful and the elite to focusing on the perspectives and contributions of the previously marginalized. Many of such

4 Tøssebro took this definition from the Norwegian government's action plan for disabled people, 1990–1993.

historical studies show that disability can be found in various, even unexpected contexts. Strong, non-disabled bodies have featured prominently in the nineteenth- and twentieth-century national discourses, as in the case of the German national gymnastic movement Turnverein, the Czech gymnastic organization the Sokol movement, or the Jewish image of the Sabra (Jews born in Israel) which, as Oz Almog notes, sought to challenge the post-Holocaust "image of the Diaspora Jew as weak in body and mind" with "the strong and healthy Hebrew" (87). This only reinforced the well-established, ableist view that disability is simply incompatible with national leadership. Thus, during his presidency, Franklin Delano Roosevelt would carefully avoid exposing his disability to the world. His public appearances were carefully choreographed so as not to show the effects of the president's paralytic illness. Even a few years ago the debate around Hillary Clinton's health issues, in connection with her running for the presidential elections, showed that many Americans still have very specific expectations from the candidates with regard to the degree of their able-bodiedness. The problem, however, does not seem to rest with the candidate, but is rather generated by the public image of the compulsory able-bodiedness of the leader of a nation. As some historical evidence shows, disability was often no longer a problem, once the person in question could afford to apply effective means to either hide his or her disability, or adjust the environment to his or her needs, which shows a close relationship between disability and the material and social status of a person. For instance, born without arms and legs, Arthur MacMurrough Kavanagh pursued a successful career as an Irish politician. Between 1866 and 1868, he held the office of MP for County Wexford and, being an affluent, skilled yachtsman, travelled to London in his private boat.

The second example of the growth of CDS in the humanities concerns the investigation into the ways in which theorizing disability as an identity category responds to critical theory's inquiry into the body's relation to subjectivity, agency, and identity. This is closely connected with the third point – namely, that framing disability in political terms reflects the post-civil rights impulse toward positive identity politics. This brings us back to the affirmative model. It completely reverses the tragic view of impairment and disability, which are seen as a value to be celebrated rather than a burden to be lifted from the person who carries it. The affirmative model highlights the various personal, social, and cultural potentials residing in alternative ways of being in the world. Thus it is strongly present in disability culture, arts, and literature, for example in disability life writing, as well as in works of fiction, such as Brian Friel's 1994 play *Molly Sweeney*, whose eponymous protagonist describes her multisensory, non-visual experience of the world as being different, and in many respects richer, than the experience of individuals with no visual impairments. Speaking about her leisure activities, she declares:

> Oh, I can't tell you the joy swimming gave me. I used to think the other people in the pool with me, the sighted people, that in some way their pleasure was actually diminished because they could see, because seeing in some way qualified the sensation; and that if they only knew how full, how total my pleasure was, I used to tell myself that they must, they really must envy me.
>
> FRIEL 19

This description of Molly's experience gives voice to the experience shared by a number of visually impaired people who use their other senses more effectively than the non-disabled.

The fourth area in which Critical Disability Studies in the humanities flourishes focuses on the integration of disability into the curriculum, and disabled people into the classroom, which corresponds to the recent humanistic commitment to serving under-represented populations. This is conspicuous in numerous universities which are striving to become more accessible, both in theory, and in practice. One of the problems to be addressed is that, in many countries, research in disability studies is mostly conducted within such fields as medicine, education, and sociology, which have not yet fully shed the limitations of the medical model. Attempts to achieve this goal are conspicuous on a number of levels, for example, in creating accessible space and eliminating architectural barriers, or in bringing disability out of the sphere of the taboo and fostering understanding, for instance, through promoting disability etiquette, and popularizing CDS.

Last is the fifth, most prominent aspect of Critical Disability Studies in the humanities derives from the fact that disability arises logically from literary theory's emphasis on discourse analysis, social constructivism, and the politics of representation. This largely consists in destigmatizing disability, including the objects related to it, which have often been metonymically viewed as indicative of a personal tragedy. A case in point is the wide range of highly aesthetic and functional prostheses, such as the ones made for Viktoria Modesta by Sophie de Oliveira Barata, the founder of the Alternative Limb Project, or the ones used by Oscar Pistorius in athletic competitions. Furthermore, as Stelarc's experiments with the third ear he had implanted on his forearm show, the role of prosthetic devices does not need to be limited to adjusting the bodily variety to normative standards, as they can creatively and functionally enhance a non-disabled human being.

To sum up, let us return to the tenets of Critical Disability Studies whose premise is that disability is a culturally fabricated narrative of the body. Operating similarly to the gender and race systems, the disability system produces subjects by way of cultural and linguistic practices that differentiate and mark bodies. This comparison of bodies legitimizes the distribution of resources, status, and power within a biased social and architectural environment. As such, disability has four aspects: first, it is a system for interpreting bodily variations; second, it is a relationship between bodies and their environments; third, it is a set of practices that produces both the able-bodied and the disabled; fourth, it is a way of describing the inherent instability of the embodied self. Disability is defined broadly to include a cluster of ideological categories as varied as the sick, deformed, ugly, old, maimed, afflicted, retarded, insane, mad, abnormal, or debilitated – all of which disadvantage people by devaluing bodies that do not conform to cultural standards. Thus, disability functions to preserve and validate such privileged designations as beautiful, healthy, normal, fit, competent, or intelligent – all of which provide cultural capital to those who can claim such status, who can reside within these subject positions. It is, then, the various interactions between bodies and the world that make disability the raw material of human variation and precariousness.

Critical Disability Studies focuses its analytical lens on the myriad sites where culture elaborates disability. It ranges across such discourses as history, art, literature, religion, philosophy, and rhetoric, by engaging critical conversations between aesthetics, epistemology, cultural studies, ethnic studies, feminism, the history of the body, and issues of identity. Disability is everywhere in culture – from Oedipus to the Human Genome Project – once critics know how to look for it. It is a narrative about the human differences which we can chart over time, an interpretation of the physiological and mental traits we can query, an exclusionary discourse we can excavate, and a fiction about bodily variation we can reveal. Most importantly, these narratives shape the material world, inform human relations, and mould our sense of who we are. In short, then, Critical Disability Studies interrogates disability; it challenges our collective stories about disability, redefining it as an integral part of all human experience and history.

Works Cited

Almog, Oz. *The Sabra: The Creation of the New Jew.* Trans. Haim Waizman. Berkeley, CA: University of California Press, 2000. Print.

Anderson, Benedict. *Imagined Communities: Reflections on the Origin and Spread of Nationalism*. Rev. ed. London: Verso, 1991. Print.

Araniello, Katherine. "Artist's Statement: 'Sick, Bitch, Crip.'" *Canadian Journal of Disability Studies* 2.4 (2013): n.pag., http://cjds.uwaterloo.ca/index.php/cjds/article/view/108/181. Accessed 3 Mar. 2019.

Araniello, Katherine. "Pity." *araniello-art*, https://web.archive.org/web/20190227081759/https://www.araniello-art.com/PITY. Accessed 3 Mar. 2019.

Bauman, Zygmunt. *Modernity and Ambivalence*. Ithaca, NY: Cornell University Press, 1991. Print.

Beauvoir, Simone de. *Second Sex*. Trans. H.M. Parshley. New York, NY: Knopf, 1953. Print.

Beller, Manfred. "Perception, Image, Imagology." *Imagology: The Cultural Construction and Literary Representation of National Characters*. Ed. Manfred Beller and Joep (Joseph Theodoor) Leerssen. Amsterdam: Rodopi, 2007. 3–16. Print.

The Bible. New International Version. London: Hodder and Stoughton, 2001. Print.

Bogdan, Robert. *Freak Show: Presenting Human Oddities for Amusement and Profit*. Chicago, IL: The University of Chicago Press, 1988. Print.

Bourdieu, Pierre. *Language and Symbolic Power*. Trans. Gino Raymond and Matthew Adamson. Cambridge: Polity, 1991. Print.

Donaldson, Moyra. "The Skeleton of the Great Irish Giant." *Miracle Fruit*. Belfast: Lagan, 2010. 19–22. Print.

Eberly, Susan Schoon. "Fairies and the Folklore of Disability: Changelings, Hybrids and the Solitary Fairy." *Folklore* 99.1 (1988): 58–77. Print.

Foucault, Michel. *The Birth of the Clinic*. Trans. Alan M. Sheridan. London: Routledge, 1989. Print.

Friel, Brian. *Molly Sweeney*. New York, NY: Dramatist Play Service, 1996. Print.

Garland-Thomson, Rosemarie. *Extraordinary Bodies: Figuring Physical Disability in American Culture and Literature*. New York, NY: Columbia University Press, 1997. Print.

Garland-Thomson, Rosemarie. "Integrating Disability, Transforming Feminist Theory." *NWSA Journal* 14.3 (2002): 1–32, https://www.english.upenn.edu/sites/www.english.upenn.edu/files/Garland-Thomson_Rosemarie_Disability-Feminist-Theory.pdf. Accessed 3 Mar. 2019.

Garland-Thomson, Rosemarie. "Roosevelt's Sister: Why We Need Disability Studies in the Humanities." *Disability Studies Quarterly* 3/4.30 (2010): n. pag., http://dsq-sds.org/article/view/1278/1311. Accessed 3 Mar. 2019.

Goodley, Dan. *Disability Studies: An Interdisciplinary Introduction*. London: Sage, 2011. Print.

Goodley, Dan, et al. "A DisHuman Manifesto." *Manifestos for the Future of Critical Disability Studies*. Vol. 1. Ed. Katie Ellis et al. Oxon: Routledge, 2019. 156–65. Print.

Goodley, Dan. "Posthuman Disability and Dishuman Studies." *Posthuman Glossary*. Ed. Rosi Braidotti and Maria Hlavajova. London: Bloomsbury, 2018. 342–45. Print.

Horkheimer, Max. "Postscript." *Critical Theory: Selected Essays*. Trans. Matthew J. O'Connell et al. New York, NY: Continuum, 2002. 244–52. Print.

Kaczkowski, Jan. "Egzamin z miłości" ["Exam in Love"]. Interview by Przemysław Radzyński. *e-eSPe* 7 Jan. 2014, http://www.e-espe.pl/temat-numeru/egzamin-z-milosci/26. Accessed 3 Mar. 2019.

Kleege, Georgina. "Blind Faith." *The National Federation of the Blind of Connecticut*, http://www.nfbct.org/html/fed-sprsum2011/blindfaith.htm. Accessed 3 Mar. 2019.

Mattingly, Kate. "The Transporter." *The Village Voice* 7 Jan. 2003, https://www.villagevoice.com/2003/01/07/the-transporter/. Accessed 3 Mar. 2019.

Skotko, Brian G., Levine, Susan P., and Richard Goldstein. "Self-perceptions from People with Down Syndrome." *American Journal of Medical Genetics* (2011): 2360–369, https://www.ncbi.nlm.nih.gov/pmc/articles/PMC3740159/. Accessed 3 Mar. 2019.

Parsons, Talcott. *Social Systems*. London: Routledge, 1995. Print.

Said, Edward. *Humanism and Democratic Criticism*. New York, NY: Columbia University Press, 2004. Print.

Said, Edward. *Orientalism*. New York, NY: Vintage Books, 2003. Print.

Shakespeare, Tom. *Disability Rights and Wrongs*. London: Routledge, 2006. Print.

Siddique, Haroon. "Scope Finds Improved Public Attitudes to Disability over Last 20 Years." *The Guardian* 24 Nov. 2014, https://www.theguardian.com/society/2014/nov/24/scope-disability-improvement-public-attitudes-discrimination-employment. Accessed 24 Apr. 2020.

Temkin, Owsei. *The Falling Sickness: A History of Epilepsy from the Greeks to the Beginnings of Modern Neurology*. Baltimore, MD: The Johns Hopkins University Press, 1994. Print.

Tøssebro, Jan. "Introduction to the Special Issue: Understanding Disability." *Scandinavian Journal of Disability Research* 6.1 (2004): 3–7, https://www.sjdr.se/articles/10.1080/15017410409512635/galley/184/download/. Accessed 3 Mar. 2019.

Warkany, Josef. "Congenital Malformations in the Past." *Problems of Birth Defects: From Hippocrates to Thalidomide and After*. Ed. T.V.N. Persaud. Lancaster: MPT, 1977. 5–17. Print.

Wood, Caitlin. "Introduction – Criptiques: A Daring Space." *Criptiques*. Ed. Caitlin Wood. Portland, OR: May Day, 2014. 1–4. Print.

CHAPTER 2

Critical Disability Studies: Sketches from Poland and the UK

Dan Goodley and Marek Mackiewicz-Ziccardi

1 Introduction

Examining the foundations of Critical Disability Studies (CDS), the chapter also presents our personal relationships with, reactions to, and thoughts alongside these foundational principles. In the first part of the chapter, Dan paints a background to the depiction of what has been described as Critical Disability Studies. In the next part, Marek provides a personal response to this very complex and complicating interdisciplinary field of activism and research. Marek's critical and subjective account sparks some very important considerations. Thus, at various times, Dan and Marek engage in a conversation about the themes, issues, and ideas prompted by Marek's account. We end with some joint reflections on the state of the field.

We choose to incorporate these personal considerations into this essentially theoretical account in order to avoid the distanced scientific perspective through which disability is persistently interpreted in the medical context. Such a scientific approach, as Małgorzata Sugiera shows in her chapter, pretends to offer a direct and objective access to biological aspects of human existence, but in fact leads to creating unreliable and ideologically biased conceptualizations of human body and humanness. Consequently, in our chapter we have incorporated Marek's personal perspectives and experiences of an insider, which can be seen as a form of autoethnography described by Laura L. Ellingson and Carolyn Ellis as a critical

> response to the alienating effects on both researchers and audiences of impersonal, passionless, abstract claims of truth generated by such research practices and clothed in exclusionary scientific discourse.
>
> ELLINGSON AND ELLIS 450

Our strategy aims to help examine the theoretical concepts in a more nuanced and accessible way. At the same time, following Ellingson and Ellis, we also hope it will "disrupt and breach taken-for-granted norms of scientific discourse"

 | DOI:10.1163/9789004424678_004

(450), blurring such binary oppositions as "researcher-researched, objectivity-subjectivity, process-product, … and personal-political" (450). Our aim is to 'crip' or disrupt the traditional distanced academic discourse, in other words, undermine its elitist foundations by using the disruptive and creative power of the lived experiences and realities of disability. On a somewhat more mundane level, cripping also seeks to unashamedly reclaim the activities that – in the normate's psyche – are reserved for non-disabled people. This is another reason why Marek chose to include those personal vignettes.

2 Part 1: Introducing Critical Disability Studies

In the first section of the chapter Dan will provide an introduction to CDS. More developed discussions of the field can be found in Goodley's article "Dis-entangling Critical Disability Studies" and his books: *Dis/ability Studies: Theorising Ableism and Disablism* and *Disability Studies: An Interdisciplinary Introduction*. For the purposes of this chapter, we unpack some of the founding principles of what has become known as Critical Disability Studies.

2.1 *Being Critical*

What does it mean to be 'critical'? What kinds of leanings are illuminated by a public declaration of 'criticality'? To be critical provokes a moment of uncertainty: to give up on what one holds (perhaps unconsciously) and to embrace possibility and opportunity (often linked to the not-yet-known). Being critical evokes reconsideration. And being critical always entails being evaluative of one's own positionality, one's politics, and one's value judgements. The critical of our Critical Disability Studies captures a response to the foundational principles of disability studies (or at least those principles founded in the UK). CDS builds on these foundations but introduces new and emerging perspectives that inevitably contest some of the origin stories of disability studies. Being critical is not the same as rejecting previous ideas. But being critical does mean asking some important questions about dominant theories, perspectives, and assumptions, and questioning doxa. In a paper presented in 2012, one of us argued that Critical Disability Studies might well:

> start with disability, we often never end with it as we engage with other transformative arenas including feminist, critical race and queer theories. Yet critical disability studies reminds us of the centrality of disability when we consider the politics of life itself. In this sense, then, disability

> becomes entangled with other forms of oppression and revolutionary responses.
>
> GOODLEY, "Disentangling" 631

What this quote alerts us to is that an encounter with disability is often also an engagement with age, class, gender, sexuality, ethnicity, and geopolitical location. Critical Disability Studies is open to these intersectional conversations and meetings. But we are getting ahead of ourselves a little here. Let us therefore turn to the foundations of British disability studies. We chose this location because this is where we met: specifically at a British university (Sheffield) some years back, in 2012. While this might sound parochial, our engagements have been pan-national. Marek comes to any conversation about disability as a Polish activist. And Dan has found any comfortable positionings around disability necessarily destabilized by Marek's political narrative. We have discovered together that we are increasingly comfortable with making one another uncomfortable in our positions on disability. And our conversations provoke difficult and troubling questions about disability, the social world, and the human condition. These conversations inevitably involve discussions of geography, community, and home.

2.2 *Finding Critical Disability Studies*

From where Dan writes, to speak of disability studies necessarily invites a conversation with 'the social model of disability.' In Britain in the late 1970s a number of physically impaired disabled people got together to politicize the conditions of disabled people's lives (UPIAS). The term 'disabled' was reappropriated from a medicalized term (disabled being equated with impairment) and made instead a marker of activism (to be disabled was to be oppressed by a society that treated impaired people as less than human). The social model sociologized disability: it made it a concern not of medics, monks, or therapists but a concern of anyone interested in making the world a more equitable place, including activists, artists, academics, and the general public (Goodley, *Disability Studies*). It also said something very simple: that mainstream society was – and is – hostile to disabled people. Disability became, then, less an afterthought of politicized people and was instead put centre stage (Oliver, *Understanding*). In order to conceptualize an equitable community, disability activists and theorists asserted that how a community treats disabled people was a barometer of how inclusive, up-to-date, and truly communitarian that community was. A large number of excluded disabled people would then indicate that a given society is essentially discriminatory. The social model made disability a topic that would spark anger: not fury at the loss of a non-disabled body but a community-shared raging at the everyday exclusion of disabled people.

Vic Finkelstein demanded a rethink of professional responses to disability. While psychologists, medics, and social workers have historically dealt with the individual problems of disability – treating and rehabilitating individuals as they adjust to their impairment (PAMs, or Professionals Allied to Medicine) – Finkelstein called for a more radical form of professional practice that was allied to the politics of disability. Moving from PAMs to PACs (Professionals Allied to the Community) demanded new kinds of professional knowledge on, for example, making the community more inclusive and thus augmenting the community participation of disabled people (cf. Finkelstein, "A Profession Allied" and "Professions Allied"). In a similarly transformative way, Jenny Morris called upon mainstream British feminists to address their disabling exclusion of disabled women from their communities. She argued that disability brings some particular challenges to the lives of women with impairments: not least considerations of physical access and a need to redress simplistic feminist rejections of care as a marker of female oppression. Morris reminded us that care is a key element of the human condition and something that we should not simply dismiss.[1] Last but not least, early contemporary British disability studies owes much to the pioneering work of Michael Oliver[2] – the first professor of disability studies in the UK – who many now see as the Godfather of the social model. His work necessarily pushed forward a materialist analysis of disability: attending to the real barriers and structures within the systems of society that led to the exclusion and oppression of people with impairments. Many disabled people became members of a group of people deemed incapable by the demands of capitalism: joining the masses of the lumpenproletariat, unable to find work, and therefore dependent on the welfare of others.

By the late 1990s in Britain, a number of university courses were starting to feel the influence of disability studies. Disability became an opportunity to 'study' the social world. When we find ourselves contemplating a phenomenon, then we discover things we had not anticipated beforehand. And often when we think of the social world, then disability is discovered. When we read of a child with autism's exclusion from primary school because they have been disrupting the learning of non-disabled children, then we find disability. When we observe that governments are signing up to the United Nations Convention on the Rights of Persons with

1 Cf., for instance, *Pride Against Prejudice: Transforming Attitudes to Disability*, "Personal and Political: a Feminist Perspective on Researching Physical Disability," and *Encounters with Strangers: Feminism and Disability*.

2 Cf. Oliver, *The Politics of Disablement* and *Understanding Disability: From Theory to Practice*.

Disabilities, then we find disability. And when you access the latest news via an app or webpage, you will read of cures for, rehabilitation of, and professional responses to impairment. Here, again, we find disability. The social model of disability necessarily sensitizes us to find disability: understood as the exclusion of people with sensory, physical, or mental impairments from everyday life.

While this social model work was going on in the UK, in the United States, and Canada (and to a lesser extent Australia), disability was being reconfigured as an opportunity to rethink culture (Goodley, *Disability Studies*). We might refer to this emerging literature as reflecting a more generic 'cultural model of disability.' The work of Sharon L. Snyder and David T. Mitchell emerged from the humanities in which the human condition was rethought through the presence of disability (cf. Mitchell and Snyder, *The Body and Physical Difference* and *Narrative Prosthesis*, and Snyder and Mitchell, "Re-engaging the Body," and *Cultural Locations*). Their research on "narrative prosthesis" has been incredibly influential, placing disability in the foreground of cultural studies. They note that disability is everywhere in popular culture but is often evoked or included in order to say something about the kinds of values that dominate our everyday lives. Disability becomes a crutch: a prop on which to hang a myriad of stereotypes, causing a paradoxical situation in which "disabled peoples' social invisibility has occurred in the wake of their perpetual circulation throughout print history" (Mitchell and Snyder, *Narrative Prosthesis* 52). The concept of prosthesis is closely connected with normalization and the illusion of normalcy: "The need to restore a disabled body to some semblance of an originary wholeness is the key to a false recognition" (Mitchell and Snyder, *Narrative Prosthesis* 6). In other words, the need to "prostheticize" "a deviance marked as improper to a social context" (Mitchell and Snyder, *Narrative Prosthesis* 53) shows itself in the overreliance on fixed narrative patterns which do not challenge the non-disabled audiences' reactionary and stereotypical understandings of disability. So, for example, an implicit cultural valuing of independence, autonomy, and self-sufficiency is upheld through an explicit pathologization of disability's association with dependency. The human condition of dependency – our reliance on others to live – jars with the capitalist imperatives of independence, self-sufficiency, and autonomy. And in order to denounce dependence society finds it in some and not in others. Disability becomes one category necessarily associated with dependency and is contrasted with the preferred category of independence (associated with non-disabled people). The cultural model of disability considers what disability does to culture and vice versa, whilst also challenging dominant disabling cultural practices.

In Canada the work of Rod Michalko continued to think about disability in the world. While disability has traditionally been viewed as a kind of psychic or physical assault on the human condition, Michalko urged us to think about the potential of disability for new ways of being in the world together, to rethink our relationships with one another, and to consider the possibilities offered by disability to live in very different ways with one another.

In the USA, the intersections of disability studies and women's studies were explored by the disabled feminist Rosemarie Garland-Thomson whose analysis has spanned considerations of disability freak shows through the offerings of disability analyses to the development of a more inclusive feminist practice (cf. Garland-Thomson *Freakery*, *Extraordinary Bodies*, "Integrating Disability," and "Feminist Disability Studies"). Disability shines new light on feminist priorities contesting, for example, a problematic view of the achievements of women in the workplace. While Garland-Thomson would of course welcome new modes of working that increase women's career progression, she is also in tune with the demands made by disabled women to work in mutual and interdependent ways with one another. This reimagining of feminist practice is offered by disability.

The intersectionality and notion that disability is an opportunity are tropes that have been taken further by a growing area of Critical Disability Studies. This approach – 'crip theory' – seeks to celebrate the disruptive potential of disability. It can be traced, largely, to the influential work of Robert McRuer (cf. "As Good as It Gets," "Compulsory Able-bodiedness," and *Crip Theory*), who yet admits that crip theory has non-academic roots. As he explains, "in general the term 'crip' and the theorizing as to how that term might function have so far been put forward more by crip artists and activists, in multiple locations outside the academy," who have proudly and defiantly "come out crip" "in response to systemic ablebodied subordination and oppression" (*Crip Theory* 34). Crip has much in common with queer, since both terms serve as examples of a derogatory stigmaphilic word being reclaimed by members of the stigmatized group and refashioned into a flamboyant and subversive identity category. Both seek to identify and disturb normative modes of production that enhance the ambitions of the powerful and threaten to further segregate those considered abnormal, troubling or peripheral to the demands of the normative centre. Disabled and queer people are often deemed to be dangerously disruptive to the workings of society. Some disabled people trouble the stereotype of a successful citizen: able, autonomous, working, and consuming. Similarly, queer people appear to live their lives in ways that are counter to the heternormative desires of mainstream society. As McRuer notes, compulsory able-bodiedness and compulsory heterosexuality are just two of the defining discourses of the mainstream, which operate in a discreet way, since both "functio[n] by covering over, with the appearance of choice, a system in which there actually is no choice" (*Crip Theory* 8). Crip theory – like queer theory – recuperates the disruptive potential of disabled and queer and seeks to elaborate on the effects of this potential.

One area of interest advanced from this crip perspective comes from Fiona Kumari Campbell and her work on ableism. Rather than focus on the deficiencies of disability, she suggests we turn the tables on the dominant: on ability. Advanced capitalist societies rely heavily on the ideology of ableism: that individuals are capable, independent, self-sufficient, and willing to work and shop for themselves, untouched by the hand of government. In neoliberal societies across the globe the self-sustaining discourse of ableism fits with the rolling back of welfare states, reductions in government expenditure, and austerity policies. Campbell urges us to contest the logics of ableism and offers disability as a necessary antidote to this mindless acceptance of ableism (cf. Campbell "Refusing Able(ness)," "Exploring Internalized Ableism," and *Contours of Ableism*).

Indeed, in some of our work at the University of Sheffield, we are wanting to celebrate the crip potential of organizations of disabled people to promote interdependence in times of austerity (http://ihuman.group.shef.ac.uk/portfolio/humanactivism-org/). This has led one of us to recently suggest that disability is *the* key arena for opposing the logics of ableism (Goodley, *Dis/ability Studies*). This means challenging taken-for-granted ideas such as:

- non-disabled bodies are beautiful and disabled bodies are not;
- austerity is economically sensible and necessary;
- only those who work can be considered valued citizens;
- educational achievement of individual pupils should be measured and assessed through rigid forms of examination;
- bright kids should be educated separately from not-so-bright kids;
- because a few people fraudulently claim welfare then a widespread revision of the welfare system should be enacted.

Crip contestations of ableism have the potential to reimagine how we want to live our lives together.

2.3 *Responding to Critical Disability Studies*

In this second section of the chapter Marek and Dan will 'crip' (think challenge, dislodge, or – with a slightly slang-ish twist – 'diss'[3]) the academic narrative, by engaging in a dialogue, whereby they share vignettes on and around disability

3 'Diss' is a word used by the English-speaking and Polish rappers alike that derives from the word 'disrespect' and denotes a clever and often multi-layered taunting of their opponents' shortcomings.

and ableism. The aim of this is to set up an affirmative discursive space that will provoke our Readers to have similar conversations – whether with their loved ones, colleagues, or even themselves.

As Dan aptly shows above, disability – or more specifically, the occurrence of disability in the world – can often be a signpost to furthering our understandings of what it means to be human. There is only one 'but' about it: for disability to become such a signpost, you, dear Readers, need to allow the 'magic' to happen. Therefore, we offer an 'intimate' narrative of thinking through and about disability. Come and 'do' crip with us, will you?

On the morning of the day that Marek received the first part of this chapter, he was laid in bed with his partner – a fellow CPee (person with cerebral palsy). This is indeed significant for a few reasons. Firstly, because they were having a discussion about anything and everything – as you often do in bed – and among the host of things that they were talking about was the Facebook post that he wrote (Mackiewicz-Ziccardi, "How is One Supposed to Find"). In that particular post Marek was trying to capture the debilitating – that is, sadly, not an exaggeration – discomfort that he had been feeling about his relationship with his own disability. The conundrum in question was the constant shifting of perspective that Marek experienced (and will likely still experience in the future) from the passive, victimized, disabled man – an attitude 'gained' while being raised in a family whose ethos originated in relatively unskilled labour rather than education, living in an eastern Poland town (Biała Podlaska, approximately thirty kilometres from the border with Belarus) – to the politicized crip 'demanding' recognition. Marek often finds himself aspiring to the latter status which he highly reveres – perhaps to the levels that are almost unprofessional. Yet, as a Polish, disabled (former) town-dweller, he finds it deeply hard to occupy. As a result of this, he often finds himself rubbing his eyes in disbelief when Dan in his appreciation calls him 'an activist.' Dan responds to this is as follows:

> Marek is very much an activist from my perspective. And he has always been at least in the time I have known him. I remember meeting him as a student on a generic MA course in Psychology and Education. On introducing him to a number of key disability studies texts I was struck by how these works resonated with Marek's own experiences of a disabling society. He was often the first to speak in lectures and classes. Quick to challenge or seek clarification. And happy to publically acknowledge if he was at all troubled by theories and provocations from the literature. This marked him as a politicized being. And one possible consequence of living in disabling society is, of course, a depoliticization of disabled and

> non-disabled people as we come to view our bodies through dominant, narrow, and individualizing narratives of medicalization and psychologization. I therefore interpret Marek's troubled relationship with the activist category as a direct reflection of disabling society and not an inherent weakness of Marek.

Growing up in eastern Poland, one can be taught, for example, that "a humble calf suckles on two mothers" (Marek's translation) – which is an actual bon mot that his father used in attempts to teach him that it is perhaps 'not' wise to be too critical – at least not openly – particularly when you are disabled, and it is reasonable to assume that your life will be 'harder than usual.' We are aware of the issues around the notion of 'reasonable assumptions,' but being conscious of space we will recommend Jenny Slater's take on those instead of elaborating ourselves (cf. *Youth and Disability*). What we will say is that being reasonable is a key element of ableism: ensuring that the normative centre of everyday life is kept in check; untroubled by the 'unreasonable' requests of those people that are deemed not capable nor welcome to occupy an ableist identity.

In these circumstances, it is not surprising at all that some of us will identify with, or internalize individualistic ideas that centre around 'overcoming' the predicament of disability. The replaying of that harmful discourse is precisely at the heart of the above-mentioned conundrum. Marek shamelessly confesses that he has internalized ableism and even though he now knows it does not serve him, it continues to have a profound impact on his life, self-image, etc. – it even makes Marek question his competency as an academic. How does one deal with that? An instinctive response is to try to annihilate the victimized part of one's identity, but Marek has not managed to do it so far, nor does he feel that it is actually possible. This complex internal conflict hardly makes one an activist material, in Marek's opinion. In his home environment, before coming to Sheffield, it has never occurred to him to campaign for social justice, or that the ubiquitous flights of stairs and scarce and badly serviced lifts are, in fact, a form of systemic oppression. One way to explain it is to say that prior to 2012 he knew nothing about ableism or disablism. Marek's current understanding of these notions is greatly influenced by Dan Goodley's *Dis/ability Studies: Theorising Ableism and Disablism* and Carol Thomas's "Disability & Impairment," which he recommends as very accessible and illuminative texts.

Nevertheless, even Marek himself acknowledges that there is little surprise in his ignorance of ableism and disablism, because as Carrie Wade – again, a fellow CPee, based in the USA – points out, even the liberal arts curricula that allegedly take on "exposing and unpacking prejudice" are oblivious to the abhorrent treatment of disability. Similarly, in a Polish high school you may learn – as Marek did – about kalokagathia, the idea that ties goodness and beauty (Weiler 11), but you will surely not come across any of the many models of disability, nor any explanation as to how disability enhances our understandings of the world around us. Dan's own memories of schooling in England reveal ableism. Many disabled children in the 1970s and 1980s were housed in segregated special schools and were therefore often not present in the local community, the shops, and sports centres. This meant that mainstream, so-called normal schools, were very homogeneous – in Dan's case white and working class – which peddled particular kinds of idealized images of the body and mind.

At the same time, Marek thinks of the Union of the Physically Impaired Against Segregation, UPIAS (1976) pioneering work that they obviously started before they had the notional apparatus that they gave us and about the anger brought about with/in the social model of disability and he finds himself asking: "Why did not I feel such anger?" The tentative answer to this question relates to two domains and readily shows us which of the many issues around genuinely including and catering for disabled people need rectifying as soon as possible. These issues are:

- Absence of an 'engaged' community – 'engaged community' is understood here as the like-minded, disabled people and their allies that are conscious of disablism and ableism getting together to provide both emotional support and a space to discuss collective action. Instead of such a community, Marek was surrounded by chiefly well-meaning and chiefly non-disabled people whose refusal to adequately address his disability has prompted Marek to internalize the overcoming narrative of disability.
- Absence of ideological critique of cultural artefacts – which has developed elsewhere as a consequence of crip theory (cf. e.g. McRuer, *Crip Theory*), the cultural model of disability (cf. e.g. Garland-Thomson, *Extraordinary Bodies*, "Integrating Disability," and "Feminist Disability Studies"; Snyder and Mitchell, *Cultural Locations*; and Mitchell and Snyder, *Narrative Prosthesis*) and the critical study of ableism (cf. e.g. Campbell, *Contours of Ableism*). For the purpose of galvanizing this point, Marek tried to remember what sort of prescribed readings he had in his school years that featured any form of disability. The only example he can actually remember is Sophocles' *Oedipus the King*. No analysis of his blindness was offered, beyond the simple assertion that it was a punishment.

Marek's work as a PhD candidate at the University of Sheffield was, in part, an attempt to mitigate the latter. In his project, he explored the cultural representations and constructions of disabled people's sexuality. Dan learned a lot from

Marek's PhD thesis not least in relation to aspects of Polish culture and their relationship with disability and sexuality. The impact of religion and the previous, communist regime are common topics of our conversations. And, of course, these are deeply complex ideas in Polish society as well as in the British classrooms in which Marek and Dan talk. One recurring theme is this: that disability and sexuality have been historically troubled and pathologized to varying extents by religion and communism. And these pathological tropes exist even today.

Indeed, religion is a crucial factor in Poland because the state takes Catholicism very seriously. So much so that one of us argued elsewhere that the church "attempts to hold on to its discursive power over bodies that it enjoyed for centuries" (Mackiewicz, "Kulturowe przedstawienia seksualności" 71, Marek's translation; see also Król and Pustułka). One way that this discursive power plays out is, for example, that some disciplines within social sciences, such as gender studies, are mistrusted and misconstrued as ideology rather than considered legitimate scholarship. This mistrust and misconstruing are perpetuated by both clergy and their lay allies (Mackiewicz, "Kulturowe przedstawienia seksualności"), including socially conservative politicians. It is also not without relevance that many such politicians form the current Polish government. For instance, this state of affairs enabled the Catholic hierarchs to exert considerable pressure on politicians to "immediately proceed" (Komunikat, point 4, Marek's translation; cf. Ogólnopolski Strajk Kobiet in English) a draft bill that, if passed, would have tightened the already harsh abortion law. It was the mass protests against the draft bill that made the government reconsider its position.

Equally, Kubicki, Bakalarczyk, and Mackiewicz-Ziccardi argue that Poland's communist past has grave consequences for the way the state approaches disability. For example, the country lags behind in terms of introducing progressive welfare and/or support system. In fact, both in 2014 and 2018 disabled people, their parents, and carers resorted to sit-in protests to draw attention to their dramatic financial situation (Kubicki, Bakalarczyk, and Mackiewicz-Ziccardi). In these circumstances, it is hard to research a topic like sexuality of disabled people in the geo-cultural context of Poland. It is so because, on the one hand, one's morality and intentions are called into question. On the other hand, one is often made to feel that there are more pressing issues to champion around disability, such as seeking better material conditions. Under no circumstances does Marek mean to say that these are not worthy or needed causes. Rather than that he suggests that focusing solely on them is detrimental to disabled people's lives. At the same time, our conversations draw in capitalism and secularism, each of which have their own problematic relationship with disability. In short, a discussion of nation state and disability brings with it a cultural analysis of the ways in which disability is constituted in these local and pan-national spaces.

The issue of disability and sexuality, which opens part two of this text, has also been raised by Marek because to the mainstream society the very possibility of disabled people engaging in romantic or – God forbid – sexual conduct remains uncanny (cf. e.g. Bonnie; McRuer, "Sexuality"; McRuer and Mollow; and Shildrick). Caterina, Marek's partner, has pointed out on a number of occasions how people stare at them if they do so much as hold hands in public spaces. Marek's contention is that the principal condition that invites such stares is the simple fact that both Marek and Caterina use wheelchairs, so their disabilities are very visible. This proves what one of us poignantly termed "the psychopathology of the normals" (Goodley, *Dis/ability Studies* 72). What Dan meant by this term was a playful consideration of the often serious implications of the ways in which non-disabled people think of, react to, and construct disability. Staring, for example, relates to what we might term the cultural disavowal of disability. When people stare at disability, then they are drawn to disability. They desire to look at disability. But we know too that people who stare often turn their eyes away. And in that moment of turning the gaze away is the potential for denigration: for ignoring or erasing disability. Hence, in the cultural disavowal of disability, disabled people are the objects of curiosity and disgust stared at and looked away from. And it is this complex cultural ambivalence that disabled people have to negotiate.

Marek also thinks that the psychopathology of the normals seems to be related to the earlier-mentioned fallacious and ableist ideology of kalokagathia. Originating in ancient Greece, it implied a supposedly unbreakable connection between the categories of "goodness" and "beauty" (Weiler 11). Palsied bodies, like his or Caterina's, are not considered conventionally beautiful. Because of this supposed 'ugliness,' their rituals of affection seem to break an unspoken decorum and thus an aura of suspicion always accompanies them, regardless of how 'innocent' their particular behaviours might indeed be. Or, to borrow a term from crip theory, they discredit what McRuer calls "compulsory able-bodiedness" ("Compulsory Able-bodiedness"). This concept captures the fact that many European and Northern American societies are organized in ways that for full access and recognition, one inevitably 'has to' be able-bodied.

These experiences also further galvanize Mitchell and Snyder's narrative prosthesis theory, outlined briefly by Dan above. If we think of a life as a narrative or a collection of stories – a premise that, in Marek's view, is close to both himself and Dan (cf. e.g. Goodley et al.) – then the presence of disabled people in every day spaces evokes feelings much similar to those invoked by observing disability on screen or in a book. Thus, disabled social actors prompt their non-disabled peers to think of tragedy, loss, and limitation – 'even' if the disabled person(s) in question do not feel those emotions themselves (sic!).

Yet, Marek would go even further, i.e. to suggest that it does not seem an overstatement to paraphrase Foucault's famous bon mot "We, the other Victorians" (2) into "We, the other ancient Greeks." In other words, regardless of many centuries our conceptualizations of what is good, nice, and, by extension, worthwhile or even worth living are still underpinned by ancient and ableist discourses.

That is Marek's (think 'a,' or 'one of many') crip response to the inherent everyday disablism of these mundane encounters. Add to this the notorious and age-old question of "Can you have sex?" – to which some of us will brilliantly answer: "Yes, but not with you" (Dremousis) – and you get a mental landscape of the normate that is as obsessive as it is disturbing. Sometimes, the only response to that can be 'laughing it out.' In her biography, Francesca Martinez – a British CPee comedienne – shares a story of how she was invited to speak at the conference dominated by PAMs on the topic of "[l]iving with cerebral palsy" (263). Exposing the inherent unfairness of defining a person by means of their lacks, Martinez proposes an experiment to her audience. She asks one of the men what is the one thing that he is not good at. In response, the man says that he cannot dance. Then Martinez proceeds to mock puzzlement and says that she has never met anyone who could not dance and she does not know how to approach such a person. The absurdity is taken one step further when she asks the man if he can have sex. This story is poignant insofar that if you genuinely consider this, the ability to dance has as little to do with the ability and/or desire to have sex as does being blind, deaf, or using a wheelchair. The embarrassment that Martinez's audience member faced has, hopefully, prompted reflection in many of his colleagues.

But this psychopathology can take on a more tacit guise too. Marek makes this argument in relation to his work on cultural location of disability in and around the Polish critically acclaimed film directed by Maciej Pieprzyca and entitled *Life Feels Good* (2013). The film tells the story of a Polish, non-verbal boy – later a man – with severe cerebral palsy. The specific impairments that the protagonist has lead the doctors to pronounce him "a vegetable" – someone who in practical terms has no concept of what is going on around him. This has grave consequences for the protagonist and the story alike. Firstly, very few of the people who surround him question the diagnosis. And even those who do are guilty of disablist treatment. Girls that Mateusz bonds with do not treat him seriously in the end. In turn, the implication for the tone of the story is this: not being considered as having severe intellectual disability is a matter of dignity; what does this say about the devaluation of intellectually disabled people? That it is routine and merciless.

During Marek's research around the film, he has come across the director-screenwriter's statement that if he did not find a suitable (non-disabled) child actor to play the young version of his protagonist, he would have rewritten the script to only require a skilled – non-disabled – actor ("Aktualności filmowe+"). Readers might wonder what is pathological about that. Well, the idea of hiring a disabled actor – whether child or adult, or both – clearly did not dawn on the filmmaker, which according to Marek is pretty pathological. Indeed, this point of representation is picked up by cultural modellists such as Mitchell and Snyder who insist on challenging the ableist frames that shape film-making and other creative industries. Clearly, if no disabled people are part of the production machinery, then disability will only ever be represented in simplistic and unrealistic ways.

Another characteristic of Marek's professional-political outlook on disability studies is a disappointment with the social model of disability. Remaining mindful of the fact that it changed and saved lives (cf. Crow), he is also aware of its problematic nature. Its inherent predilection towards materialistic account of the social system that excludes disabled people is both its biggest strength and weakness (cf. Shakespeare and Watson). It is a strength insofar that it allowed organizing to push for more rights, recognition, and inclusion (Oliver, *Understanding Disability*; Shakespeare and Watson; and Goodley, *Disability Studies*). Moreover, the focus on real material barriers associated with poverty, unemployment, inaccessible housing, exclusionary school systems, and unrepresentative political organizations necessarily politicizes disability. However, towards this end, the social model adapted an obscure, malestream version of 'the social,' that related mainly to the question of employment, access, and external world. At the same time, even Colin Barnes and Mike Oliver – the chief heralds and defenders of the hard-line social model – acknowledge that the changes in British disabled people's collective situation were, in fact, "more apparent than real" (9). In light of the last assertion, it seems relatively safe to say that the social model has *not* achieved what it was supposed to achieve. Thus, its exclusion of the personal aspects from the narrative of disability seems to have been a pointless intellectual exercise. More importantly though, this kind of approach quite simply does not do justice to the myriad of emotions that are brought about by *both* impairment and disability. But it has been made clear by 'the founding fathers' of the social model that they do not intend to revise their positions (Oliver, *Understanding Disability*; and Barnes). Thus, it seems to Marek that the social model of disability masquerades as yet another grand narrative.

That is where the cultural model comes in handy. As Goodley argues, it rejects the firm distinction between disability and impairment because it posits that these categories influence one another (*Disability Studies*). More importantly still, it turns our gaze towards cultural artefacts. This is useful, particularly although not exclusively, with regards to disability, because a proportion of non-disabled population will draw most of their knowledge about this phenomenon, from pop/cultural depictions. What we view on the TV, check out in the pictures and capture in music will substantively impact on the kinds of referent points that are available to disabled people and their non-disabled peers alike.

Other useful practical tools also come from the crip theory. 'Crip' is, in fact, something that we do in this chapter. Crip encourages prioritizing, valuing, and amplifying the sorts of discourses that elevate the otherness of disabled people. It prescribes proudly manifesting our differences, instead of trying to minimalize them, in attempts to fit in, or emulate the norm (cf. Adams, Reiss, and Serlin). For an identity that has, as we demonstrated, been historically devalued, the processes of reclaiming and pampering are very important and can indeed be healing. But having been raised in a socially conservative setting, where fitting in was greatly valued, Marek continues to struggle with unapologetically claiming his cripness.

3 Conclusions

In this chapter we briefly sketched some of the offerings of disability to the understandings of the social and cultural realms. We hope that we have managed to show Readers that disability is 'not' some insular matter that affects only those considered and/or constructed as disabled. Disability is a matter of not only human curiosity but also human activism. Indeed, as Dan has been exploring with disabled people's organizations in Britain, when disabled people fight for recognition of their human rights, they do so in ways that extend the category of human (see http://ihuman.group.shef.ac.uk/portfolio/human activism-org/). Disability studies has never been more needed than today.

Works Cited

Adams, Rachel, Reiss, Benjamin, and David Serlin, eds. *Keywords for Disability Studies*. New York, NY: New York University Press, 2015. Print.

"Aktualności filmowe+" ["Film news+"]. *Canal+Film* 2 Oct. 2013. Television.

Barnes, Colin. "Social Model of Disability: A Sociological Phenomenon Ignored by Sociologists." *The Disability Reader: Social Science Perspectives*. Ed. Tom Shakespeare. London: Continuum, 1998. 65–78. Print.

Barnes, Colin, and Michael Oliver. "Disability Politics and Disabled Movement in Britain: Where did It All Go Wrong?" *Centre for Disability Studies: University of Leeds*, Jul.

2006, http://citeseerx.ist.psu.edu/viewdoc/download?doi=10.1.1.464.6659&rep=rep1&type=pdf. Accessed 3 Mar. 2019.

Bonnie, Selina. "Disabled People, Disability and Sexuality." *Disabling Barriers – Enabling Environments*. Ed. John Swain et al. 3rd ed. London: Sage, 2014, 138–45. Print.

Campbell, Fiona Kumari. *Contours of Ableism: Territories, Objects, Disability and Desire*. London: Palgrave Macmillan, 2009. Print.

Campbell, Fiona Kumari. "Exploring Internalized Ableism Using Critical Race Theory." *Disability & Society* 23.2 (2008): 151–62. Print.

Campbell, Fiona Kumari. "Refusing Able(ness): A Preliminary Conversation about Ableism." *Media and Culture* 11.3 (2008): n. pag., http://journal.media-culture.org.au/index.php/mcjournal/article/viewArticle/46. Accessed 3 Mar. 2019.

Crow, Liz. "Including All of Our Lives: Renewing the Social Model of Disability." *Encounters with Strangers: Feminism and Disability*. Ed. Jenny Morris. London: Women's, 1996. 206–26. Print.

Dremousis, Litsa. "Yes, I'm Disabled. But I Still Love Sex." *Washington Post* 17 Oct. 2016, https://www.washingtonpost.com/national/health-science/yes-im-disabled-but-i-still-love-sex/2016/10/13/06d9e7de-792a-11e6-beac-57a4a412e93a_story.html?noredirect=on&utm_term=.dedc80c5376c. Accessed 3 Mar. 2019.

Ellingson, Laura L., and Carolyn Ellis. "Autoethnography as Constructionist Project." *Handbook of Constructionist Research*. Ed. James A. Holstein and Jaber F. Gubrium. New York, NY: Guilford, 2008. 445–65. Print.

Finkelstein, Vic. "A Profession Allied to the Community: The Disabled People's Trade Union." *Disability & Development: Learning from Action and Research on Disability in the Majority World.* Ed. Emma Stone. Leeds: The Disability, 1999. 21–24. Print.

Finkelstein, Vic. "Professions Allied to the Community (PACs I)." *Centre for Disability Studies: University of Leeds*, https://disability-studies.leeds.ac.uk/wp-content/uploads/sites/40/library/finkelstein-pacall.pdf. Accessed 3 Mar. 2019.

Foucault, Michel. *The History of Sexuality: The Will to Knowledge*. London: Penguin, 1998. Print.

Garland-Thomson, Rosemarie. *Extraordinary Bodies: Figuring Physical Disability in American Literature and Culture*. New York, NY: Columbia University Press, 1997. Print.

Garland-Thomson, Rosemarie. "Feminist Disability Studies." *Signs: Journal of Women in Culture and Society* 30.2 (2005): 1557–587. Print.

Garland-Thomson, Rosemarie, ed. *Freakery: Cultural Spectacles of the Extraordinary Body*. New York, NY: New York University Press, 1996. Print.

Garland-Thomson, Rosemarie. "Integrating Disability, Transforming Feminist Theory" *NWSA Jorurnal* 14.3 (2002): 1–32. Print.

Goodley, Dan. *Disability Studies: An Interdisciplinary Introduction*. 2nd ed. London: Sage, 2016. Print.

Goodley, Dan. *Dis/ability Studies: Theorising Ableism and Disablism*. London: Routledge, 2014. Print.

Goodley, Dan. "Disentangling Critical Disability Studies." *Disability & Society* 28.5 (2013): 631–44. Print.

Goodley, Dan, et al. *Researching Life Stories: Method, Theory and Analyses in a Biographical Age*. London: RoutledgeFalmer, 2004. Print.

"Komunikat z 378. Zebrania Plenarnego Konferencji Episkopatu Polski" ["An Announcement from the 374th Plenary Assembly of the Polish Episcopal Conference"]. *Konferencja Episkopatu Polski*. 14 Mar. 2018, https://episkopat.pl/komunikat-z-378-zebrania-plenarnego-konferencji-episkopatu-polski/. Accessed 29 Mar. 2019.

Król, Agnieszka, and Paula Pustułka. "Women on Strike: Mobilizing Against Reproductive Injustice in Poland." *International Feminist Journal of Politics* 20.3 (2018): 366–84. Print.

Kubicki, Paweł, Bakalarczyk, Rafał, and Marek Mackiewicz-Ziccardi. "Protests of People with Disabilities as Examples of Fledgling Disability Activism in Poland." *Canadian Journal of Disability Studies* 8.5 (2019): 141–61, https://cjds.uwaterloo.ca/index.php/cjds/article/view/569/838. Accessed 9 Mar. 2020.

Mackiewicz, Marek. "Kulturowe Przedstawienia Seksualności Osób Niepełnosprawnych: Zarys Problematyki" ["An Introduction to Cultural Representations of Disabled People's Sexuality"]. *Studia de cultura* 10.1 (2018): 71–83. Print.

Mackiewicz-Ziccardi, Marek. "How is One Supposed to Find…" *Facebook* 10 Dec. 2014, https://www.facebook.com/search/top/?q=marek%20mackiewicz%20How%20is%20One%20Supposed%20to%20Find%20&epa=SEARCH_BOX. Accessed 3 Mar. 2019.

Martinez, Francesca. *What the **** Is Normal*. London: Virgin, 2014. Print.

McRuer, Robert. "As Good as It Gets: Queer Theory and Critical Disability." *GLQ: A Journal of Lesbian and Gay Studies* 9.1–2 (2003): 79–105. Print.

McRuer, Robert. "Compulsory Able-bodiedness and Queer/Disabled Existence." *The Disability Studies Reader*. Ed. Lennard Davis. 2nd ed. New York, NY: Routledge, 2006. 301–08. Print.

McRuer, Robert. *Crip Theory: Cultural Signs of Queerness and Disability*. New York, NY: New York University Press, 2006. Print.

McRuer, Robert. "Sexuality." *Keywords for Disability Studies*. Ed. Rachel Adams, Benjamin Reiss, and David Serlin. New York, NY: New York University Press, 2015. 167–70. Print.

McRuer, Robert, and Anna Mollow, ed. *Sex and Disability*. Durham, NC: Duke University Press, 2012. Print.

Michalko, Rod. *The Difference that Disability Makes*. Philadelphia, PA: Temple University Press, 2002. Print.

Mitchell, David T., and Sharon L. Snyder, eds. *The Body and Physical Difference: Discourse of Disability*. New York, NY: Verso, 1997. Print.

Mitchell, David T., and Sharon L. Snyder. *Narrative Prosthesis: Disability and the Dependencies of Discourse*. Ann Arbor, MI: The University of Michigan Press, 2000. Print.

Morris, Jenny, ed. *Encounters with Strangers: Feminism and Disability*. London: The Women's, 1996. Print.

Morris, Jenny. "Personal and Political: A Feminist Perspective on Researching Physical Disability." *Disability, Handicap and Society* 7.2 (1992): 157–66. Print.

Morris, Jenny. *Pride Against Prejudice: Transforming Attitudes to Disability*. London: The Women's, 1991. Print.

Ogólnopolski Strajk Kobiet. "#SolidarityWithPolishWomen…" *Facebook.* 16 Mar. 2018, https://www.facebook.com/ogolnopolskistrajkkobiet/photos/a.1540520529307273/2357347334291251/?type=3&theater&ifg=1. Accessed 29 Mar. 2019.

Oliver, Michael. *The Politics of Disablement*. Basingstoke: Macmillan, 1990. Print.

Oliver, Michael. *Understanding Disability: From Theory to Practice*. London: Macmillan, 1996. Print.

Pieprzyca, Maciej, dir. *Chce się żyć* [*Life Feels Good*]. Perf. Dawid Ogrodnik, Kamil Tkacz, Dorota Jakubik, and Anna Nehrebecka. Kino Świat. 2013. Film.

Shakespeare, Tom, and Nicholas Watson. "The Social Model of Disability: An Outdated Ideology?" *Research in Social Science and Disability* 2 (2001): 9–28. Print.

Shildrick, Margrit. "Sex." *Keywords for Disability Studies*. Ed. Rachel Adams, Benjamin Reiss, and David Serlin. New York, NY: New York University Press, 2015. 164–66. Print.

Slater, Jenny. *Youth and Disability: A Challenge to Mr Reasonable*. Surrey: Ashgate, 2015. Print.

Snyder, Sharon L., and David T. Mitchell. "Re-engaging the Body: Disability Studies and the Resistance to Embodiment." *Public Culture* 13.3 (2001): 367–89. Print.

Snyder, Sharon L., and David T. Mitchell. *Cultural Locations of Disability*. Chicago, IL: University of Chicago Press, 2006. Print.

Thomas, Carol. "Disability & Impairment." *Disabling Barriers – Enabling Environments*. Ed. John Swain et al. 3rd ed. London: Sage, 2014. 8–15. Print.

UPIAS. *Fundamental Principles of Disability*. London: Union of the Physically Impaired Against Segregation, 1976. Print.

Wade, Carrie. "Telling Myself the Truth: 5 Strategies for Fighting Internalized Ableism." *Autostraddle* 19 Sept. 2016, https://www.autostraddle.com/telling-myself-the-truth-5-strategies-for-fighting-internalized-ableism-350528/. Accessed 3 Mar. 2019.

Weiler, Ingomar. "Inverted Kalokagathia." *Representing the Body of the Slave*. Ed. Thomas Wiedemann and Jane Gardner. London: Frank Cass, 2002. 11–28. Print.

CHAPTER 3

Making Sense of Bodies: Normalizing Power of Models and Metaphors in Sciences and Arts

Małgorzata Sugiera

The last few decades have seen Critical Disability Studies (CDS) become a recognizable and recognized part of the academic world, and, at the same time, a widely used critical term in an on-going discussion on today's most important issues. This point has been convincingly proven by Lennard J. Davis in his preface to the fourth edition of *The Disability Studies Reader* (cf. 1–14). As he argues, it suffices to take a look at the rapidly diminishing interim period between the consecutive editions of this volume: ten years between the first and the second one, four years between the second and the third, and only three between the third and the fourth which was published in 2013.[1] During that time the medicalized (or even over-medicalized) notion of disability, passed down from the twentieth century, was replaced by a much broader and multi-layered concept covering the legal, social, and cultural aspects of the issue.[2] As a consequence, disability came to be recognized as a complex phenomenon, requiring different levels of analysis and intervention, ranging from the medical to the sociopolitical. Disability is not to be ascribed to a universal and unchanging essence, but is rather a phenomenon that has its own cultural and historical specificity, which has given rise to a variety of diverse, yet in many ways complementary, models and theories of disability that have been discussed in the first two chapters of this volume.

What is even more important is that Critical Disability Studies not only examines the construction of disability, but also the construction of 'normalcy,' because the concept of 'the norm' implies the notions of deviation and extremes. Such a constructionist approach lies at the foundation of contemporary CDS. It is, for instance, conspicuous in Rosemarie Garland-Thomson's concept of "the normate" which, as we have been reminded in Chapter 1, denotes "the veiled subject position of cultural self, the figure outlined by the array of deviant others whose marked bodies shore up the normate's boundaries" (Garland-Thomson 8). It is also visible in the second chapter of Lennard Davis's

1 The fifth edition was published after this chapter had been written, in 2017.

2 To learn more about different models of disability, see Garland-Thomson and Ojrzyńska's chapter in this volume.

 | DOI:10.1163/9789004424678_005

book *Enforcing Normalcy: Disability, Deafness, and the Body*, in which the historical study of 'the norm' mostly concentrates on symbiotic relationships between statistical science and eugenics or other regulative concerns such as, for instance, the concept of 'the norm' and 'normalcy' in psychoanalysis. In this way, medicine and biology have been reintroduced into conceptualizations of disability as specific post-Enlightenment models of embodiment. In what follows, I would like to take a step further in reintegrating sciences into Critical Disability Studies.

I will demonstrate how ideas about 'normalcy' in medicine and biology could be researched not only in order to bring to the foreground the relationship between the normative and the non-normative, but also to highlight the historically and culturally situated concept of the body as part of nature, an idea born in the mid-seventeenth century. For the natural philosophers of that period it was evident that the natural body could be directly and objectively assessed by means of increasingly accurate instruments. The idea has not changed until today. The introduction of more and more sophisticated technologies and machines has only strengthened the belief that the so-called natural sciences have worked out an ideologically unbiased concept of the human body. That is why it seems important to raise once again the question so rightly asked by Evelyn Fox Keller in her *Making Sense of Life* (cf. 1–9): what counts as a legitimate scientific explanation of biological phenomena? This problem should be taken into account not only in biology, which at the turn of the twenty-first century outflanked physics as the leading natural science, but also in the field of disability studies. Therefore, I will take a closer look at several lessons in anatomy and their artistic representations from different historical periods, ranging from the famous painting by Rembrandt *The Anatomy Lesson of Dr. Nicolaes Tulp* to a 2012 multimedia installation *Somabook* by contemporary artist Jill Scott. I intend to show how tightly the techniques, instruments, models, and metaphors used by both scientists and artists were interwoven at a given time to make sense of a natural body and materialize it in a performative manner, thus shedding light on the arbitrariness and constructedness of 'the norm.'

Art historians agree that the widely known *The Anatomy Lesson of Dr. Nicolaes Tulp* is Rembrandt's first masterpiece. The painting was commissioned in a traditional way by the guild of surgeons in Amsterdam as their collective portrait. It represents eight figures of natural size during a lecture by Nicolaes Tulp, a doctor of medicine and *praelector anatomiae* (i.e. a reader in anatomy), during the public autopsy of a thief named Adriaenszoon, who had been hanged the day before. The autopsy was carried out on 31 January 1632, and Rembrandt depicted it in a realistic fashion. The scene is skilfully conveyed, as though it was taken straight from real life. Each of the doctors surrounding the corpse, which occupies a central position in the painting, is taking an active part in the lesson and they react differently to the sight of the muscles, tendons, and nerves of the left forearm, held up in Tulp's forceps. For this reason Rembrandt's painting is not only part of art history, but it also belongs to the history of medicine. It is often used as a plausible, or sometimes even historical testimony to the anatomical theatre, a place where seventeenth-century education was combined with entertainment. However, during a thorough conservation of *The Anatomy Lesson* carried out between 1996 and 1998, it was discovered that the painting conceals a significant secret.

The conservators became interested in the thick layer of paint in the spot where the second hand of the corpse lies. An X-radiograph of the painting showed that, instead of an elegantly drawn hand, initially there was only a stump. The stump was probably seen by the original viewers in the *theatrum anatomicum*. Documents related to Adriaenszoon testify that he was sentenced by the authorities of his hometown, Leiden, to having his hand cut off. What made the painter change his mind? This question was so intriguing to a young American writer, Nina Siegal, that she spent six years searching for an answer. She studied scholarly works on Rembrandt and their conservation, seventeenth-century Dutch history and customs, the literature of the epoch, and the archives of Amsterdam. She presented the results of her research in her novel entitled *The Anatomy Lesson* (2014) which, in the rhythm of hours announced by the newly built Westerkerk, presents Adriaenszoon's last day. It is also another day in the lives of his contemporaries: not only historical figures like doctor Tulp, Rembrandt, and Descartes, who by that time lived in Amsterdam, but also fictional characters, such as the heavily pregnant Flora from Leiden, who to no avail comes to Dam Square to save the convict's life (cf. Siegal 263–64). Although Siegal introduced a traditional omniscient narrator into the text, she often lets the characters tell the stories of their lives. These are interwoven with transcripts of the dictated notes of a conserver who becomes the author's alter ego. Thanks to her commentaries written in a different font, with every passing hour we get to know the fate of the characters and, step by step, resolve the mystery of Rembrandt's painting. Late at night Rembrandt changes the initial concept of *The Anatomy Lesson* and decides to "remove the exterior signs of his malfeasance" so that "no one would try peering into his organs to detect evidence of his soul's corruption" (Siegal 243). In other words, he does not want the corpse to be perceived through the prism of the moral model, according to which, as Garland-Thomson and Ojrzyńska explain in their chapter, a body that does not fit in 'the norm' "is seen as indicative of a moral flaw and uncleanness" (21).

In her *The Anatomy Lesson*, Siegal, from a contemporary point of view, answers the question of whether Rembrandt's painting only has a realistic and documentary value. She assumes that he not only took part in the lecture, but also drew sketches in the adjacent room where the corpse was stored. She deliberately widens the gap between that which the painter could see with his own eyes, and that which he represented on canvas, disregarding the rules of the guild and the conventions. She aptly describes the aesthetics of Rembrandt's painting, inspired by the Italian masters both in terms of perspective and chiaroscuro. Furthermore, using the Italian concept of *disegno* (drawing),[3] it is possible to explain the new arrangement of sensory data according to the artist's idea and his assumptions that preceded the actual experience (cf. Alpers 222–28). *The Anatomy Lesson* can then be regarded not only as Rembrandt's first masterpiece, but also as the symbolic moment when art bid farewell to medicine. They went in different directions and their paths crossed four centuries later in such currents of contemporary art as bioart (wetart) or neuromedia. This is confirmed by a different autopsy, carried out thirty years later, with which Carl Zimmer opens his 2004 book *Soul Made Flesh*.

Let us imagine a room in one of the buildings in Oxford, in Beam Hall in Merton Street, where on a summer day in 1662 a group of local philosophers of nature gathered around a long table. The one who was most important among them was Thomas Willis, who has just opened a skull. In this room, filled with the odour of turpentine and decaying human and animal flesh and resembling a combination of a laboratory and butcher's shop, we witness the first anatomical dissection of a human brain and the nervous system. This was a true revolution in medicine, which gave birth to the science that Willis called (with a Latin neologism): neurology.

In order to realize what the scene described by Zimmer looked like, we can refer to a different and relatively unknown painting produced by Rembrandt a few years earlier, in 1656. It was commissioned by the guild of surgeons and was entitled *The Anatomy Lesson of Dr. Deijman*. In the centre of the painting there is a corpse, drawn in sharp foreshortening and covered with a white cloth. It lies in a position that is reminiscent of Andrea Mantegna's *Lamentation of Christ*. The table seems to go out of the frame, and the exaggerated, large feet, pointing in the direction of the viewer, occupy the foreground. Clearly, we are witnessing an autopsy at an advanced stage, because above the cover we can see the empty space of an open abdomen. Doctor Deijman is now carrying

3 As Alpers explains, 'disegno' is "the notion of drawing that refers not to the appearance of things but to their selection and ordering according to the judgment of the artist and in particular to the ordering of the human body" (39).

out a brain autopsy. He is standing in the background with an assistant who is holding the upper part of the skull like some kind of a vessel. Unfortunately, only this part of the picture survived the fire. A preserved sketch, in ink, proves that the original painting could have presented a scene similar to the one described by Zimmer. This, however, is only a speculation. What is more, because of the defacement of the painting, the work is less known than the famous *The Anatomy Lesson of Dr. Tulp*. However, it is not without a reason that I took interest in the earlier Rembrandt's depiction of an anatomy lesson, the one carried out by Nicolaes Tulp. One object represented in it helps demonstrate convincingly the nature of the Copernican revolution that took place in medicine in the period that separates these two paintings.

In the bottom right-hand corner of *The Anatomy Lesson of Dr. Tulp*, by the feet of the corpse, on a stand lies an open book and the physician standing next to Tulp and facing us with his right profile is holding a piece of paper that shows a visible anatomical drawing of a forearm. This does not mean, however, that *praelector anatomiae* is metaphorically reading this particular body, or that he is learning and teaching others from his experience. Quite the opposite, his lecture focuses on the topic of the written records of ancient authorities, and the corpse is merely an illustration that in no way subverts the dominant knowledge. The testimony of the eye cannot go against the canon of learning. It is determined by the standards set by the scholarly drawing which provides a normative point of reference for the lecturer.

The open book in Rembrandt's painting may be the famous anatomy atlas *De humani corporis fabrica libri septem* by the Flemish anatomist Andreas Vesalius to whom Tulp often referred in his writings. By the mid-1500 Vesalius was the first to question Galen's findings. He corrected the gross mistakes committed by the Roman physician and, at the same time, proved that his great predecessor did not conduct autopsies on human corpses but described and drew human tissues and organs on the basis of autopsies carried out on domestic animals. A hundred years later when doctor Tulp referred back to Vesalius's works, he did not belong to the avant-garde of contemporary medicine (cf. Kooijmans). *The Anatomy Lesson of Dr. Tulp* presents medicine in the period before the scientific revolution. By contrast, the later painting by Rembrandt depicts the autopsy of the brain, 're-invented' in the form that is now seen as informed by the ideas expressed by natural philosophers who thus eliminated the mediation of anatomy atlases. It depicts doctor Deijman in the process of reading the anatomy straight from the open body, straight from nature.

Small wonder that Descartes from Siegal's novel, a character who regularly buys animal corpses from a butcher and conducts autopsies, attends doctor Tulp's lesson only as a social courtesy. Tulp reads the world through the prism of Vesalius's atlas, whereas Descartes is looking for a soul, the cardinal difference between humans and animals, in the mechanics of their muscles and bones. However, it was not enough to repudiate the ancient authorities for modern medicine to be born and establish its new normative standards. Willis, the founder of neurology, would not have been capable of changing the dominant views on the brain if he had not modified the method of conducting autopsy. Having opened the skull, his predecessors would have cut into the brain layer by layer, at the same time destroying its delicate tissue and thus wasting the opportunity to examine its structure. Willis took the entire brain out and only then studied its structure. He would not have been able to do this, however, if in the meantime a new substance had not been invented, one that made it possible to harden and conserve the brain tissue. Willis was also aided by another invention, the microscope, which let him see that which was invisible to the naked eye. Such new advances prove the claim that when philosophers of nature rejected the authority of scholarly books, they did not gain immediate access to nature itself.

In her *Screening the Body*, Lisa Cartwright rightly points out that the image which is visible under the microscope was decidedly different from the previous artistic and scientific representations of nature (81–106). There was no way to verify this except through direct, unmediated sensory experience. By the turn of the seventeenth century, this problem led to serious epistemological doubt and scientific uncertainty. The magnifying glass also mediated between the eye and the object under scrutiny, but in the microscope the image was produced between two lenses, which complicated the relationship between the viewers and the object that they looked upon. The person could adjust the distance between the lenses, change the sharpness of the image, and enlarge a detail, but the image itself underwent a series of uncontrollable distortions caused by the instrument. By the same token, the lenses, the eye, and the objects under scrutiny became elements of a composite, self-correcting technological apparatus, which did not have any centre. This apparatus took over the agency of sight and dispersed this agency onto its component parts. Moreover, the image produced in this way was not only virtual, but also could, at any moment, turn out to be a simple artefact when a scratch on the glass or a speck of dust became part of the image. Therefore, we cannot claim that the image is faithful to nature if we disregard the technology that not only produces, but also disciplines and regulates it. From this point of view, nature, treated by the naturalists as the only true source of knowledge, turns out to be a product of technology. It is mediated like the knowledge gained by watching the body through the prism of the treatises of ancient philosophers and physicians. Technology only changed the manner of gathering data about nature, which have been used, among other things, as seemingly objective grounds for diagnosing humans and defining the medical bodily 'norm.' This claim can be supported by the second autopsy that Zimmer describes in his *Soul Made Flesh*.

This time we have to go down to the basement of Green Hall, one of the buildings of Princeton University where, in 1999, Joshua Green was studying the nature of our ethical judgment by means of magnetic resonance imaging. This non-invasive method of producing images of the brain and its internal functioning does not require a corpse, or the sweet smell of blood and the odour of turpentine. Plastic tubes and colourful wires are sticking out of the body of a young man, who is "loosely corseted" with special straps. His two fingers rest on buttons. There is nobody around. Three people are waiting in the adjacent room. Sitting on wheeled chairs, they move from one monitor to another, constantly supervising the examination and comparing the results of the measurement. By means of a computer mice or keyboards they change the position of the slab. A contrasting fluid allows them to see how different areas of the brain are activated when the subject is looking for answers to questions about moral and immoral conduct (Zimmer 262–63). Graphic inscriptions show the internal processes that could not otherwise be registered by human senses. The organoleptic assessment of a corpse is now replaced by the use of sophisticated instruments and data analysis. There are no witnesses to the procedure who, according to Robert Boyle, should have an important role in the process of scientific fact-making (Shapin and Schaffer 55–60). People can only become familiar with the results of 'the reading of the anatomy' in the form of images, graphs, and numbers. They can only be virtual witnesses. Hardware and software entirely eliminated wetware from the field of sensory perception.

This conclusion has been inspired by the scene from *Soul Made Flesh* that took place at the turn of the twenty-first century in Green Hall, "where a machine eavesdrops on the moral circuits crackling inside a man's head" (Zimmer 295). Zimmer used this scene only to remind us that it was Willis who invented modern neurology. For this reason, when describing Green's experiment, Zimmer emphatically draws an analogy between the practices initiated by Willis and the neurology of the early twenty-first century. However, when Green tried to establish whether the difference between good and evil in the human brain is the same as that between blue and red, did he still examine the same brain that Willis represented as the alchemists' wondrous alembic? After all, it is not only technologies that mediate between ourselves and the world. Our perception is also regulated and disciplined by the metaphors and concepts that we use, and they are just as authoritative as the ancient treatises.

In *The Anatomy Lesson*, in a letter to the French polymath Marin Mersenne, Descartes recollects Tulp's demonstration, which he watched on the same evening. He pays particular attention to the moment when the surgeon's forceps took hold of a tendon in such a way that the fingers of the hand moved, as if the corpse had come back to life. However, as Descartes affirms, Tulp was only playing the puppeteer who pressed the right switch. He adds: "It was proof that the body is a machine and that muscle and bones all act in accordance with mechanical principles" (Siegal 206). Willis was familiar with the alchemic tradition, but he transposed its mysterious workings onto material connections in the brain. He did not treat the human body as a set of cogs and gears which function like a piece of clockwork. Rather, he treated it like a chemical factory in a constant state of fermentation and transformation, where particles of air and food are combined to create new substances and forms. Just as these two metaphors cannot be reconciled, it is impossible to make a seamless transition from them to the concept of the body as a database extended by specialist instruments in order to transform them into inscriptions that our senses can register. Therefore, as it seems, the story told in *Soul Made Flesh* should be completed with one more stage of transition that can even be symbolically situated on a time axis.

In 1895, brothers Lumière patented their cinematographer, an ameliorated version of Thomas Alva Edison's kinetoscope, and William Roentgen discovered mysterious X-rays, later called by his name. A year later Edison publicly announced that he could use these rays to show the cross-section of a human brain without opening the skull. As Cartwright writes, the Lumières quickly gave up filmmaking and started laboratory research on tuberculosis and cancer with the use of Roentgen's machine. Their own apparatus turned out to be a revolutionary invention for the dynamically developing physiology, which replaced anatomy because it could grasp the dynamic processes inside the body. It also helped to establish 'the norm' and detect 'pathologies.' Three years later, Ludwig Braun of Vienna opened the chest of a dog and filmed the contractions of its beating heart. In 1907, Julius Ries prepared fourteen hours of footage presenting the process of the insemination and development of an egg cell of a sea urchin. He shortened the film to two minutes with the help of the technique that we know from David Attenborough's films. Not only did he let his viewers see that which the naked eye could not register, but he also moved away from naturalist imagery towards virtual simulation which only presented selected excerpts from the original documentation. No one questioned the scientific credibility of his film, because he selected the material from the original footage in accordance with the dominant views of scientific authority.

Ries's *Fertilization and Development of the Sea Urchin Egg* anticipates the anatomy lesson of Dr. Green, which Zimmer depicted as a follow-up to Willis' neurological investigations. Therefore, Kirsten Ostherr, who in her *Medical*

Vision analyzes the process of reshaping patients' bodies through new imaging technologies, is right to point out that

> even the most powerful imaging techniques of the twenty-first century, such as live cell MR fluoroscopy, still employ a significant element of selective interpretation based on how the leading experts imagine things would look, if only we could see them directly.
>
> OSTHERR 50

To a large extent, this selective process still determines the ways in which non-normative bodies and disability are conceptualized according to the medical model, described in detail by Garland-Thomson and Ojrzyńska in their chapter. It plays an important role in the practice of teaching doctors how to see and analyze a patient's body and its possible pathologies in an institutionalized and standardized manner, at the anatomical and neurological levels.

1895 was not only the time when the contemporary concept of human body and its visibility (life) came into being, but it was also the moment when medicine and art met again – and I do not mean only popular art. In *Screening the Body*, Cartwright convincingly argues that the possibility of taking a look inside a body and thus exposing its private and intimate insides influenced the Italian futurists, Marcel Duchamp and Germane Dulac, not to mention Thomas Mann's *Magic Mountain*. At this juncture, I would also like to refer to a lesser known product of the cooperation of an artist and a doctor: a short, merely twelve-minute long film *Fall of the House of Usher*, based on Edgar Allan Poe's short story. It was made in 1928 by James Sibley Watson Jr., a film director and radiologist, in cooperation with the art historian and poet Melville Webber.

It is quite obvious why Watson and Webber chose this short story. The reason for the eponymous fall of the house of Usher lies in the guarded secret of an incestuous love which is discovered by the narrator who visits the mansion. His sight resembles an X-ray machine, which in the film is shown through a series of images, sometimes difficult to decipher because of the multiple shades and reflections. Significantly, in the beginning we see pages from the short story, including the title and the first sentences. Then a misty landscape appears against the background of which a silhouette of a man on a horse is visible. He rides towards a castle with a few towers. Their shadows become flat, two-dimensional staircases superimposed on each other like in a cubist painting. The screen resembles film tape with a crack in the middle. The tape is broken and, like an opened abdomen, reveals the inside of the house. The consecutive sequences are also reminiscent of an autopsy. For a moment, two hands are visible on the screen and their position resembles that of the hands of operating surgeons. A similar perspective is used a few more times: different layers or planes of the image shift apart and we can see deeper and deeper into the mysteries of the house. The film ends with the image of two bodies of siblings and lovers. Like an X-ray scan, it shows us pathology, a deadly moral illness in the house of Usher.

The cultural meaning and use of medical images produced by X-ray scans at the beginning of the twentieth century prove the falseness of the hypothesis that the intense dialogue of art with medicine ended in the seventeenth century only to begin anew at the turn of the twenty-first century. We can argue that already in the case of *The Anatomy Lesson of Dr. Tulp* a number of details were omitted because of artistic strategies and the conventions of *disegno*, as well as the principle of idealizing the bodies presented in anatomy atlases. Their images and interpretations were standardized and turned into an object of scientific study. Therefore, unnecessary details had to be eliminated in order to increase the clarity and readability of the images. Rembrandt, working for the guild of surgeons, may not have been driven by the noble intentions that were ascribed to him by Siegal in *The Anatomy Lesson*. He may just as well have used an idea that he borrowed from Vesalius' treatise. He may have simply wanted to focus the viewers' attention on the opened forearm, and therefore omitted the significant detail, that is the missing right hand bearing the marks of earlier autopsies and scars. Even if both of these interpretations remain hypothetical, it is worth remembering that their equal status strengthens the role of Rembrandt's *The Anatomy Lesson* in both art history and the history of medicine. This is especially worth remembering today, when arts and medicine are closely involved with one another and influence each other in a number of ways (cf. Stollfuss).

This is most conspicuous in computer-generated images that fulfil all the requirements of photographic realism, seemingly establishing an indexical and iconic homology with their referents to reality. However, their referentiality is entirely fictional, because they are not materially linked with the world, as is the case with photography. Moreover, digitally produced and edited images can be endlessly manipulated. Some elements can be added or removed, but these changes do not destroy the real character of the image. This is caused by the fact that unreal, that is referentially fictional, images can still be realistic at the perceptual level, if they are adjusted to the visual and social experiences of the viewers (cf. Prince 27–37). I am not only referring to a series of educational films entitled *Inner Life of a Cell*, produced since 2006 for the students at Harvard University, and the influence that they exert on medical practices, such as endoscopy, in which the image on a computer screen provides the basis for surgical intervention. I am also concerned with the image of medicine and its cultural meaning, which is spread by computer-generated images in Hollywood films watched by millions of viewers worldwide (cf. Kirby). In this context we can go back to bioart and particularly to neuromedia which is situated at the crossroads of neurobiology, physiology, and media art. It should now be clear why interactivity is so significant for neuromedia, having in mind the cultural image of science and the virtual testimony offered by Hollywood movies.

I would like to finish my analysis of a handful of anatomy lessons by taking a look at a project by Jill Scott (Scott and Stoeckli 23–55) which is particularly relevant to my analysis because of what it presents and how it presents it, using the book as both a material object and an ambiguous metaphor. Jill Scott is a professor for Art and Science at the Zurich University of the Arts, where she runs the Artists-in-Labs programme in which artists cooperate with scientists. They take part in research and prepare installations which tackle the most significant problems of contemporary science in an interactive way. They focus particularly on the biological processes of their own bodies. The artist herself admits that the concept for her installation *The Electric Retina,* presented for the first time during the Neuromedia exhibition in Zurich in 2012, was born when she was diagnosed with glaucoma. The interactive sculpture that I have chosen for analysis was produced in the same year and has a meaningful title: *Somabook*. Its main theme is connected with the brain and the nervous system 'invented' by Willis, although today it is represented in a more contemporary vein, at the level of molecular biology.

The basic idea for *Somabook* was born in a lab at the Institute of Molecular Life Science at the University of Zurich, where inseminated chicken eggs were used as a material to study the development of the nervous system in embryos. The method called RNA interference was used to damage chosen groups of cells. The scientists observed the pathological consequences of the damage which is the same as in the case of, for example, Foetal Alcohol Syndrome. Drawing from these studies, Scott produced an animation of the development of the nervous system, while a dancer, Merit Schlegel, filmed dance sequences that demonstrated 'normal' and 'pathological' movement at various stages. Both types of images were superimposed on each other and complemented with graphs and a voiceover that explained the processes shown in the images. They were divided into five groups, according to the basic representational maps which they formed in the brain in order to properly recognize and process the sensory stimuli. The viewers could 'direct' the axons or regulate the level of ethanol and witness the damage that it does to a healthy organism. At that point, the artist still lacked a concept for the sculpture that was to give the viewers access to the material that she had gathered.

Scott came up with the idea when she got to know one of the techniques for opening the spinal cord by dissecting it at the dorsal midline. The spinal cord can then be flipped open like a book. Hence the name of the procedure: 'open-book preparation.' The sculpture, *Somabook*, resembles an open book, but instead of pages it has two interactive screens and its spine resembles a backbone with the spinal cord. It has narrow ribbons on both sides. They look like steel nerves and are bent upwards, leading straight to the screens, as if they conducted sensory stimuli and made them visible on the screen. Surprisingly, Scott managed to create a link between the anatomy lessons that I addressed, traditional media and representations, and new methods of generating digital images, in other words a link between the sensory experience of reading and the virtual world. Significantly, this link was made possible by a laboratory technique which metaphorically alludes to old-day practices, but still belongs to the world of technologically advanced molecular neurobiology. Scott inadvertently did even more. By identifying a page from a book with a touch screen, she showed that today, just like in the past, our access to nature is always mediated not only by instruments and practices that have their own agency, as well as the assemblages of instruments and practices, but also through the authority of models and metaphors. All of the above-mentioned elements have been playing a crucial role in determining our perceptions of the human body and what has been defined as the bodily 'norm.'

Thus, taking into account the historically and culturally situated process of mediation, the analysis of the contribution of all the agents involved in it seems to be important for questioning the idea of 'the norm' and 'normalcy' in the field of Critical Disability Studies. More specifically, it is particularly relevant to the examination of the role of science in the construction of disability in line with the medical model as well as the study of prevalent, often metaphorical representation of disability which serve the function of what Sharon L. Snyder and David T. Mitchell call "narrative prosthesis" (see Goodley and Mackiewicz-Ziccardi's discussion of Mitchell and Snyder's work in their chapter), often depicting impairment as individual tragedy, medical pathology, or biological deficiency that needs to be heroically overcome. The analysis of various works of art, from Rembrandt's masterpieces to Jill Scott's *Somabook*, offering different, yet in some ways strikingly consistent lessons in anatomy, facilitates the examination of the myriad of technical and conceptual factors that have been involved in the medical study of the human body. It sheds light on the ways in which these works help challenge the belief in the unbiased and objective nature of the medical 'norm.'

Works Cited

Alpers, Svetlana. *The Art of Describing: Dutch Art in the Seventeenth Century*. Chicago, IL: University of Chicago Press, 1983. Print.

Cartwright, Lisa. *Screening the Body: Tracing Medicine's Visual Culture*. Minneapolis, MN: University of Minnesota Press, 1995. Print.

Davis, Lennard J., ed. *The Disability Reader*. 4th ed. London: Routledge, 2013. Print.

Davis, Lennard J. *Enforcing Normalcy: Disability, Deafness, and the Body*. London: Verso, 1995. Print.

Garland-Thomson, Rosemarie. *Extraordinary Bodies: Figuring Physical Disability in American Culture and Literature*. New York, NY: Columbia University Press, 1997. Print.

Keller, Evelyn Fox. *Making Sense of Life. Explaining Biological Development with Models, Metaphors, and Machines*. Cambridge, MS: Harvard University Press, 2002. Print.

Kirby, David A. *Lab Coats in Hollywood. Science, Scientists, and Cinema*. Cambridge, MS: MIT, 2010. Print.

Kooijmans, Luuc. *Niebezpieczna wiedza. Wizje i lęki w czasach Jana Swammerdama*. Trans. Robert Pucek. Warszawa: Aletheia, 2010. Print.

Mitchell, David T., and Sharon L. Snyder, *Narrative Prosthesis: Disability and the Dependencies of Discourse*. Ann Arbor, MI: The University of Michigan Press, 2000. Print.

Ostherr, Kirsten. *Medical Visions. Producing the Patient through Film, Television, and Imagining Technologies*. Oxford: Oxford University Press, 2013. Print.

Prince, Stephen. "True Lies: Perceptual Realism, Digital Images, and Film Theory." *Film Quarterly* 3 (1996): 27–37, http://fq.ucpress.edu/content/49/3/27. Accessed 3 Mar. 2019.

Rembrandt. *The Anatomy Lesson of Dr. Deijman*. 1656. Oil on canvas. Amsterdam Museum, Amsterdam.

Rembrandt. *The Anatomy Lesson of Dr. Nicolaes Tulp*. 1632. Oil on canvas. The Mauritshuis Museum, The Hague.

Scott, Jill. *The Electric Retina*. 2008. Installation. Premiered at Parcours des Wissens, The Brain Fair, University of Zurich, 8–16 Mar. 2008.

Scott, Jill. *Somabook*. 2010–12. Interactive media and sculpture. Premiered at the 16th Annual Meeting of the Swiss Society for Neuroscience, University of Zurich, 3 Feb. 2012.

Scott, Jill, and Esther Stoeckli, eds. *Neuromedia. Art and Neurosciences Research*. Berlin: Springer Verlag, 2012. Print.

Shapin, Steven, and Simon Schaffer. *Leviathan and the Air-Pump: Hobbes, Boyle and the Experimental Life*. Princeton, NJ: Princeton University Press, 1985. Print.

Siegal, Nina. *The Anatomy Lesson*. New York, NY: Anchor, 2014. Print.

Stollfuss, Sven. *Digitale Körperinnewelten. Endoskopische 3D-Animationen zwischen Medizin und Populärkultur*. Marburg: Schüren Verlag, 2014. Print.

Zimmer, Carl. *Soul Made Flesh. The Discovery of the Brain – and How It Changed the World*. New York, NY: Free, 2004. Print.

PART 2

Disability Film Festivals: The Politics of Representation and Participation

CHAPTER 4

Disability Cinema: Charting Alternative Ethical Maps of Living on Film

David T. Mitchell and Sharon L. Snyder

1 Introduction: An Alternative Ethical Map of Living

The topic with which we would like to begin is a contemplation of some overarching modes and methods operational in international in(ter)dependent disability films – particularly within the genre of disability documentary; although it is important to point out that we believe one cannot fully understand the form of disability documentary alone without a necessary juxtaposition alongside disability fiction films. Thus, we will move back and forth between two genres throughout this analysis.

Independent disability films, when contextualized and screened in a meaningful way within international disability film festivals, allow for a crucial alternative approach to imagining disability: namely, these visual works provide opportunities for not only raising public awareness about inclusion (i.e. the sharing of public space) but, even more importantly, global disability cinema (i.e. the filmic portrayals of disability from around the globe) now provides viewers with an alternative ethical map of living interdependently with each other. It thus challenges the ableist, neoliberal model of a "capable, independent, self-sufficient" individual about which Dan Goodley and Marek Mackiewicz-Ziccardi write in their chapter (41) and serves as what the editors of this volume call Rancierian "art of dissensus" which, in Steven Corcoran's words,

> cuts across forms of cultural and identity belonging and hierarchies between discourses and genres, working to introduce new subjects and heterogeneous objects into the field of perception.
>
> CORCORAN 2

Being part of the key shift in representational approaches to disability, this increased cultural and social visibility of disabled subjects has the potential to exponentially escalate audience understanding of disability as a productive social identity in its own right – one that complicates previous social model efforts to merely argue disabled people should be able to live as non-disabled people do (Mitchell and Snyder 4). Further, unlike policy focused efforts to

 | DOI:10.1163/9789004424678_006

restructure the physical terrain of barrier-ridden communities, independent disability films seek to change audience mindsets about the value of disabled lives; not merely by arguing for including them in the normative rituals of able-bodiedness, but through explicating lives that alternatively demonstrate the desirability of living interdependently with others. In other words, independent disability films do not tend to argue for Western-based norms of independence and productivity as the barometer of disabled peoples' successful integration; instead, they emphasize radically progressive intimacies made available through the explication of non-normative lives. Such portraits reveal an alternative ethical map of living that disability helps to unveil.

2 The Founding Sexual Prohibition

For instance, one fiction film by Stephen Lance called *Yolk* (2008) explores the narrative of a post-adolescent girl with the Down syndrome moving toward maturity and exploring her own sexuality. One of the ways we introduce this film to students and general audiences is to explain that the film is about the sexual prohibition of pursuing active experiences of pleasure – particularly for cognitively disabled women. A primary point to understand about the social management of people with disabilities in Western cultures revolves around sexual prohibition as a foundational cultural exclusion. As Tobin Siebers argues, reproductive withdrawal of sexual opportunities serves as a key impetus for most socially perpetuated violence against disabled people: it is one reason why disabled people are institutionalized, why marriage laws develop at the end of the nineteenth century, and why disabled people are coercively sterilized by nations practicing eugenic beliefs (38). The argument of eugenics, in the most straightforward gloss of its structure as a discriminatory belief system, was for states to remove forcibly disabled people from the reproductive pool of the country (Snyder and Mitchell 98).

During an audience Q&A at the 2015 DisArts Film Festival in Grand Rapids, Michigan (April 19–22, 2015), an individual made the earnest observation that he did not see *Yolk* as about the sexual oppression of disabled people. Instead, he only saw a film about a mother naturally concerned about her daughter's naïve interest in becoming sexually active. This comment seemed completely right except for the fact that the film only shows up at disability film festivals and is informed by the historical sexual prohibition of disabled women as the cultural backdrop against which its narrative unfolds. We also point out that the comment distorted the fact that we framed the film with respect to explorations of 'sexual prohibition' and not 'sexual oppression.' Those are different magnitudes of order for us and we had to make that correction. We said that

> this could be a film about sexual oppression, there is plenty of sexual oppression experienced by disabled people (disabled women in particular), but this film is not the vehicle for that topic.

Yolk is more in the family melodrama genre of film that requires one to bring the content of sexual prohibition to its story.

But, nonetheless, this exchange reminded the audience that the stakes are very high in these films. One key to understanding in(ter)dependent disability film is to recognize that these works understand serious social dangers and attempt to imagine more habitable worlds for members of multiple marginalized communities (racial, queer, female, cognitive, sensory, psychiatrically and physically disabled people). A pressing need to diminish feelings of audience alienation with embodied differences serves as their foundational political platform. There is an urgent social background against which all of these films develop. This recognition, we believe, is incredibly important to acknowledge in part because it is easy to miss this facet of their politicized objectives beneath the surface of their aestheticized presentations.

3 A 'Lack' of Cinematic Urgency

When viewing independent disability film one does not necessarily get a sense of that urgency. In general, the degree of desperation they conjure up within their plots exists on a relatively small scale. One can critique and/or feel dissatisfied with this absence of urgency given the violence of current circumstances, but disability film tries to ease audiences into a comfort with non-normative functionality and the appearance of socially excluded bodies. Each film brings audiences into the lives of their disabled characters and helps us negotiate these difficult social questions brought on by the historical exclusion of disabled people from social participation in a fairly gentle way. This is what independent disability film offers us at this historical moment of which we write (i.e. largely films made between the years 2000 and 2014). Expressing the desperate circumstances of many disabled peoples' lives is not the terrain that disability film inhabits. But, perhaps paradoxically, this desperation forms the complete background of the film narrative they generate.

So, for instance, in a film such as the Russian documentary *O Lubvi* (*About Love*, 2003) directed by Tofik Shakhverdiev, we are introduced to a cast of cute disabled children going to school in a segregated special education environment. The subjects talk about the relationships between boys and girls (both heterosexual and 'agnostic'), define their understanding of 'love' and sexuality, etc. But like many in(ter)dependent Russian disability films, *O Lubvi* is a celebration of Russian culture because the film features a celebration of their special education programmes; one could easily argue that *O Lubvi* is, in fact, about the love of devoted teachers and extended family caregivers. The film captures scenes of teachers carrying children who cannot walk to the chalkboard where they have to write their letters like everybody else. In portraying these scenes the film offers a truly beautiful vision of a supportive educational system focused, appropriately, on pedagogy and socialization for disabled children.

Yet, as the film unfolds, one might suddenly say to oneself, "Oh, I understand, the content here is actually about the abandonment of disabled children and how common that neglectful situation has become." Also, there is the fact that nations – this happens in the US as well as Russia – have to create these massive support systems in order to take up care for disabled children rejected by their families. Such children are commonly left at hospitals and in orphanages by their parents, or the parents just cannot provide the level of care needed, given the lack of social support and the economic demands placed on their lives: abandonment can now be recognized as part and parcel of contemporary austerity measures under neoliberalism, which we broadly define elsewhere, using Henry Giroux words, as "the arrival of … 'hyper-market-driven societies [that] organize identities largely as consumers'" (*Biopolitics of Disability* 4), whose constraints produce "a tightly limited form of inclusion for 'diverse' citizens" (*Biopolitics of Disability* v). Likewise, *O Lubvi* also helps audiences take into account the commonality of men who leave relationships as a result of the birth of a disabled child.

On 28 December 2012, Russia's President Putin signed a law that stated the country would no longer allow people in countries such as the United States to adopt Russian children … with the exception of disabled ones. Disabled children could continue to be adopted but all other Russian children were off the international adoption market block. So everywhere in these films one finds an incredibly urgent, desperate situation informing their materials. And yet despite this hazardous social terrain, these films ease us into their materials with little fanfare; you could watch them without ever taking note of the desperate circumstances to which they give voice. In many ways these works encourage viewers to feel free to watch their narratives without attending to the alarm of social neglect and violence residing in the background. But, at bottom, independent disability cinema wants the seriousness of materials to slowly emerge and make an impression on audiences without throttling them, so to speak: this is their deal with the social devil of ableism in many ways. The urgency of the issues is downplayed in order to secure a wider general audience and/or to depend upon the knowledgeable investments of their audiences across in(ter)dependent disability film networks.

Since these films are often financed by nationally sponsored arts funding organizations, they are, to a certain extent, expressions of the state's desirability. When we speak of in(ter)dependent disability films, we refer to predominantly video-based works created on low budgets (less than USD $100,000 but in many cases below USD $10,000) and without the backing of multi-national corporations that often promote other minority film festivals. Independent disability films derive largely from local community contexts but speak globally to people with disabilities living around the world. To some degree, one could extrapolate their collective message as a voicing of paternalistic states; they seem to say, "We even take care of our disabled populations no matter how little they have to contribute to the robust life of the citizenry."

The tenuous line that must be navigated between personal story and public critique is exemplified most powerfully in documentary films such as *goodnight, liberation* (2003) by the African American filmmaker Oriana Bolden. *goodnight, liberation* serves as an example of what we refer to as the 'Introduction to My Disability' films. Many films screened at disability film festivals are about introducing audiences to disability conditions through discussions of symptom clusters and the negotiation of stigmatizing public responses. Collectively these works offer an entré into the unique experiences of living within non-normative bodies by saying, "here's what it's like to exist in my particular kind of body." Consequently, these films have an unabashedly diagnostic impulse behind them. Effectively they argue that if we understand a particular disability from the point of view of the bearer, audiences will have an easier time relating with and accepting other disabled people who share a particular medical label.

This journey into a certain level of medical complexity represents a significant impulse in in(ter)dependent disability documentary films. Except that in the case of *goodnight, liberation*, Bolden's film gives you a taste of the 'Introduction to My Disability' genre only to turn the tables on the scenario completely. The documentary uses a search for the diagnosis of what is troubling the narrator physically (bleeding gums, unexplained bruises on her abdomen, chronic stomach upset) in order to expose a lack of systemic access to public healthcare in the United States. So once again a film such as *goodnight, liberation* reverses its more individualistic trajectory while having a serious message couched in minoritarian social justice terms.

4 Alternative Disability Universes

A significant alternative to the 'Introduction to My Disability' genre (nearly always an expression of documentary form) are disability films that use all-disabled ensembles of actors. The employment of disabled actors proves highly uncommon in the US but, for instance, in the UK there is now a stipulation that companies may not hire a non-disabled actor to play a disability part. Among all of the things that such an employment practice allows is the creation of film worlds wherein the exclusionary isolation most people with disabilities experience is inverted. One may think this practice leads to the portrayal of significant stories about collective action (and this does happen to an extent such as in the first film discussed below). However, the works about alternative disability universes tend to narrate the tensions and fissures that exist across and between disability groupings.

For instance, in the ensemble cast of Louis Levacher's short French fiction film, *Sang Froid* (*Cold Blood*, 2002), one views deaf people cast as animalistic predators chasing a hysterical able-bodied human prey across a snowy landscape. The prey and predators arrive at a church near the end of the chase, the person being pursued hides behind a life-sized Jesus crucified on the cross, and much mayhem ensues. The deaf vampires are stopped at the sight of the cross as if the overwhelming Christianity of the symbol halts them from their pursuits (this is also a law of vampire films). After realizing that the place is being protected, the once-pursued hearing character begins to laugh hysterically at the deaf vampires' inability to continue their attack. In the middle of a 360-degree shot things change and the vampires begin pointing and laughing at the Christ-like figure on the cross, who comes to life with fanged teeth and devours the figure of their pursuit from above.

So no sanctuary within the religious setting is allowed and the church – which has been historically presumed as a social sanctuary for disabled people – turns out otherwise in this reversal of fortunes (and able-bodied to disabled bodies performance ratios). In fact, the film goes on to show other people asleep in their beds in a nearby rural village also being attacked in a similar way by smaller bronze-and-silver Jesuses. The now animated statues jump in commando-like fashion from their stations on tiny wooden crucifixes nailed above their beds for protection. The horrified shrieks of unsuspecting villagers fill the night air. There is nothing made of the fact that the vampires are deaf in the film but they survive while the hearing world continues to experience the assault of their own imprisoning religious tradition.

In general what one comes to understand about disability films is their primary emphasis on the removal of stigma from disabled bodies and the transfer of that social debasement onto those who would perpetuate it. They are, in other words, about depathologization at their most basic level. Within such an effort to gather up those on the margins of the margins, the alternative disability universes on display in in(ter)dependent disability films expose cultural norms (and the models of disability that they give birth to and perpetuate) for what they really are: inelastic standards of homogeneity incapable of accommodating a wide array of human diversity. In contrast, international in(ter)-dependent disability film festivals have become new spaces of social collectivity-making: as people with disabilities find themselves denied ways to narrate viable futures for themselves, in(ter)dependent disability cinema allows an exploration of alternative modes of transmission and the creative exploration of non-normative modes of being (Kafer 2). In this sense, it could well be said to work in accordance with the egalitarian principles of the Rancierian aesthetic regime of the arts, as described by the editors in their introductory chapter. At their best, in(ter)dependent disability films themselves may be seen as acts of dissensus that challenge the unjust, exclusionary status quo, as they acknowledge and validate alternative ways of being in the world, and lead to the subjectification of non-normative collectivities.

In a UK short such as Martin Taylor's *Berocca* (2005), the main story is told through interactions of an all-disabled cast. This genre of film (almost always fiction but usually drawing upon disabled actors who share congregate settings) often shows up at disability film festivals in the form of a plot puzzle. It is hard to say what many of these films are about as they thrive on the experimental, the allegorical, and the mysteries of unfamiliar, non-normative life forms. *Berocca,* for instance, forwards a plot about a disabled man with cerebral palsy who is illegally selling after-market Viagra to a pharmacist who also happens to be parenting a young boy. The young boy – who turns out to be the son of Kohl, the film's disabled protagonist – has been removed by the state to live with a foster family due to a charge of negligence on the part of Kohl who has no legal gainful employment to support him. In undertaking this plot, the film also points out that parenting a disabled child provides the basis for state removal of children from the home.

Near the conclusion Kohl and his mute companion (one is tempted to read the child as a symbolic fragment of the adult protagonist's psyche) arrive at the coast of the British Isle. The differences between the two characters prove intense: the father's neurological differences contrasting with the son's intensity of introspection and muteness (some reviews of the film identify the boy as autistic). Ultimately the film turns out to be about the struggle to identify, communicate, and establish some meaningful connection between these two divergent disabled bodies. The two characters inhabit distinct, and certainly not automatically overlapping, neuroatypical worlds and the challenge is to see if the film can create a bridge between them. This connection fails in some significant ways and one is left contemplating the degree to which disability film is about incomplete, imperfect, and missed opportunities for connection between non-normative human actors.

The matter of minority group solidarity is at stake with respect to disabled people, disability communities, and everyone who cares and works on these issues. The issue now plaguing various social movements is – and we want to argue this must be recognized as an alternative strength within crip/queer collectivities – the degree to which we can search for unity across differences without jettisoning their content-specific cargo. For instance, in the Scottish autism film *I'm in Away from Here* (2007) by Catriona MacInnes, the audience awakens with Archie, suddenly and without warning along a Scottish beach. Signalled by distortions on the audio and video tracks, the world crashes in upon viewers as well as the protagonist; we cannot interpret the story amidst these sensorial intrusions coming from every direction. Disability films employ experimental narrative techniques such as these as ways to 'simulate interior subjectivities' that offer access to disabled people's ways of experiencing the world directly. They are, in effect, disability simulation stories and their phenomenological content attempts to place the viewer within the confines of a developed disability subjectivity.

The alternative disability universe of *I'm in Away from Here* helps to underscore a key element in the earlier film *Berocca*, in that they both attempt to situate audiences within the perspectives of their disabled characters. So, for instance, in the latter film we experience sensory events through the autistic protagonist, Archie, in order to understand his life through a series of interruptions he experiences throughout his daily travels. Thus, the best way to describe the plot of this film might be through our exposure to the discomfort of the myriad intrusions that enter into his personal space. His inability to control these unwanted interruptions of his personal space become part of our own annoyance and hindrance to pleasure, but they also provide an alternative simulation of embodiment as an opportunity to widen audience perspectives on this corner of disability experience.

Early on in the film Archie takes up with a friend named Bruno, who also has a disability (likely CP and he uses a wheelchair), and they spend most of their days together within the limited options offered by life in a Day Centre. The two grow frustrated with the adherence to arbitrary rules, incomprehensible social cure, and the deadening pursuits prescribed by the Day Centre staff. Rejecting these limited options, they go off to pursue more adventurous worlds on their own – such as life at a nearby pub that includes Archie gambling on a brightly coloured Lotto machine and sex with a prostitute for Bruno. As in the earlier films mentioned above, the two characters struggle to make a connection and at the conclusion they roll off toward the harbour with the sun glinting in the background and tell each other in a simple, yet reassuring manner something that the outside able-bodied world refuses to say: "You're all right." This sentiment is echoed by Archie's mother waiting anxiously at the Day Centre when they return worried that her autistic son has walked off and the staff has no idea of his whereabouts. When his mother sees him return safely, her relief is spoken by words that echo Bruno's words: "It's all right, Archie."

In other words, the film asks us to contemplate whether a strictly regulated form of institutionalized care is necessary to protect disabled participants. Like the other characters in the film, audiences are also reassured that Archie has his own strategies for navigating a turbulent life as others must negotiate them. Rather, a socially paternalistic protectionism seems to be acting more on behalf of protection for the able-bodied world rather than the other way around.

5 Who Owns Disability Representations?

Even in mainstream media it is very uncommon to find stories about the relationship between mothers and daughters. As an example of the immersion and exposure to atypical lives that in(ter)dependent disability films offer, Norah McGettigan's short fiction film *What It Is Like To Be My Mother* (2007) uses a family drama to stage a now common political conflict between disabled people and non-disabled image-makers about the necessity of policing the borders of disability representation. In the film, a non-disabled daughter makes a film about the life of her newly disabled mother who has become a double amputee. The film gets selected for screening at 'the last minute' by a disability arts festival in Warsaw and the story unfolds based on the mother's ensuing reluctance to allow her to screen her naked double amputee body for a public audience. A debate erupts about who owns the disability image and whether or not even an intimacy such as the one between a mother and daughter is enough to allow respectful entry into the disabled character's life.

During the festival screening of the film, the mother hastily rolls out of the theatre and decides to manually propel herself home (hundreds of miles away from the theatre) in a torrential rainstorm. Whereas the mother's character appears relatively unlikable to this point of the film (both a bit tyrannical and exhibitionistic), she tells the daughter that she became upset while watching the film. The reason for this emotionality is that she realizes how mature the daughter is becoming (certainly capable of telling her story in a moving way) and that she inevitably will have to leave her someday to pursue her own adult life.

As with all of the independent disability films discussed to this point, a real-life urgency at the bottom of the film emerges in that many disabled people – like the mother – need caregivers to navigate their lives and that care is often most effectively and comfortably provided by family members. The mother's prospects of developing her own romantic relationship appear slim. For instance, she tells her daughter a story about a disabled female friend of hers who is rejected by a male partner because "he cannot trust himself to not leave her in ten years." If she were not disabled, he explains, he would never have had this thought. Thus, the mother becomes suddenly more sympathetic in revealing these personal details and making herself vulnerable to the daughter.

In turn, the daughter – through whose eyes we have watched the action unfold – uses the opportunity of this private revelation to reject the mother's efforts at renewed intimacy between them. She calls her a "stupid cow" and tells her taxi-cab driver, Jurek, that he should refuse to drive her around Poland in the future. In the culminating scene in the mother's bedroom after the emotion-filled night, the mother removes her prosthetic legs with great delicacy for the audience and asks the daughter to hug her. The daughter grows stiff and refuses to return the show of affection. A stalemate develops and the film ends in discomforting irresolution.

One of the things that disability film allows audiences to do is to comprehend the degree to which they allow us to sit with non-normative bodies in public spaces. Such an opportunity remains relatively rare in that we usually do not get to share public space with those with severe impairments. The fact that film is the kind of imaginative site where one can gain intimacy with people who inhabit different bodies and that opportunity, in and of itself, is a very powerful political emphasis within disability film. If you go to disability film festivals you quickly realize that these works are global vehicles; they do not simply originate in the US or the UK or Australia, the usual triumvirate of disability 'savvy' Western nations. Instead, in(ter)dependent disability cinema represents a global phenomenon where disabled people think about what people within one national boundary have done to make their lives more manageable and then attempt to export some of those strategies to their home towns in order to affect transformations in their own local arenas.

We want to think about this wider principle of disability access and the creation of multiple accessible spaces as the advent of more habitable forms of living and environments for disabled people. Consequently, we have been arguing that we need to understand disability as a baseline model of interdependency rather than a tangential or exceptional situation. The kinds of inclusion on display in in(ter)dependent disability films are much more than outside efforts to include four or five more people in a culture; rather they help us think about disability as a foundational dissensual cultural model for re-imagining how human beings might inhabit the Earth together. In early April 2015, during a presentation to a Chinese disability delegation at George Washington University (where we teach) we explained to the gathered dignitaries that

> [w]e're not particularly good at getting along with each other in the world, inhabiting the world with other human beings is not particularly our forte, and we think disability culture has something to teach us about that because of the degree to which interdependency is an in-built, consciously created, intergenerational necessity.

That value of in(ter)dependency is what disability culture has to teach us in a much wider sense about better inhabiting the Earth with each other. Thus, this unveiling of alternative possibilities within disability universes turns disability into not only a target of oppression, attitudinal prejudice, and exclusions through the imposition of social barriers, but rather a productive value of non-normative embodiment. Audiences discover alternative ethical maps by which to live their lives in contrast to the majority of others pursuing normative habitudes.

6 Afficionados of Human Variation

This innovative, alternative cultural value of interdependency also plays a key role in films about disability dance. We call the primary thematic of these films, 'disability in motion.' The works within this category prove significant in the sense that one often hears, "Well, disabled people they don't move and they certainly don't dance! We all know that." In other words, this is a foundational paradox at the heart of much independent disability film. One of the best examples of films sharing this central concern about disability movements is the UK film *The Cost of Living* (2004) directed by Lloyd Newsome. *The Cost of Living* was made by the UK mixed disabilities theatre and dance company DV8. All of the primary dancers and performers in DV8 have significant disabilities and that fact in and of itself makes DV8 an incredible originator. This film is one of the most powerful and interesting films to come out of the independent disability cinema movement in the past two decades.

When we originally viewed this film, we had the good fortune of watching it in the company of disability performance studies professor Carrie Sandahl from the University of Illinois at Chicago. As we were watching the film, we were asking ourselves, "Why is this film so amazing?" Carrie made this insightful comment:

> Watch the way the film uses the alternative bodily movements, rhythms, and flows of the disabled performance artists rather than the other way around [i.e. disabled peoples' bodies mimicking the movements of the more graceful able-bodied performers around them]. The plane of disabled existences and the movement of very disabled bodies sets the rhythm, the score, the shape, the texture of the film itself.

And that is one of the truly powerful things about the film.

The other thing we want to argue is that we began this chapter with an observation about the rare instance of inhabiting public space with disabled bodies. This observation is at the basis of most independent disability film. These events are now held all over the world in nearly every major urban cosmopolitan urban centre: Helsinki, Milan, London, Paris, Brazil, New Zealand, and there are several in the United States, Canada, Australia, and Japan. In other words, independent disability film is a serious global phenomenon. And when you go to other disability film festivals, just like other events, they are like marathon events – events that no disabled person can quite do successfully! Three days of film programming, screening disability film after disability film for eight, nine, ten hours at a time, and by the end of the day one has to try to rest in order to struggle and endure the following day of programming.

But we think that spending that much time with disabled bodies in a theatre for this expansive space of time has a powerful effect. By the end of this continual exposure to non-normative bodies at the disability film festival one becomes a connoisseur of bodily difference. One starts to think of oneself as a kind of aficionado of human variation in much of its dissimulated richness in the outside world. One comes away from the disability film festival thinking: "One of the values I took away from this experience was getting incredibly comfortable with the massive variation that human bodies show up in."

For instance, Christian Von Tippelskirch's disability documentary film *Invitation to Dance* (2014) tells the story of the life and times of US disability scholar, activist, and dance advocate, Simi Linton. One of the most important things about a film such as *Invitation to Dance* is that filmmakers allow us to consider the fact that in many ways we do not know how to do this awkward, world-fragmenting dance of disability. Linton's film allows us to admit that and yet keep going with this invention as a guiding value. There are so few things in the world of able-bodiedness that can help disabled people more effectively manage their own lives. As Alison Kafer says in the film, "We're all uncomfortable with the way our bodies move."

At the 2010 SDS (Society for Disability Studies) conference a flash dance erupted out in the main intersection of the campus. The impromptu event stopped traffic in order to allow disabled people to celebrate their bodies. What struck us about the conference participants is that the world of disabled people continues to be experienced as the violation of powerful taboos about displaying the disabled body in public on disability terms. It is not an artefact of the past – this was the year 2010. And the event led to an incredibly complex, uncomfortable, harassing situation. This response accompanied, at the same time, an organization of disabled people trying to create an alternative public space, a way of life that might prove more sustaining, creative, and enjoyable than anything that non-disabled culture would provide for them. The flash dance offered nothing less than a glimpse at an alternative way to be disabled in the world. *Invitation to Dance* takes up this very project in a serious, unfinished, imperfect pursuit of crip/queer bodies, almost like a Cubist experiment. As Rosemarie Garland-Thomson says on screen, "This is broadest invitation to dance that has ever been issued in the history of the world!." Yet it turns out to be an incredibly fraught subject in so many ways.

Disability movements (including the independent international film festivals they help spawn) have to re-imagine exclusionary public spaces including alternative theatre seating layouts, presentation formats and projection techniques. Yet, ultimately, what independent disability film seeks to target is the domain of public consciousness. It is one thing to be able to get on the bus and enter into public space – this is a huge innovation of global disability rights movements – but it is another to change the attitudinal reception of disabled peoples' entry into the world. Film, ultimately, tries to transform the realm of public consciousness. The medium tries to change our perspective by giving us access to disabled peoples' subjectivities. It is this targeting of the attitudinal domain that is so difficult to get at from anywhere other than film art. Getting disabled people into the public is definitely part of this transformation; just the fact of getting us to share public space in a way that has rarely happened in history is part of the change of our moment. This is the reason why the disability rights movement is so significant to the way we live now (to borrow the theme of Germany's 2007 disability short film festival) in that it helps reconfigure

Rancière's distribution of the sensible.[1] However, in and of itself, that is not enough. There is an entire other domain that is often off limits to us: how do we affect peoples' belief systems, the attitudes, their ideas, and their conceptualization of people with disabilities? That is where we see film's most significant, potential innovation.

One last point on which to end regarding the accessibility of film festivals to disabled people. Films, like other products such as books, once one produces them, have a life of their own. They go out into the world without you, like children or students, and you do not always know how they will turn out or how they will be received. Getting disabled people to a film festival, such as the April 2015 DisArts extravaganza in Grand Rapids, Michigan, is very difficult. Many people cannot travel; if you travel on airlines they commonly break power wheelchairs due to inadequate handling procedures – there is a great deal one has to exchange in order to participate in such global events. One of things about film is that it travels in a rectangular box on a round disc. So it goes really easily without the participants in an envelope. We think this is one of the key reasons why disability film festivals have become so significant – they offer a kind of tiny mobility across national borders that disabled people themselves do not enjoy. If you try to move across borders as a disabled person, as we did recently in early March 2015 with a group of students studying Action T4 in Germany, you could find yourself pulled out of line by a guard suggesting a BiPAP machine might have a bomb in it. You might find yourself (as we did) taken off into an interrogation room and nearly made to miss your flight. Disability film festivals serve as a key way in which disabled people might be able to communicate through the physical barriers of mass transit inaccessibility, heightened police security, intensive immigration restrictions, and poverty.

But even all of those hassles aside, we would rather see the world and participate in it than observe it from the sidelines where so many disabled people are sequestered. That risk of going out into the world is worth it, but it is highly draining at the same time. So when that cannot happen, film also does that for us. It gets disabled people into the space with an audience and gives us access to their lives. An intimacy with disabled persons' perspectives becomes available even when they live in radically divergent corners of the globe.

1 As the editors of this volume explain in their introductory chapter, distribution of the sensible "is a system of rules that both assigns the roles and functions that people have in a society and determines what can be said and seen" (3).

7 Conclusion

While each film discussed wrestles with its own particular struggles with ableist nationalist practices and beliefs, its own ensnarement within neoliberal orders of reproductive sameness resulting from more meagre forms of inclusion, the ensemble of films available for viewing across the space of multi-day international film festivals significantly pluralize encounters with human variations. They tend toward a diminishment of audience alienation with embodied differences while avoiding the alternative problem of flattening the field with platitudes of claims to universally shared identities in disability. We suggest, in drawing upon these multivalent media portrayals of disability in various global locations, that the exploration of subjectivities wrought within neoliberalism unveils alternative possibilities for an ethics of living interdependently with others developed within disability subcultures.

Such explorations of experiential navigations involve the opening up of formerly prohibited interactions based on sexuality, body care, arts/cultural programming, shared access to public and private spaces, intrusions upon bodies, and the ambivalences of disability inclusion projects. In each of the examples provided, disability's 'failures' to meet ableist expectations result in dissensual inversions that challenge the assumed positivity of heteronormative practices, beliefs, and capacities provisioned for able bodies.[2]

Works Cited

Corcoran, Steven. "Editor's Introduction." *Dissensus: On Politics and Aesthetics*. By Jacques Rancière. London: Continuum, 2010. 1–24. Print.

Kafer, Alison. *Feminist, Queer, Crip*. Indianapolis, IN: University of Indiana Press, 2013. Print.

Mitchell, David T., and Sharon L. Snyder. *The Biopolitics of Disability: Neoliberalism, Ablenationalism, and Peripheral Embodiment*. Ann Arbor, MI: University of Michigan Press, 2015. Print.

Siebers, Tobin. "A Sexual Culture for Disabled People." *Sex and Disability*. Ed. Robert McRuer and Anna Mollow. Durham, DC: Duke University Press, 2012. 37–52. Print.

2 The chapter was originally published as "Global In(ter)dependent Disability Cinema: Targeting Ephemeral Domains of Belief and Cultivating Aficionados of the Body" in *Cultures of Representation: Disability in World Cinema Contexts* by Benjamin Fraser, ed.

Snyder, Sharon L., and David T. Mitchell. *Cultural Locations of Disability*. Chicago, IL: University of Chicago Press, 2006. Print.

Filmography

Bolden, Oriana, dir. *goodnight, liberation*. 7 minutes. USA, 2003.
Lance, Stephen, dir. *Yolk*. 14 minutes. Australia, Head Pictures, 2008.
Levacher, Pierre-Louis, dir. *Sang Froid* (*Cold Blood*). 6 minutes. France, 2002.
MacInnes, Catriona, dir. *I'm in Away from Here*. 16 minutes. Scotland, 2007.
McGettigan, Norah, dir. *What It Is Like to Be My Mother*. 30 minutes. Poland, 2007.
Newsom, Lloyd, dir. *The Cost of Living*. 35 minutes. UK, DV8 Films, 2004.
Shakhverdiev, Tofik, dir. *O Lubvi* (*About Love*). 26 minutes. Russia, 2003.
Taylor, Martin, dir. *Berocca*. 13 minutes. UK, 2005.
Von Tippelskirch, Christian, dir. *Invitation to Dance*. 86 minutes. USA, 2014.

CHAPTER 5

Disability Film Festivals: The Spaces where Crip Killjoys Take Action

Maria Tsakiri

In this chapter I examine disability film festivals as the spaces where the representations of disability in films, and more specifically in documentary films, work towards a change that is required to develop new understandings of disability. I claim that the representations that lead to this change are representations of "crip killjoys" (Johnson and McRuer). I also argue that disability film festivals combine arts and activism, bringing together crip killjoys, giving them the space to take action, and challenging notions of normative aesthetics and compulsory able-bodiedness. I mainly focus on the Emotion Pictures – Documentary & Disability International Festival where I undertook my fieldwork at the beginning of my research. This case study will be placed in the bigger picture of other disability film festivals which I examined in my doctoral project.

1 The Emotion Pictures – Documentary & Disability International Festival

Emotion Pictures – Documentary & Disability International Festival was the first festival in Greece that focused on disability and was part of a worldwide artistic movement. Held in Athens, it became one more node in the disability film festivals network, among other popular festivals such as: The Other Film Festival in Melbourne, Picture This … Film Festival in Calgary, Breaking Down Barriers – International Disability Film Festival in Moscow, The Way We Live – International Short Film Festival in Munich, and London's Disability Film Festival. Some of the above-mentioned events are still running, taking forward issues related to disability, art, access, and inclusion. Some of them though fell victim to funding cuts and their functioning is currently suspended.

The Emotion Pictures – Documentary & Disability International Festival was organized by the Secretariat General of Information and Communication, in collaboration with the Greek Film Centre. It was funded and promoted by various organizations and cultural foundations, such as the John F. Costopoulos Foundation, the Institut Français d'Athènes, the British Council, the Goethe

 DOI:10.1163/9789004424678_007

Institute, and the Beijing Film Academy. The festival was hosted at the new Benaki Museum building and entrance was free of charge. During daytime, screenings took place at the amphitheatre of the museum, capable of seating three hundred people, whereas at night the courtyard, which covers a space of 850 sq. m., was used, giving a sense of a summer cinema. Viewers had a chance to watch as many films as they wished. The programme included three-day screenings, followed by discussion panels with filmmakers, disabled people who were the main characters of the documentaries, and the festival organizers. Special screenings on the themes of "Disability & Environment," "War and Disability," and "Autism" were organized with the support of the High Commission of the United Nations (UN), the World Wide Fund for Nature (WWF), Greenpeace, and Médecins sans Frontières (Doctors without Borders). Special events also took place during the opening and closing ceremonies of the festival with guests who were well-known for their involvement in the international disability community. On the last day of the screenings, the International Annual Conference "People with Disabilities and Mass Media" started in connection with the Emotion Pictures Festival, funded and organized by the Greek Secretariat General of Information and Communication.

It is important to mention that the festival made a significant impact well beyond the borders of the Greek capital. In 2010 and 2011, numerous municipalities and associations organized events hosting screenings of films that had earlier been shown at the festival. The festival organizers also collaborated with the University of Thessaly, the Technological Educational Institute of Crete, and the Aristotle University of Thessaloniki, where educational screenings took place. The Primary Education Department of the University of Crete included screenings and workshops from the Emotion Pictures Festival in the programme of an international symposium attended by two hundred scholars and teachers. The list of collaborators also includes universities in the USA and Europe, such as the University of Pennsylvania, Bryn Mawr College, Swarthmore College, Brown University, and the Aix-Marseille Université. Links with other film festivals around the world were developed through support and participation, aiming at a collaboration that would empower disabled people's voice and promote social dialogue. One of the major actions undertaken as part of the festival was the distribution of an educational package, with the award-winning films being circulated to three thousand schools in Greece and abroad in collaboration with the Greek diaspora (the USA, Canada, and Australia). This project was sponsored by the Stavros Niarchos Foundation, with the support of the UNESCO.

As stated on the official website of the event, the festival's aim was:

> to bring to prominence, using the documentary as the medium, the concern of artists from all over the world on disability issues and to encourage the development of a fruitful social dialogue in Greece with art – the common language of us all – as the starting-point.
>
> "Festival"[1]

The organizers characterized the festival as: "a cultural event, a meeting place, and a celebration" ("Festival"). Trying to communicate a clear message to the audience, they adopted the slogan: "Diversity is the only truth that unites us all" ("Festival").

Sharon L. Snyder and David T. Mitchell argue that corporate backing is not usually established at the early stages of the development of major disability film festivals and that the "concept of disability collectivity is elusive" within these developing organizational structures (12). The main action is directed towards destigmatization. The sponsors that support the organization of disability film festivals vary depending on the size and the objectives of each event. State funding in some cases helped festivals get established and grow, but in other cases proved to be problematic as these events did not receive consistent financial support and therefore had to end their functioning. Collectivity grows when the festivals grow and pursue their inclusive, political, and activist goals. Either in their formative stages or as established events, disability film festivals bring an element of change. In a sense, they serve as what the editors of this volume in their introductory chapter describe as vehicles for Rancierian dissensus, which help rethink and restructure the existing social status quo in a more egalitarian fashion and facilitate the subjectification of disabled people.

This change has an impact on different levels. Firstly, in the context of disability film festivals which "operate as active filters for forging new ways of 'being disabled'" (Snyder and Mitchell 13), the arrangement of a public space has to accommodate all viewers' needs. Reimagining and redesigning public space for the needs of film festivals help raise the awareness of the necessity of providing accessibility to all bodies. Secondly, the multiple functions of the festivals and the audience's exposition to various representations tease out identity issues. According to Sharon L. Snyder and David T. Mitchell, "[d]isability film festivals actively disrupt static boundaries of disability identity – even with respect to disabled peoples' concepts of their own collective make-up" (14). All attendees go through an experience that causes various reactions as it leads to a change. As Catherine Frazee warned the audience at the

1 The official English translation published on the Festival's website.

Unruly Salon sessions, which was a series of events related to disability arts, culture, and studies, held at the University of British Columbia in Vancouver, Canada,

> There will be turbulence and majesty, encounters with the profane and the divine, illuminations that both affirm and unsettle. There will be nervous laughter, gut wrenching howls, pin-drop silence and riotous enthusiasm. There will be bafflement, resonance and revelation. And you will be changed.
>
> FRAZEE 8

Similarly, disability film festivals are the spaces where all of the above-mentioned reactions take place. People with or without experience of disability are exposed to stories and images that may reaffirm or challenge their views, shock and surprise them, make them laugh, and give them new information. This impact is the first step to becoming aware of disability and its complexities. Snyder and Mitchell see disability film festivals as "depathologising contexts" that contribute to the destigmatizing efforts of disability communities. Sharing their views after participating in a few festivals as disability studies scholars and independent filmmakers, the authors describe their function quite clearly: "[t]his agonistic, cross-cultural, and cross-disability space becomes the site where the social implications of rights and policy-based initiatives are worked through for locals" (Snyder and Mitchell 12).

Disability film festivals are also the spaces where viewers are introduced to disability aesthetics and new ways of looking, so all the actions taken in these spaces should be coordinated towards their fundamental mission. It can be argued that changing the ways of looking at disability and becoming familiar with disability aesthetics can lead to the development of inclusive thinking. Tobin Siebers, in his introduction to disability aesthetics, notes that reinforcing the influence of disability in arts requires a revision of traditional conceptions of aesthetic production and appreciation. This process will also challenge established aesthetic presuppositions (Siebers 71).

The organizers of The Other Film Festival, a biennial event held in Melbourne, officially established the provocative question of "What are you looking at?" as the subtitle/slogan of the festival. This aims to challenge all of the uncomfortable looks that disabled people have been receiving in their encounters with non-disabled people. The interesting thing is that disability film festivals can expose a variety of looks through the point-of-view perspective employed in some of the screened films and educate their participants about the ways of looking. According to Mitchell and Snyder,

> multiple ways of viewing disability made available to audiences participating in disability film festivals play a key role in what could be called the politics of atypicality – the refusal to remain within the strict boundaries of medically and socially prescribed categories of sameness.
>
> Mitchell and SNYDER 14

The viewers are exposed to a variety of depictions that are devoid of didactic or medical undertones. Disabled people come on the screen with their stories that usually offer close-ups of numerous human conditions. Disability film festivals offer space for engaged staring encounters where disabled people guide the viewers on how to look at them. As Rosemarie Garland-Thomson notes in her analysis of staring, "the impulse to stare at novel sights … can move the audience towards a 'newness' that can be transformative" (188). In February 2003, Harriet McBryde-Johnson, an American author, attorney, and disability rights activist, stated in "Unspeakable Conversations" written for *The New York Times Magazine*: "It's not that I'm ugly. It's more that most people don't know how to look at me." Disability film festivals engage viewers with a range of 'tutorials' on different ways of looking at disabled bodies, bringing disabled people's life stories closer to the audience. This interaction, although virtual and mediated, allows viewers to become more familiar with the presence and actions of disabled bodies.

2 Crip Theory and Crip Killjoys

Combining disability studies and queer theory, Robert McRuer's crip theory, whose tenets Dan Goodley and Marek Mackiewicz-Ziccardi examine in Chapter 2, accentuates that access should be understood "both very specifically and very broadly, locally and globally" (McRuer, *Crip Theory* 71). One of crip theory's main principles refers to constructing an accessible world in opposition to neoliberalism. Another principle insists "that the disabled world is possible," as a counter-argument to the leftist movements tied to "liberationist models that need disability as the raw material against which the imagined future world is formed" (McRuer, *Crip Theory* 71). Neoliberalism brought changes to the role of the welfare state and government intervention (Owen and Harris). Neoliberal approaches prioritize the development of the free market and economy, rather than social rights, and this had an impact on benefit provision policies: reassessing the criteria for eligibility and introducing employability plans for disabled people. There was a wave of welfare reform in the UK from 1997 to 2010, based on the motto "no rights without responsibilities" (Owen and Harris).

This came along with the re-entrenchment of social rights, which affected disabled people, fitting in well with what Garland-Thomson and Ojrzyńska in their chapter call "the contemporary capitalist logic of disposability" (22). As Randall Owen and Sarah Parker Harris state,

> The impacts of the neoliberalism can be summarized by considering that neoliberalism embodies the recommodification of labor; that is, market participation is required for an individual to meet their needs and be considered a citizen. While governments have adopted this approach to varying degrees, individual needs are now the responsibility of the individual and they receive minimal government assistance.

Flexibility in the labour market was introduced as a motivation for disabled people to go into employment, and employers, according to equality and diversity policies, should make reasonable adjustments to accommodate equal opportunities. This concept of flexibility, though, proved problematic and disabled people's rights were retrenched as a result of neoliberal practices reconceptualizing human rights.

The notion of a "crip killjoy" is a recent development that combines feminist and crip theories. Merri Lisa Johnson and Robert McRuer draw upon Sara Ahmed's work on feminist "killjoys" and "willfulness" to create the ideas of "crip killjoy" and "crip willfulness." Ahmed examines happiness and sociocultural instructions for acting happy in an oppressive context where individuals' (particularly female individuals') positioning is imposed, fixed, and ordered, according to society's perceptions of different social categories. She specifically notes that

> [t]he figure of the feminist killjoy makes sense if we place her in the context of feminist critiques of happiness, of how happiness is used to justify social norms as social goods (a social good is what causes happiness, given happiness is understood as what is good).... Not to agree to stay in the place of this wish might be to refuse the happiness that is wished for. To be involved in political activism is thus to be involved in a struggle against happiness.
>
> AHMED, "Feminist Killjoys"

Crip killjoys also refuse to fake satisfaction and happiness to justify social norms that are actually oppressive for disabled people. According to Johnson and McRuer, disabled people are called to deal daily with "[t]he inter-implications of capacity and debility," which, as in the authors' cases, lead them to "crip willfulness." As they explain,

> It is a refusal to insist – a refusal to act in accordance with the system of compulsory able-bodiedness – that requires individuals to mask, suppress, and disregard discomfort in the process of determining what is possible, of what we are capable.
>
> JOHNSON and MCRUER 136

Social norms create particular social expectations, resulting in the fact that that individuals need to deal with the discrepancy between how they feel and how they should feel. Ahmed explains that

> [w]illfulness as a judgment tends to fall on those who are not compelled by the reasoning of others. Willfulness might be what we do when we are judged as being not, as not meeting the criteria for being human, for instance.
>
> AHMED "Feminist Killjoys"

The importance of "willfulness" is the transformation of being, when not being (not being white, not being male, not being straight, not being able-bodied) is coming up against being. When crip killjoys act and become "willful" against the oppressive, ever-present comfort and happiness imposed by compulsory normalcy, it is a conscious political decision "to be unstable, incapable, unwilling, disabled," and this decision "opens up a world of possibility" (Johnson and McRuer 137).

3 Cripping Representations: Killjoys in Action!

Two documentary films that were screened during the Emotion Pictures – Documentary & Disability International Festival and invite the viewers to have a good look at the social actors who proudly expose themselves, their personal stories, and their unruly bodies in order to make a claim are: *MasterPiece – Part 1* and *Including Samuel*. All individuals presented in these films act as killjoys and stand in the way of stereotypes and visual representations of compulsory normalcy, expanding the viewers' understandings of beauty, bodily aesthetics, and the political rights of disabled individuals, be it in relation to education, employment, sexual relationships, or promoting disability culture.

3.1 *MasterPiece – Part 1*

Stelios plays along with the iconic representations of James Bond, starting his autobiographical crip story with this popular stereotype of handsome masculinity:

> My name is Payias. Stelios Payias. I was born on 20 February 1971 in Thessaloniki. Do you understand me when I speak? Make an effort. I'll also try to speak more clearly.
>
> MONDELOS

Stelios introduces himself as a person with spastic quadriplegia, a medical term frequently used in Greek diagnostic categorization. His impairment was caused by *icterus neonatorum* which began developing in nuclear jaundice five days after his birth. He starts his personal narration by presenting his academic accomplishments, which include a master's degree in Informatics and Management, speaking foreign languages, IT skills, and other distinctive achievements. Stelios informs the viewers that he is not as independent as he would like to be because he cannot find a job, but this does not put him off being active. He has a number of interests, including adapted skiing and sailing, and expanding his knowledge on IT and programming. The image of Stelios dressed in his tuxedo and holding a big toy gun is accompanied with the sound of a gunshot. He also talks about his interest in cinema. He likes adventure, spy, war, and science fiction films. He is into James Bond stories with fast cars, high technology, gadgets, beautiful women, and Bond's irresistible charm. This challenges the viewers to expand the established representations of the James Bond icon and appreciate a new version of it performed by Stelios. Can the viewers recognize the irresistible charm of Stelios' face? Filmed in a studio with a white background this time and a woman's shadow on it, Stelios talks about women:

> Women are very tender to me and it seems that they like me. If this proves that I am charming?! Maybe they think that they are not in danger and therefore they feel free. However, I am equally dangerous for them as any other man.
>
> MONDELOS

In a close-up shot, Stelios asks the viewers: "I don't know if I am handsome. What do you think?" (Mondelos). In order for the viewers to think about his question, a sequence of Stelios's different posed facial expressions follows. He gives his answer again in a close-up shot, keeping a straight face: "Beauty is in the eye of the beholder" (Mondelos). Just after this line is uttered, the title *Master-Piece – Part 1* comes on the screen, apparently as a provocative answer to Stelios's question. This short documentary clearly plays with notions of constructed beauty and aesthetics and by depicting Stelios in many close-ups, familiarizes the viewers with new images of disability and its aesthetics. Stelios challenges the viewers' perceptions of beauty and charm, and with Mondelos's technical support, this challenge functions as a response that parallels McBryde-Johnson's earlier-mentioned statement.

Stelios seems to be in control of his story. In his autobiographical narration, he addresses the camera and, by extension, the viewers directly. In addition, by quoting the lines from Jonathan Livingston Seagull: "Don't let them spread silly rumours about me," (the screen fills with a close up on Stelios' face) "or make me a god. O.K. Fletch? I am a seagull. I like to fly, maybe" (Mondelos), Stelios accentuates the fact this is clearly 'his' story and it is told by 'him.'

The main question that *MasterPiece – Part 1* asks is if we can see disability as having an aesthetic value. The director addresses the problem that in our society there is a specific aesthetic dogma that disability does not fall in line with because it is seen as non-eligible. With his film, Mondelos highlights the fact that in order to define the position of disability in the present aesthetic order, society may either change the aesthetic rules to include disability, or preserve the existing order and exclude it. Thus, through his documentary, Mondelos asks the viewers if they can change and widen their aesthetic criteria.

The fact that Stelios, a person with quadriplegia, was the social actor of the documentary had an impact on the filming process. Mondelos was aware of the fact that Stelios's facial expressions are not those that people deal with daily, since the majority of the viewers do not interact with any persons with quadriplegia, and thus he focused on Stelios' face. He saw his character as a living sculpture, as a 'masterpiece.' The director used Stelios's sense of humour and sarcasm as tools for challenging stereotypes. This is where the idea of presenting Stelios as James Bond comes from (Mpoutsi). For decades James Bond has predominantly been portrayed as a perfect male icon, so how does our society perceive it when a man with quadriplegia takes Bond's place? Stelios has the right, as every individual, to represent himself and talk about matters of his life the way he wants, even if he uses irony, sarcasm, and humour. Mondelos chooses this approach against the romantic 'feel-good' or 'superhero' models created by Hollywood.

Stelios seems to keep himself busy with a number of interests and hobbies, most of which he pursues at home. Adapted skiing, sailing, and photography are the most significant activities he is involved in outside home. He lives with his parents because he is unemployed and this affects his independence. Even though he talks about meeting women, he is not in a relationship and he does not share any information about his social life or friends, apart from his interest in going out and socializing. As we learn from his self-narrative, the protagonist's connections are mostly built around family life and outdoors activities. It becomes quite clear though that the obstacles against his independence are caused by societal restrictions and fixed ideas about disabled people, which conceptualize disability in terms of deficit and are deeply rooted in the medical model, which Garland-Thomson and Ojrzyńska discuss in detail in their chapter.

3.2 *Including Samuel*

Including Samuel addresses the issues of educational inclusion and transition from primary to secondary education. *Including Samuel* turns the eponymous Samuel's story into a disability rights matter, probing into parents' concerns as well as giving space to different voices: disabled and non-disabled students, disabled activists, teachers, parents, and academics. Examining Samuel's case, the film promotes the discourse of inclusion, making the personal political. Dan Habib, Samuel's father and the director of the film, states in a voice-over that his son brought disability rights movement into his life and this triggered new questions about perceptions, policies, and practices related to disability, education, and inclusion.

Samuel attends the Beaver Meadow Elementary where all students share the same classroom and participate in an inclusive educational programme. Samuel's teacher Mrs O'Brien, one of the voices that contribute to the discourse of inclusion, recognizes the benefits of inclusive education and approaches it as a civil right in a democratic society. She states:

> I don't think inclusion builds community. I think not having inclusion takes away community. When children leave the classroom and don't come back for hours, I don't think you have that community anymore.
>
> HABIB

However, she also sees the challenges of the transition to a higher educational level, when she states: "Inclusion is easier in our grade level. I think when you get up to the higher grade levels, it's much more difficult" (Habib).

A few other voices confirm Mrs O'Brien's concerns. The challenges that put inclusion at stake are reflected in the testimonies of the teaching staff of the Pembroke Academy, a public high school in New Hampshire, which works towards inclusive education in partnership with the University of New Hampshire's Institute on Disability. The testimonies reflect a mixture of positive attitudes and frustration, as some believe that inclusive education gives them the freedom to apply new teaching methods that benefit all students in class, whereas others feel unprepared to find the right balance between the demands of delivering the mandatory sections of the curriculum and disabled students' individual educational needs, claiming a discrepancy between these two teaching requirements. Cheryl Jorgensen and Jan Nisbet, two of the academic voices in the documentary, who represent the Institute on Disability at the University of New Hampshire, stress that the demands for teachers have changed, but the definition of inclusion has also changed and this requires additional planning in terms of curriculum design, instructions for delivery, the use of technology, and classroom management. Considering the pressure on planning, imposed by the neoliberal approach which privileges cost-effective practices, Nisbet notes that "students with disability are charged as the most expensive in education but as [they are] citizens of America, this becomes a civil rights issue" (Habib). Undoubtedly, inclusion is a civil right issue, but the application of educational inclusion has been quite problematic. Julie Allan mentions that inclusion has almost become discredited for causing confusion, frustration, guilt, and exhaustion in the world of education (3), and this seems to be an international issue. Inclusion has been interpreted and implemented in so many different ways with no support or training for teaching staff, lack of provisions, and failure in creating effective interdisciplinary teams of professionals. Another problem is the failure in the transition from primary to secondary education, and from secondary to further education. Roger Slee argues that "for many, inclusion connotes a linguistic adjustment to present a politically correct facade to a changing world" (131). Derrick Armstrong, Ann Cheryl Armstrong, and Ilektra Spandagou add that the actual factors that make the implementation of Education for All (EFA) problematic include: "the economic disparity between countries" and "cultural imperialism which often means that countries of the North dictate the pace and direction to countries of the South" (36). In other words, policies, strategic plans for education, and curricula are introduced in the countries of the South, while equity in distribution of resources is not secured. Thus, inclusion, before becoming an educational practice, should start with a political will to change educational systems at country levels and secure provisions for implementing and supporting this change.

Including Samuel also represents crip killjoys and this is the consequence of the fact that Habib shifts the personal to the political and acts as a killjoy himself. Seeking answers to his questions, he gets involved with disability activists Keith Jones and Norman Kunc, both of whom represent strong voices of the disability rights movement, taking action in public spaces. They are both "willful" and unseated, getting in the way of the others by claiming the places they want to access and challenging discriminatory notions of belonging. Talking to the camera about his experience, Keith Jones criticizes the low expectations that society has of disabled students:

> People really did not have high expectations for students with disabilities. How the hell do I develop a positive self-image if from the time I get off the bus to the time I leave, I am being told because of my physical presence, because of the physical condition of my being, that I have to be secluded, and stashed away and talked to in a demeaning manner or talked to in a way where there are no expectations about me doing anything?
>
> HABIB

Norman Kunc touches upon the thorny matter of building a sense of belonging without relying on prejudice:

> What do we do to get that sense of belonging? Well that's when I think we rely on prejudice. Because if I hate the same guy you hate, we must be friends, if we call someone retarded or stupid or fat or faggot, we're on the same side. How do you build a sense of belonging without relying on a common enemy? And without simply trying to be nice to each other. How do we authentically build a sense of belonging in our schools and our community?
>
> HABIB

In Habib's film, killjoys voice their support for disability rights by challenging prejudice and exclusionary practices. The viewers are guided from a personal story to a political matter.

Including Samuel uses an interactive mode of representation, including material evidence such as Samuel's personal photographs taken at various moments of his life, black and white photos from equal rights protests, newspaper articles, and interviews with people that have taken significant action towards inclusion. The documentary has a tight structure and is organized by chapters. Questions posed by Dan, who is Samuel's father and the filmmaker, and his wife Betsy determine the structure of the film. The narrative starts with Samuel's story but it continues with other disabled students' stories, disabled activists' statements, and teaching staff's views, which all contribute to the discourse of inclusion. The documentary is a puzzle of home videos, interviews, and scenes filmed in schools and classrooms.

Samuel is depicted as taking action in various spaces outside school and home, enjoying the full benefits of social life and different fun activities. His family's approach is different from the approach of other people who find themselves in a similar situation, as they seem to have access to more resources. They expand Samuel's and their own connections as they become killjoys through their involvement with the disability rights movement. They do not just get in the way as killjoys refusing to be seated where the oppressive practices of 'happiness' dictate, but they also pass on the message that the implementation of education for all and, by extension, society for all requires a shared responsibility of involvement, participation, and cooperation, like every application of a democratic procedure.

The majority of the films' social actors are presented as living rich lives that include a wide range of personal and familial relationships, careers, professions, artistic and political actions, and athletic and scientific achievements. A complex representation as such counters the stereotypical motifs of disqualification, damaged bodies, and invalid lives. It affirms disability as a valued human condition that can have a powerful role in art and life. The films *MasterPiece – Part 1* and *Including Samuel* negotiate various dimensions of disability discourse. They focus on the complexities of disability and successfully shift the narrative context from personal to political.

4 From the Film Festival to Disability Activism: Crip Killjoys Take Action in the Post-festival Era

Even though the Emotion Pictures – Documentary & Disability International Festival is no longer held, it managed to plant the seeds of strong collective political activism, and this certainly defines it as an essentially dissensual space where crip killjoys take action. In June 2011, nine disabled people occupied the Central Department of Social Security Institute in Athens for two days. They refused to leave until the Federal Minister agreed to meet them to discuss their demands. The Social Security Institute, the largest, state-based, social security organization in Greece, had published Bulletin 37/2011 that announced 50 per cent cuts in allowances for assistive devices. McRuer notes that "[a]usterity ... generates extravagant abjection" (*Crip Times* 101), wounding and devaluing bodies and minds. The process of wounding and devaluation follows a necropolitical[2] logic, as the bodies and minds in question are marked as those that are unproductive and have no value and as such they are disposable. According to the report on poverty and social exclusion that the Greek National Confederation of Disabled People published in 2017, 26.7% of the disabled population within the 16–64 age range were at risk of poverty. The unemployment rates for disabled people in Greece reached 32.2%, where the EU average rate for the year 2016 was 19.6%.

2 Necropolitics is understood here as biopolitical control over life and death.

Anna Carastathis, who examined the relationship between austerity and hostility, introduces, drawing on Ahmed's *The Cultural Politics of Emotion*, the concept of "affective economy of hostility" that naturalizes the production of living conditions that lead to social death, imposing the status of "living dead" on large groups and even entire populations of people (75). The affective economy of hostility manifests and materializes itself in the politics of disgust and resentment (Soldatic and Meekosha; Hughes) that constructs disabled people as scapegoats, thus justifying their abjectification and dehumanization. In the case of the Greek crisis, hostility against disabled people was also supported by extreme ideologies. The far-right party Golden Dawn (Χρυσή Αυγή), which first entered the Parliament in 2012, has publicly used eugenic propaganda promoting euthanasia and sterilization of disabled people so that the Greek nation remains "clean" of those that will never be able to become "soldier-citizens" due to their heavy burden of hereditary "defects." This propaganda against disabled people's lives resembles the Nazi propaganda that lay the groundwork for implementing Action T4,[3] the systematic killing of disabled people during the Second World War.

The new economic and social realities of Greece required a different way of action and resistance from disabled people. The occupation of the Central Department of Social Security Institute in June 2011 marked the beginning of a series of actions taken by two activist groups that were formed by disabled people in response to austerity and exclusion. In both cases, the founding members had been actively involved in the organization of the Emotion Pictures – Documentary & Disability International Festival either as key members of the organizing team and jury or as participating artists. The dissensual ferment that emerged at the festival continued in the times of austerity, motivating disabled killjoys and other disability activists to take further political action. The Movement of Disabled People for Emancipation – Zero Tolerance[4] was formally founded in 2011 after the death of a man who breathed with the support of an iron lung. His untimely demise was a result of the power company cutting off electricity in his house due to an unpaid power bill. A year earlier the Movement of Disabled Artists[5] was founded. The aim of this group

3 Useful basic information and resources on Nazi eugenic propaganda can be found in *The Holocaust Encyclopedia* which is available on the website of the US Holocaust Memorial Museum (see e.g. https://encyclopedia.ushmm.org/content/en/article/eugenics and https://encyclopedia.ushmm.org/content/en/gallery/propaganda-for-the-euthanasia-program).

4 To learn more about the movement, visit their Facebook profile: https://www.facebook.com/mideniki.anoxi/.

5 To learn more about the movement, visit their Facebook profile: https://www.facebook.com/DisArtMove/.

was to bring together disabled artists and all those who have historically been marginalized, because they did not fit in the criteria of compulsory normalcy and able-bodiedness, in order to promote their artwork. The group also aims to secure access to art and to spaces where disabled people take action and participate in disability-related activities or events. In their statement, members of the group underscore the fact that through their work as disabled artists they support political and social rights for disabled people.

During the austerity years, "disability commons," in other words "campaigns, activism and other interventions produced through recognizing common humanity and interdependence" (Runswick-Cole, Curran, and Liddiard 49), were shaped through and for crip resistance. This is most conspicuous in various forms of activism and actions of solidarity. Silvia Federici suggests that communal relations offer "an increased capacity for resistance but also, a path to transform our subjectivity and gain the capacity to recognize the world around us" (kindle loc. 1631). The discourse of commons is central to societies when neoliberal practices lead to a crisis of the state. Katherine Runswick-Cole and Dan Goodley invoke the notion of "disability commons" when they refer to disabled people's acts of resistance and agency that work the spaces of neoliberalism. Disabled people reject and resist being constituted as disposable humans, as this justifies abjection and social death. The Movement of Disabled People for Emancipation – Zero Tolerance and the Movement of Disabled Artists have shaped and supported the development of disability commons in Greece through various tactics of crip resistance, "a range of collective projects that speak back, in critically disabled ways, to a globalized politics of austerity" (McRuer, *Crip Times* 92). Both groups have followed traditional tactics of activism such as anti-austerity protests, open public discussions and film screenings about the impact of austerity and disablism on disabled people, participation in festivals and events against racism, fascism, and injustice, and participation in Pride Athens in order to promote the visibility of crip sexuality. One of their important actions was the testimony of a prominent founding member of the Movement of Disabled People for Emancipation – Zero Tolerance as a prosecution witness at the trial of Golden Dawn where the prosecution charged sixty-nine members of the far-right party, following the murder of the Greek rapper Pavlos Fyssas and violent attacks against refugees, migrants, activists, and the party's political opponents. The major accusation was based on Article 187 par. 1 of the Greek Criminal Code, which defines a criminal organization. Still ongoing after five years, the trial has been seen as crucial for Greek democracy, while the disabled activist's testimony was an action of crip resistance to the fascist propaganda against disabled people in Greece.

The crip killjoys of the Movement of Disabled People for Emancipation – Zero Tolerance and the Movement of Disabled Artists have also followed certain crip tactics to stop their dehumanization caused by neoliberal practices and austerity. "Crip camp" (McRuer, *Crip Times* 101–05) and filming were their tactics for exposing the inhumane conditions at a state-run institution in the town of Lechaina where disabled children were locked in cages and tied to their beds. The Movement of Disabled People for Emancipation – Zero Tolerance has also supported disabled refugees. In view of the lack of any official action initiated by the state, the movement took the initiative. They collected personal details of the disabled refugees, which were later passed on to NGOs and other organizations who could provide these individuals with provisions and support, particularly after their first arrivals. The members of the movement have also acted as the mediators and helped reconnect the family of a disabled refugee child. This act of solidarity can be seen as a crip tactic of "the conscientious objection, the materialization of an excessive 'we' that austerity policies cannot fully negate" (McRuer, *Crip Times* 115).

The Movement of Disabled Artists has also been applying the tactics that Robert McRuer calls theatricalization (*Crip Times* 123–24), cripping arts and activism in the field of education. The exclusionary Law 370/1983 that required that all students of the Greek Higher Schools of Drama be able-bodied with no physical or learning impairments was abolished in February 2017 and this was an outcome of collective action. When the State School of Drama did not apply the law at the entry exams in September 2017, crip killjoys affiliated with the Movement of Disabled Artists occupied the entrance of the school and staged short improvised performances in order to protest against the discriminatory policies of the school.

The Movement of Disabled Artists includes different groups of disabled artists-activists who work towards the development of disability arts and draw public attention to the political and social disability-related matters in Greece. They take action by cripping the arts, transforming film screenings, concerts, and other performances into fully accessible artistic events. This is a process that promotes the right of access to art and changes the approaches of non-disabled event organizers, artists, and audiences. The members of the movement also support and claim the disabled artists' right to have access to the different art platforms enabling them to show their works so as to provoke political and social debate. In 2016 ΘΕ.Α.Μ.Α. (Theama, Theatre of Disabled People),[6] the only professional disabled theatre company that is part of the Movement of Disabled Artists,

6 In order to learn more about the company, visit their website: http://www.distheater.gr/index.php?option=com_content&view=featured&Itemid=103&lang=en.

presented the ancient tragedy *The Persians* by Aeschylus as part of their programme. The choice of this particular tragedy, which is well-known for its anti-war message and which juxtaposes a desire for supremacy and control, on the one hand, and a desire to exercise free will, on the other, to be performed by a group of disabled actresses and actors is not only an action of crip resistance to the economic and social realities, but also to the limitations and stereotypical features attributed to disabled artists and people, in general. Crip resistance can thus be seen as an act of dissensus which, as Ojrzyńska and Wieczorek suggest, "makes it possible for those who were neither heard nor seen to be validated, to be recognized as speaking beings who have the right to fully partake in the life of the community" (3).

5 Conclusion

The Emotion Pictures – Documentary & Disability International Festival was definitely a space where crip killjoys showed their actions in a cross-disability and cross-cultural context. It became the starting point for the emergence of the disabled artists' and activists' collectivity in Greece. The resulting sense of solidarity and the rise of activism are most needed in the post-festival era when austerity has put disability and human rights at stake. Clearly, the Emotion Pictures – Documentary & Disability International Festival and other disability film festivals offer the space for crip killjoys to take action, either through representing them in films or by encouraging "crip willfulness" and crip resistance through artistic and political activities. All in all, disability film festivals have a significant contribution to disability culture and politics, and this definitely makes them a space to keep an eye on.

Works Cited

Ahmed, Sara. *The Cultural Politics of Emotion*. Edinburgh: Edinburgh University Press, 2004. Print.

Ahmed, Sara. "Feminist Killjoys (and Other Willful Subjects)." *The Scholar and Feminist Online* 8.3 (2010): n. pag., http://sfonline.barnard.edu/polyphonic/ahmed_01.htm. Accessed 30 Mar. 2019.

Allan, Julie. *Rethinking Inclusion: the Philosophers of Difference in Practice*. Dordrecht: Springer, 2008. Print.

Armstrong, Derrick, Armstrong, Ann Cheryl, and Ilektra Spandagou. "Inclusion: By Choice or by Chance?" *International Journal of Inclusive Education* 15.1 (2011): 29–39. Print.

Carastathis, Anna. "The Politics of Austerity and the Affective Economy of Hostility: Racialised Gendered Violence and Crises of Belonging in Greece." *Feminist Review* 109.1 (2015): 73–95, https://link.springer.com/article/10.1057/fr.2014.50. Accessed 10 Jun. 2019.

Federici, Silvia. *Re-Enchanting the World*. Oakland, CA: PM Press, 2019. Print.

"Festival." *The Emotion Pictures – Documentary & Disability International Festival*, http://emotionpicturesfestival.gr/en/node/67. Accessed 30 Mar. 2019.

Frazee, Catherine. "Unleashed and Unruly: Staking Our Claim to Place, Space and Culture." The Unruly Salon series profiling disability performance and scholarship, 2008, Green College, University of British Columbia, Vancouver. Keynote address. *Review of Disability Studies: An International Journal* 5.1 (2009): 7–10. https://www.rdsjournal.org/index.php/journal/article/view/227/0, Accessed 30 Mar. 2019.

Garland-Thomson, Rosemarie. *Staring: How We Look*. New York, NY: OUP, 2009. Epub.

Habib, Dan, dir. *Including Samuel*. Institute on Disability-UCED, 2008. Film, https://www.includingsamuel.com/. Accessed 12 Apr. 2019.

Hughes, Bill. "Disabled People as Counterfeit Citizens: The Politics of Resentment Past and Present." *Disability & Society* 30.7 (2015): 991–1004, https://www.tandfonline.com/doi/abs/10.1080/09687599.2015.1066664. Accessed 10 Jun. 2019.

Johnson, Merri Lisa, and Robert McRuer. "Cripistemologies: Introduction." *Journal of Literary & Cultural Disability Studies* 8.2 (2014): 127–47. Print.

McBryde-Johnson, Harriet. "Unspeakable Conversations." *The New York Times Magazine* 16 Feb. 2003, https://www.nytimes.com/2003/02/16/magazine/unspeakable-conversations.html. Accessed 30 Mar. 2019.

McRuer, Robert. *Crip Times*. New York, NY: New York University Press, 2018. Print.

McRuer, Robert. *Crip Theory: Cultural Signs of Queerness and Disability*. New York, NY: New York University Press, 2006. Print.

Mondelos, Stefanos, dir. *MasterPiece – Part 1*. Stefanos Mondelos, 2007. Film, https://vimeo.com/32735970. Accessed 12 Apr. 2019.

Μπούτση, Μυρτώ [Mpoutsi, Mirto]. Συνέντευξη του Στέφανου Μονδέλου. *Ελεύθερος Τύπος* [Interview with Stefanos Mondelos]. Eleftheros Tipos. Aug. 2007. *www.shortfilm.gr*. http://www.shortfilm.gr/new.asp?id=273. Accessed 30 Mar. 2019.

National Confederation of Disabled People. *10 Δελτίο Παρατηρητηρίου Θεμάτων Αναπηρίας Της Ε.Σ.Α.Μεα. "Φτώχεια Και Κοινωνικός Αποκλεισμός Στα Άτομα Με Αναπηρία."* National Confederation of Disabled People, 2017, https://www.esamea.gr/publications/others/3647-10-deltio-paratiritirioy-thematon-anapirias-tis-e-s-a-mea-atoma-me-anapiria-oi-ftoxoteroi-metaksy-ton-ftoxon. Accessed 3 Jun.2019.

Owen, Randall, and Sarah Parker Harris. "No Rights without Responsibilities: Disability Rights and Neoliberal Reform under New Labour." *Disability Studies Quarterly* 32.3 (2012): n. pag., http://dsq-sds.org/article/view/3283. Accessed 30 Mar. 2019.

Runswick-Cole, Katherine, and Daniel Goodley. "Disability, Austerity and Cruel Optimism in Big Society: Resistance and 'The Disability Commons.'" *Canadian Journal of Disability Studies* 4.2 (2015): 162–86, https://cjds.uwaterloo.ca/index.php/cjds/article/download/213/399/. Accessed 3 June 2019.

Runswick-Cole, Katherine, Curran, Tillie, and Kirsty Liddiard. "The Everyday Worlds of Disabled Children." *Disability, Normalcy and the Everyday*. Ed. Gareth M. Thomas and Dikaios Sakellariou. Basingstoke: Palgrave, 2017. 41–60. Print.

Siebers, Tobin. "Disability Aesthetics." *Journal for Cultural and Religious Theory* 7.2 (2006): 63–73. Print.

Slee, Roger. "The Politics of Theorising Special Education." *Theorising Special Education*. Ed. Catherine Clark, Alan Dyson, and Alan Millward. London: Routledge, 1998: 125–35. Print.

Snyder, Sharon L., and David T. Mitchell. "'How do we get all these disabilities in here?': Disability Film Festivals and the Politics of Atypicality." *Canadian Journal of Film Studies* 17.1 (2008): 11–29. Print.

Soldatic, Karen, and Helen Meekosha. "The Place of Disgust: Disability, Class and Gender in Spaces of Workfare." *Societies* 2.3 (2012): 139–56, https://www.mdpi.com/2075-4698/2/3/139. Accessed 10 Jun. 2019.

PART 3

Between the Real and the Reel

∵

CHAPTER 6

Disability, Gender, and Innocence: Russ Meyer's *Mudhoney* and *Faster Pussycat! Kill! Kill!* and Problems of Signification in Cinema

Murray K. Simpson

As Slavoj Žižek observed, the interpretation of film must be approached "in the way one has to interpret a Chinese political poem: absences and surprising presences count" (125). The same is true of the 'deviant' body and for the body out of place. Disability weaves its way through cinema and culture in multifarious, and often unexpected, forms. There have been various efforts to theorize disability and cinema – though, immediately, we must distinguish between theorizing disability in cinema and an attempt to produce a more general theory of disability and cinema. For the most part, these efforts have come from disability studies, rather than cinema studies, gender studies, semiotics, or sociology, although these areas of study inform them to greater or lesser degrees.

This chapter will look at the narrative construction and deployment of three characters with disabilities from two films by exploitation moviemaker Russ Meyer: *Mudhoney* (1965) and *Faster Pussycat! Kill! Kill!* (1966), in order to explore the various ways in which different impairments link with gender, sexuality, and moral culpability, avoiding a simplistic assessment of these representations as one-dimensional and revealing their complex semiotic structure. The ultimate purpose of this is to consider the vexed question of signification and the body, particularly the disabled body, building on the seminal contribution by David T. Mitchell and Sharon L. Snyder of the concept of "narrative prosthesis" (*Narrative Prosthesis* 15), which has already been addressed in the chapter written by Dan Goodley and Marek Mackiewicz-Ziccardi. This article takes disability studies as its starting point, though its purpose is not to produce or contribute to a general theory of disability in cinema, but to critique monolithic approaches. The key contribution of the chapter is to demonstrate, through the application of basic elements of semiotics, that it is rarely meaningful or useful to consider characters with specific body differences as 'representing' disability. In other words, the chapter will demonstrate that abnormal bodies rarely, if ever, signify disability as an entire category or paradigm. Also, it will highlight the paradox of considering corporeal difference as representing

 | DOI:10.1163/9789004424678_008

abstract concepts whilst simultaneously taking those very concepts as signifiers of that non-standard embodiment. Of course, within a complex economy of signs it is likely that all elements will perform multiple functions as signifying and signified components. However, it is precisely this infinitely mutually sustaining nature of language that highlights the impossibility of a meaningful, yet entirely self-contained, sign. By assuming a broadly post-Saussurean semiotic approach based on a dyadic,[1] complex, and arbitrary model of signs (cf. Deely), the analysis will show that bodily difference itself generally performs the function of signifier, and that the interplay of disability, gender, and age in the signification of moral coding highlights the error of privileging any one corporeal dimension as a narrative signifier.

At this point, it is worth making a few comments on the theoretical orientation of the chapter. First, the study considers the 'overdetermination' of corporeal signification, wherein a wide range of semi-autonomous factors, none of which is uniquely causal or essential, contribute to the production of signs. This avoids reductive approaches to the films' symbolic systems focused on any single dimension, or regarding them separately – deformed, deviant, and hypersexualized bodies, as well as cars, music, and dusty landscapes all play a part, and even the emphasis in this chapter on corporeal signs is driven purely by present interest and not because they are discrete. Overdetermination is understood in two distinct ways in semiotics. Firstly, there is the overdetermination of the sign itself and its existence *qua* sign, that is to say, the production of a sign through the repetition of a range of symbolic and non-symbolic factors results in a signifier capable of sustaining a signified concept such that the sign can be used in symbolic exchange. Floyd Merrell locates this understanding of overdetermination in Peircean semiotics, identifying it with the very earliest stage of sign formation: a "pre-Firstness, [or] pure vagueness, before there is consciousness *of* a sign" (35). For Merrell, then, overdetermination refers to a stage before intersecting flows, marks, and exclusions achieve the degree of stability necessary for meaningful signs to emerge. The formation of signs is perhaps more akin to a primordial evolution from a range of random and arbitrary conditions than it is to a clear and restricted causal determination by those conditions. For the purposes of this analysis, then, 'overdetermination' is taken more in a Freudian-inspired sense to refer to the 'accomplishment' of signs through the repetition of multiple and varied linguistic and non-linguistic

1 Semiotics involves the division of signs into two, sometimes three, component parts. In the dyadic model, taken here, a sign can be theoretically divided into a 'signifier' – a written or spoken word, a symbol, a picture – and the 'concept' that is 'signified.' Triadic approaches also include actual material 'objects' being referred to.

moments, avoiding recourse to accounts of causality completely. The second consideration, then, is implicit in the first, and that is to understand the functioning of signs themselves as factors in the overdetermination of other signs and practices. To put it simply, all signs affect the production and meaning of other signs within the same context. Understanding the semiotics of the films, therefore, demands attention to the relationality of signs and their interplay within and beyond symbolic systems. The analysis of disability in the two films considered here must also attend to gender, the mise-en-scène, the revving of car engines and of libidos, since everything contributes to the films' overall excessive symbolic economies. However, the cinematic audience must be culturally and linguistically pre-prepared for the signs, if not their precise arrangement, before the films even begin if they are not to be overwhelmed by the production of new signs. For this reason, the chapter has two main points of focus. The first of these is to look at how the films recapitulate the production of familiar signs, and the second is to analyze how the films' corporeal signs contribute to overdetermination.

This approach contrasts sharply with the dominant emphasis on 'representation,' as opposed to signification, in the study of disability and cinema. Most commonly there are interrogations of how film and other cultural media use disability as a physical or narrative representation of moral concepts, with the implication that this morality, in turn, becomes socially definitive for disabled people. Benjamin Fraser's recent collection on *Cultures of Representation: Disability in World Cinema* is a case in point, with none of the chapters adopting a semiotic approach.

In the case of director Russ Meyer, best known for his work in 'exploitation' cinema, although an undoubted auteur and innovator, the corporeal emphasis for which he is most commonly remembered is his highly sexist use of pneumatic female actors. His films were generally low budget and, whilst aimed at the grindhouse market, have become cult classics in many cases. There have been a number of studies of his films, although there has not been any real exploration of his portrayal of characters with disabilities, and this is precisely where the focus of this chapter is directed. These portrayals rely heavily, if implicitly, on social normativity in order to produce fantastical, queered landscapes of grotesques and bizarre beings. As Susan Flynn observes,

> Hollywood celebrates normativity as the oil that greases the wheels of progress and thus utilizes difference as a narrative tool. The body is used as the terrain on which the battle for power and autonomy is fought. Films replete with the threat of danger take us on a journey of cinematic escapism, which facilitates our release from "imperfect" bodies.
>
> FLYNN 6

The relevance of cinematic presentations of impaired and deviant bodies is, therefore, of central importance, not merely for disabled people, but for all. Film contributes to the biopolitical governance of human life and, as a result, becomes a site of resistance to it.

1 Eula

The first character the chapter will discuss is that of Eula, played by Rena Horten, who appears in *Mudhoney*, released in 1965. Set in Prohibition-era Missouri, the story takes place in the small town of Spooner through which the film's protagonist, Calif McKinney (John Furlong), is travelling en route to California, carrying a secret from his past, namely that he accidentally killed a strike-breaker in a fight. Instead, he finds love in the arms of the wife of the film's villain, Sidney Brenshaw (played superbly by Hal Hopper).

Eula is the deaf-mute[2] sister of Clara Belle (Lorna Maitland) and daughter of Maggie Marie (Princess Livingston) who runs a brothel and drinking den in which the two daughters are apparently the only prostitutes. What makes Eula most interesting is that she is seemingly completely unaware of the social world around her – the context, morality, and implications of what she does. Moral dissipation and turpitude surrounds Eula, whilst she remains innocent throughout.

Although much of the depravity centres on, or is in keeping with, her own sexually promiscuous behaviour, Eula is protected from its significance because she is presented as lacking in the comprehension of language. She hears and speaks no evil, and that which she sees she is unable to recognize as such. Language is presented as the medium necessary for the transformation of amoral natural proclivities into social acts, capable of being judged against moral codes. If Eula can read, we have no clue about this, and it would seem disruptive of the moral texture of the narrative if she could. She is a child of nature – a fact signified at several points by her play with a kitten – physically present in the social world, but simultaneously absent from it because she is outside of the linguistic community.

Nowhere is Eula's pre-linguistic state of moral purity made clearer than when the film's protagonist, Calif McKinney, goes to visit Maggie Marie's house. In the scene, we find Calif drinking homemade spirits. Touching the record player beside him, Eula is sensing the vibrations of a Strauss waltz through her fingers, standing in a state of ecstatic reverie with her eyes closed – further

2 I use this term to emphasize a literary trope, rather than any actual embodied existence.

focusing her senses on touch. Calif seems captivated by her. Though it is not Eula he loves – Calif has already fallen for Brenshaw's wife, Hannah (Antoinette Cristiani) – he is transported by her appearance. Calif takes Eula's hand and holds it to his throat whilst he hums the waltz himself. She smiles, feeling the vibrations. Somewhat drunk, he then dances with her around the room, an expansive and energetic waltz, before collapsing backwards through the bead-string door and onto her bed laughing. Eula pauses at the door, halfway through the strings of beads, which hang around her face and neck, before following him. She begins to undress Calif, before taking off her own dress and standing before him naked, completely lacking in self-consciousness, which the camera captures from Calif's perspective. Eula is unembarrassed by the spectator, which is to say the audience who occupy Calif's position. The vulgar intrusion of Brenshaw then interrupts the scene.

The dance itself is a curious spectacle. Sarah Whatley notes that "[a] condition of 'otherness' associated with disabled people tends to be emphasized by pairing disabled with nondisabled dancers" (50). However, as the music continues and the dancers move around the room, we forget that Eula is neither hearing the music, nor picking up its vibrations. For that moment, the scene effectively normalizes Eula for the audience.

As the scene moves from the public room to the bedroom, Calif's disposition changes in a way we would perhaps expect. Moving from his initial captivation, his happiness changes from the *joie de vivre* exhibited whilst dancing, to the seriousness of carnal anticipation captured in close-up, and, finally, to embarrassment and anger towards his tormentor, Brenshaw, which is again highlighted in a facial close-up. For Eula, however, the scene plays very differently. Whilst, again, she fails to register Brenshaw's malevolent derision, mainly directed at Calif, the more interesting aspect is the way in which, for her, the movement of the scene, from her initial euphoria to the bedroom scene, is almost completely seamless. Eula does not move, as Calif does, from a higher state of joy to a baser plane of animal desire and then anger. For her, it is all one, a continuous state of serene happiness, interrupted only by surprise at the intrusion of Brenshaw – for whom she does, curiously, cover her breasts, though not her pubic area. The bead curtain door, which is all that separates the public room from her bedroom, also highlights this continuity. The divisions of visibility that generally mark the social world do not exist for Eula, since they rest on knowledge of privacy and shame, and Eula knows neither.

Eula finally has her innocence and, as a telling marker, her silence shattered at the end of the film. Confirming her status as a child of nature, Eula, again playing with the kitten, somehow senses violence unfolding in the town, though she can neither see nor hear it, as the lynch-mob closes in on the increasingly desperate and mad Brenshaw. Running to the scene, her lack of comprehension of human violence and brutality is brought to an abrupt end with the sight of the preacher, Brother Hansen (Frank Bolger), kicking a barrel from beneath the feet of the noosed Brenshaw. The sight of the hanged Brenshaw requires no linguistic intercession to make her aware of the viciousness of the townspeople. She utters her only sound, as the film closes around her scream.

Eula's deafness isolates her from the moral corruption that immerses her. Her sexuality is an active one, which is conspicuous in the fact that she follows, without inhibition, her natural proclivities and desires, also she is very assertive in approaching men with whom she wishes to copulate. However, it is also passively feminine in that her place is to 'receive,' however willingly, aggressive male sexuality. A reversal almost happens in *Faster Pussycat!* with the case of a male character with intellectual disability, where seduction is attempted by a sexually aggressive woman. However, this cannot come to fruition precisely because, ultimately, he fails in his manhood.

Despite her amorality, or, rather, because of it, Eula's body is even more publically displayed than her sister's is. Her bra-less cleavage reaching almost to the navel is constantly on display, except when she is completely naked. Even when showering outside, Eula only smiles at the arrival of the leering Brenshaw and the apocalyptic puritan, Brother Hansen, making no effort to cover her nudity. The viewer is to understand that Eula, lacking the language to formulate the basis for embarrassment, is unable to comprehend either Brenshaw's odious lust, or Hansen's hypocritical seething moral condemnation. Whilst Eula is undoubtedly presented as the Other, it would be too simplistic to call it an 'inferiority' and there is no obvious narrative desire to restore "an originary wholeness [or] to institute a notion of the body within a regime of tolerable deviance" (Mitchell and Snyder, *Narrative Prosthesis* 6–7). Instead, her body as signifier is much more complex, with gender, beauty, sensuality, deafness, and so forth, all contributing to its overdetermination, as we shall see below.

2 The Old Man and the Vegetable

The other two characters appear in Meyer's next and arguably best (McDonough 175–76; Waters 42), film, *Faster Pussycat! Kill! Kill!*, released in 1966. The film, which has become something of a post-feminist cultural icon, centres on the rampaging exploits of three go-go dancers, led by the curvaceous and deadly Varla (Tura Satana). Having kidnapped a young socialite, Linda

(Susan Bernard), after dispatching her insipid boyfriend, the trio wind up on a broken down ranch with the lure of hidden money. The ranch is inhabited by "the Old Man" (Stuart Lancaster, who also appeared in *Mudhoney* and numerous other Meyer movies) and his two sons, Kirk (Paul Trinka), the elder son, and his younger son, known only as "the Vegetable" (Dennis Busch).

We get our first proper introduction to both the Vegetable and the Old Man as they sit at the kitchen table. Like Eula, the Vegetable is playing with a kitten when we first meet him. The scene emphasizes both his musculature and gentleness. He is redolent of Frankenstein's monster in his play, and the spectacle balances on the cusp of horror in the stark contrast between his gentle play and his muscular frame, which could crush the kitten in an instant. The Old Man injects sufficient menace into the proceedings to make the viewer consider that as a serious possibility.

The Vegetable has some kind of intellectual disability, which ultimately is the source of his innocence, but, unlike Eula, he has some degree of knowledge of right and wrong – though not enough for autonomous moral existence. His pliability and knowledge, albeit conflicted, of his wrongdoing in the brutalization of young women at his father's behest lead ultimately to a redemption that demands a trade with his freedom, as Kirk lovingly assures him of institutional care. Language as a mark of moral culpability also features for the Vegetable. For the most part, he says little and when he does, his words falter.

Entirely different to Eula, the Vegetable seems almost asexual, despite being a model of masculine physical perfection. When Varla and Rosie (Haji), another gang member and Varla's lover, strike provocative poses, the Vegetable munches unconcernedly on an apple, awaiting his next instructions from the Old Man. Later, as Billie (Lori Williams), the third of the Amazonian outlaws, tries to seduce him, he seems more intent on his weight training, almost uncomprehending of Billie's intentions. In both psychophysiological and Butlerian senses, he is unable to "perform" a masculine sexuality, and has no "gender coherence" (Butler 24). The Vegetable has no existence other than as a functional extension of his father and an object of Billie's lust until the film's final scenes.

The Old Man is a wheelchair user, with a violent unyielding misogyny fuelling his psyche following an incident in which he acquired his impairment helping a young woman to board a moving train. The film makes various allusions to the Old Man, aided by the Vegetable, inflicting sexual violence on young women. As the Old Man says, "When you hurt somebody the authorities get aroused. But what do they know about hurting and pain? We're payin' 'em back, boy. Each woman, a payment." The Old Man has a contradictory relationship to the Vegetable. On the one hand, he is completely dependent upon him for all his physical needs, including the acquisition of women. At the same time, he loathes and resents him, not only for his dependence upon him, but because his wife died giving birth to him. Though never to his face, the Old Man is open to others about the contempt he has for his younger son, "a blob of flesh."

We see the Old Man's raging madness finally boiling over as the Vegetable gives chase to the escaping Linda. The Old Man clambers out of the truck and starts dragging himself towards the low angled static camera, and to where the Vegetable has caught up with the screaming victim. The Old Man is simultaneously powerful in his violence and his ability to exercise it through his son, and emasculated and pathetic, heaving himself through the dust towards his prey, against whom he would be completely ineffectual on his own. Central to his character throughout the movie is his impaired sense of agency, which is limited by his dependence on others, a point that Tom Shakespeare believes to be common to disabled characters in cinema (58–69). The landscape through which he crawls is as barren, fruitless, and terrifying as he is. As he steadily bears down on the camera, and thus the audience, he shouts maniacally to his son, egging him on:

> The Old Man: C'mon boy let's get her. Don't let her get away this time.
> C'mon boy, we know what to do now, just like before.
> That's it boy. We got her now.
> Go on boy, get her, get her!
> Don't let her scream, and get something in her mouth. Hit her head, boy. Tell her yer daddy is paid, boy.

In his moment of need, the repudiation of his son vanishes. The Old Man is completely dependent on the Vegetable to form a fully functioning, sexually violent unit.

By this point, Linda has capitulated. With the camera alternating between the Vegetable's perspective above her – showing the tired and pained resignation in her face – to low camera shots from behind Linda and the Vegetable's menacing frame hulking towards her, Linda says: "Go ahead. I don't care. Get it over with. Just leave me alone. Leave me alone." It is at this point that the Vegetable finally breaks down and some innate sense of right and wrong takes over, superseding the authority and instructions of the Old Man. Covering his face with his fists, he begins to cry, dropping to his knees and putting his hands then head on Linda's thigh just as Kirk arrives:

> The Vegetable: I can't do it.
> I… I… I… I don't mean to

I'm... sorry
Kirk: Easy brother, everything's going to be alright.
You're doing fine, you're doing just fine.
The Vegetable: I'm sorry
you... believe me?
I... don't know.
nothing... right
nothing's ever right.
Kirk: You're going to be alright.

The co-dependence between the Old Man and the Vegetable is irreparably broken. The Old Man looks on disgusted, still lying in the desert sand.

The shifting of the camera perspective from behind Linda, looking up at the Vegetable, to the Vegetable's perspective looking down directly mirrors that of Eula and Calif in the bedroom. However, where the Vegetable's intellectual disability and masculine body create a terrifying sexual menace, Eula's deafness and feminine form produce a powerful allure. Linda surrenders, resigned to her defeat, and Calif surrenders willingly to Eula's charms. Only by introducing a pathological female hypersexuality, in the form of Varla and company, does Meyer encourage the audience to contemplate a reversal of the gender roles in the first scenario. A reversal in the second would be virtually impossible.

3 Im/moral Bodies

For the Vegetable, then, his intellectual disability diminishes his moral culpability, but although, like Eula, he is unable to formulate moral precepts, he demonstrates an innate sense of right and wrong in the end. Unlike Eula, however, he is forced to recognize the wrongness of his own actions, and he is required to perform various redemptive acts: demonstrating sorrow, killing Rosie (whom he appears to blame for the death of Billie), battling Varla, and accepting institutionalization.

Impairments aside, whilst both the Vegetable and Eula embody, and are presented as, ideals of masculine and feminine bodily perfection, the Vegetable remains sexually emasculated. Although Billie's charms begin to take some effect on him, he ultimately lacks the requisite male aggression to 'give' Billie the sex she desires, whereas Eula merely has to 'receive' the sexual advances of men. Instead, the Vegetable allows the maddening sound of a passing train – the same train that was the source of his father's injury – to interrupt him just as he is yielding to Billie's seduction, which is also one of the clearest signs that all of his violence is rooted in his unquestioning obedience to his father (cf. Mollow 286).

The Old Man is a more hackneyed symbol of moral decay. He has all of the carnal aggression that the Vegetable lacks, coupled with a deep-seated lust for violent revenge against women, and, in this respect, he embodies what Shakespeare refers to as the cultural linkage of "sexuality with disability, and sexuality with mortality" (59). It is of no consequence that his body became impaired during an act of helping; he is the architect of his own inescapable judgment. Although thoroughly rooted in his impairment, the Old Man has chosen a life of hatred: to hold all women responsible for what happened to him, to blame his younger son for his wife's death, and to use him as an instrument for his malevolent designs.

Of the three, only the Old Man and, as a signifier, his broken body, are presented as morally and physically repellent. The hidden nature of Eula's and the Vegetable's impairments mean that their externally 'normal' bodies can still conform to dominant aesthetic ideals of human beauty and also highlight the linkage between physical and moral goodness – though more akin to amoral 'noble savages' than the 'civilized' goodness discussed by Goodley and Mackiewicz-Ziccardi in their chapter. In the bedroom scene with Eula and Calif, both Calif and the audience are invited to share in the spectacle of Eula's naked body. We can see in Calif what Rosemarie Garland-Thomson calls the "visual magnetism of breasts [which] can make both starers and starees anxious" (143). He experiences the delicious erotic anxiety at the prospect of what is about to happen. Again, however, Eula has no such experience because her eroticism has an entirely different register. There is, however, an implicit devaluing of Eula, in that she is unwittingly a siren around whose rocks the moral wreckage of men floats. Calif is a free man, and, whilst the audience are not exactly enjoined to condemn his moment of desire for Eula, we have sympathy for his love of Brenshaw's wife and anticipate, correctly, that it is there that he will ultimately find happiness. Men have only lust for Eula, whilst she has pure erotic desires for them, free from the moral disapprobation implied by 'lust.' Conversely, whilst it is not possible for others to love Eula, neither can she truly give love, condemned as she is, by her deafness, to a series of sexual couplings that cannot provide the symbolic depth necessary for a truly loving relationship. For Eula, only the viewer can (choose to) see her social oppression; she herself lacks the conceptual apparatus, and neither does she enjoy any aesthetic sensibility beyond that which gratifies her.[3]

---

3 In similar vein, Jessica Berson comments on the way in which the casting of Deaf actors in female Shakespearean roles, metaphorically representing concepts and dramatic relations, has the (unintended) effect of further diminishing their agency as women (47).

4 Disability and the Problem of Representation

Mitchell and Snyder's work provides a clear starting point for the analysis of signification in the two films:

> Our thesis centers not simply upon the fact that people with disabilities have been the object of representational treatments, but rather that their function in literary discourse is primarily twofold: disability pervades literary narrative, first, as a stock feature of characterization and, second, as an opportunistic metaphorical device.
>
> *Narrative Prosthesis* 47

This leads them to assert the near ubiquity of disability in cinema and literature, on which they base their theory of "narrative prosthesis." One of the key aspects of the approach, evident here, is that the issues of oppression and resistance lie primarily in the textual reading, which always offers multiple possibilities, rather than in taking fixed positions about the nature of the texts themselves. In other words, the act of reading any text, as well as producing it, can create an act of resistance, though neither resistance nor oppression is ever fully complete. Thus, Michael T. Clarke's objection that even documentary cinema made by disabled film makers and giving direct voice to disabled people can be corrupted by the internalization of ableist cinematic conventions, thereby undermining Snyder and Mitchell's position, seems to miss the point. The potential for texts to provide opportunities for the opening of new spaces for resistance to imposed subjectivities is still compatible with the continued existence of oppressive tendencies in those same texts. In fact, both continually weave themselves through texts. Narrative prosthesis, then, is as much a committed practice of critical engagement as it is a theory of how disability functions in literary and cinematic texts.

Elsewhere, Mitchell and Snyder give a useful typology, chronologically traced, of approaches to theorizing cultural representations of disability: early efforts, focused on "negative imagery"; "social realist"; a more critical "new historicist" approach, and "biographical criticism" ("Representation and its Discontents" 196, 199, 201, 205). However, there is a problem with how representation itself is being used, pointing two ways. Mitchell and Snyder outline what they regard as the three most commonly identified stereotypes of disability – Melville's Captain Ahab, Dickens' Tiny Tim, and Shakespeare's Richard III – which are used to critique the way in which disability is represented in literature. However, confusion arises because actually none of these characters 'represents' disability. What they represent are moral concepts: hubris, pathos, and iniquity. To become confused on this point means pressing disability into double-facing service in relation to signification; the signifier is the specific impairment, or other bodily difference, that which is being signified is the, usually moral, concept it operates to denote. That which is signified cannot, therefore, function simultaneously as a signifier for the impairment.

In the case of Eula, her deafness is used to signify her natural state of amorality. It does not, however, follow that ingenuousness can serve to represent deafness, and nor is there any evidence that naivety is being equated with sensory impairments. Similarly, taking the specific character of Old Man with his physical impairment, his paraplegia signifies greed, malevolence, and his vengeful hatred. Again, however, there are problems in expecting the various elements of the sign to function 'simultaneously' as both signifier and signified. The Vegetable's intellectual disability is a different kind of marker to Eula's for innocence, but, nonetheless, innocence cannot 'by virtue of this sign' come to signify intellectual disability, a point that would be true on either a Saussurean dyadic model, or a Peircean triadic model of the sign (Deely *passim*).

We can see a clear example of this in an early exchange between Varla and the Old Man. As they confront each other in a dialogue, the camera position switches from behind Varla, foregrounding her curvaceous hips and derriere, as the Old Man talks, to a view that foregrounds a rear-shot of his wheelchair when Varla is the interlocutor. In a visual synecdoche, the Old Man talks to Varla's hips and thighs as the literal embodiment of female sexuality, whilst Varla talks to the Old Man's wheelchair, which carries his derelict body and turns out to be the location of the hidden money, as the symbol of his depraved character. But, whilst Varla's behind signifies a wanton sexuality, and the partial view of the Old Man's body and wheelchair signifies his moral corruption, those signified concepts cannot be reversed to infer those particular signifiers. The concept of dangerous femininity is not linked essentially or uniquely to the image of a woman's behind and nor is moral turpitude exhaustively and inextricably linked to wheelchair use.

However, this is a rather different point to the observation of Mitzi Walz in relation to the "looping effect" (103), in which negative, principally medical, 'representations' of disability become culturally propagated, only to be internalized by disabled people themselves and reproduced in their own narratives. This looping sequence, if indeed it can be said to exist in any substantial way, does not involve self-referential signs. Furthermore, in any system of signs, multiple loops could always be found that would bring the signified back to the signifier through the process of overdetermination, often very quickly. However, the model of looping implies a high level of passivity on the part of spectator, disabled or otherwise, and a high degree of consistency and stability in the meaning of signs and economy of semiotic elements in order to produce this self-perpetuating looping effect.

Mitchell and Snyder discuss disability in relation to its function as "a linguistic 'signifier'" ("Representation and its Discontents" 214). However, firstly, disability per se is almost never a signifier, that is, as a general concept or social category, only specific characters and precise bodily differences. Moreover, in such instances, when a particular impairment or difference exists as a signifier, 'disability' is rarely the concept signified. When it is the concept of 'disability' that is signified, something else must act as the signifier. The question in those events is: What is representing disability? Rather than the reverse: What is disability representing? 'Disability,' in other words, does not represent anything, because other than as a word – written or spoken – or probably the only other example, the universally recognized, if problematic, wheelchair logo, the entirety of 'disability' cannot be presented in a single character or situation. Signifiers are restricted to each unique instance of corporeal variance: Eula's deafness, the Vegetable's intellectual disability, or the Old Man's paraplegia, each of which signifies very different concepts, none of which could be interchangeable and all of which are variable even in other literary characters with similar impairments – highlighting the basic semiotic premise of the arbitrariness of the sign, i.e. the lack of a natural link between the signifier and the signified. The exact operations of signification become lost amidst less precise references to 'representation.' Kate Ellis renders an even more crude approach, suggesting that, "[a]n influential social barrier for people with impairments is the representation of disability in films because cinema is a powerful cultural tool in shaping society's opinion of disability" (2). However, as noted, no single disabled character, such as Eula, can be said to 'represent' disability. What Eula's body signifies is an overdetermined moral concept, or cluster of concepts, of which her deafness forms only one part of the signifier, along with her voluptuous female body, open and active sexuality, and her plunging cleavage, when she is dressed at all. In other words, this presents us with a corporeal nexus of signification, in which disability, gender, race, and sexuality are all merely dimensions.

In fact, there is a prevalence of this kind of disordered analysis of signs in most of the literature, largely stemming from an initial focus on disability, coupled with a poorly theorized understanding of representation and signification. Angela Smith, for example, also illustrates the typical difficulties with this approach when she suggests that

> [t]he narrative and metaphoric construction of disability in classical myth, folklore, and literature has invested certain impairments with particular symbolic meanings. Blindness, for instance, often figures an absolute helplessness or dependency.... Alternatively, blindness indicates, or is compensated with, inner sight and wisdom.
>
> SMITH 83

Again, the arbitrariness, and plurality, of the sign is evident, as is the impossibility of inverting the sign to make dependency or inner sight signifiers for blindness. The meanings are being invested with 'reduced' bodies, rather than the reverse.

We also need to consider whether the ways in which impaired and abnormal bodies perform signifying functions in essentially different ways to other bodies. In *Faster Pussycat!*, for example, danger does not come only from the two disabled characters; indeed, the most dangerous individuals are Varla and her two accomplices. As the opening (moral) narrator says,

> While violence cloaks itself in a plethora of disguises, its favorite mantle still remains … sex. Violence devours all it touches, its voracious appetite rarely fulfilled.… Let's examine closely that most dangerously evil creation, this new breed encased and contained in the soft suppleness of woman. The softness is there, the unmistakable smell of female, the surface shiny and silken, the body yielding yet wanton.

Immediately, without even seeing any flesh, the primacy of the female body as a surface for the eruption of sexual violence is established. The first scene shows the three go-go dancers at work in a nightclub, leering men egging them on; they are the first victims of ruinous feminine power. The ostensibly unimpaired bodies of the three outlaw women function as sites of signification as much as any of the three disabled characters considered here – a surface for the inscription of wanton lust and the murderous consequences of an assertive female sexuality. Similarly, Clara Belle, Eula's sister, is thoroughly aware of, and an active participant in, the monetary sale of her voluptuous body. This certainly shifts her moral status, but her body is no less involved in a signifying relationship with the moral concepts that it signifies than Eula's is. In the case of most of Meyer's women, and many of the men, corporeal difference 'not' constituting disability functions in signification in precisely the same way, if for other concepts, as do abnormal bodies. The bodies of Varla and her band may be extreme, but they are by no means even 'abnormal,' let alone impaired. This suggests that the recognition of the importance of the body as a site of cultural signification cannot privilege any one dimension such as disability, as Snyder and Mitchell do in claiming that "[b]ody genres are … dependent on disability as a representational device" (162).

5 Conclusion

The deployment of impaired and otherwise aberrant bodies in the two films discussed creates a tense interplay of semiotic elements. The primary signifying functions in both are performed by corporeality. However, they evince multiple and shifting relations to the moral codes that they signify. Nowhere, however, is that process of signification reversed for corporeality itself to become the signified element. This is certainly not to suggest that body concepts cannot be signified, merely that such signification cannot be assumed to be present in every case of bodily difference and must be established specifically.

Grindhouse cinema always had an ambiguous and contradictory relationship towards its own narratives and characters (Mathijs and Sexton 97). The nature of exploitation cinema was such that it had to be seen to condemn the very thing that it sold. This was a consistent theme since the early days of the morality films from the pre- and post-War period, such as *Reefer Madness* (dir. Louis J. Gasnier, 1936), *Sex Madness* (dir. Dwain Esper, 1938), or *Test Tube Babies* (dir. W. Merle Connell, 1948). The original title for *Mudhoney* was *Rope of Flesh*, a reference to the origins of Brenshaw's demise in his own carnality. Condemnation and denigration of wildly deviant characters, therefore, is not a straightforward matter. In this respect, grindhouse presents an ideal vehicle for the study of complex signification and corporeal deviance. It fetishizes bodily and behavioural deviance such that normalcy is safely circumvented before being ultimately assured.

The problem of theorizing bodily signification in cinema becomes even more pronounced in relation to the 'fantastical' body, particularly in the horror and super-hero genres. These comprise, on the one hand, the 'preternatural' body – vampires, werewolves, zombies, angels, and so forth – and, on the other, the hyper-endowed, 'super'-body – whether hero or villain. The latter category is slightly more complex insofar as, first, many such characters, such as Daredevil or Professor X, have bodies that would conventionally be considered 'impaired' – and, second, the distinction between technologically enhanced 'cyber'-bodies – Robocop, Iron Man – and the physically altered or different, those who have or acquire superhuman powers – Spiderman, Superman, the Hulk – is difficult, and perhaps impossible to draw. However, neither the preternatural nor super-body is routinely incorporated into cinematic or literary analysis from the perspective of disability studies – with the very notable exception of the analyses which Angela Smith offers in her book. This problem is usually evinced in the opposite direction where general cinematic studies of the fantastical body are invariably impoverished in relation to any demonstrable awareness and use of insights from disability studies.[4] The various offerings on the narrative of Frankenstein are almost the only regular point of mutual contact.

4 For example, see the otherwise excellent Judith Halberstam.

In spite of this, we do not have to look far in order to see the potential for fruitful crossover. In a review of Paul Verhoeven's *Robocop,* Julie Codell observes,

> Robocop's body is the nexus of hi-tech production and of consumerism as an end-in-itself. His body focuses a wide range of literal and metaphoric body imagery, expanding into the total corpus: the human body, the corporate body, the body politic, the social body.

Although the character of Murphy and his monstrous incarnation as Robocop rest on his massively impaired, not to say dead, body, Codell's comment points to the possibility of an elaborated view of narrative prosthesis. Firstly, however, any such approach would not favour any one dimension of corporeality over any other. Secondly, it would incorporate a more semiotically informed approach, in which bodily difference is much more commonly a signifying than signified element. Thirdly, such an approach would recognize in its symbolic analyses the theoretical identity of putatively 'real abnormality,' as well as the fantastical and monstrous. Fourthly, it would avoid the generalizing temptation to produce theories that take as their premise the assumption that all instances of portrayed bodily difference would fit a single pattern. And, fifthly, it would anticipate the overdetermination of signified elements.

Works Cited

Berson, Jessica. "Performing Deaf Identity: Toward a Continuum of Deaf Performance." *Bodies in Commotion: Disability and Performance*. Ed. Carrie Sandahl and Philip Auslander. Ann Arbor, MI: University of Michigan Press, 2005. 42–55. Print.

Butler, Judith. *Gender Trouble*. New York, NY: Routledge, 1990. Print.

Clarke, Michael T. "Disability, Spectatorship, and *The Station Agent*." *Disability Studies Quarterly* 34.1 (2014), http://dsq-sds.org/article/view/3310/3522. Accessed 7 May 2019.

Codell, Julie. "Robocop: Murphy's Law, Robocop's Body, and Capitalism's Work." *Jump Cut* 34 (1989): 12–19, https://www.ejumpcut.org/archive/onlinessays/JC34folder/RobocopCodell.html. Accessed 7 May 2019.

Deely, John. "Semiotics 'Today': The Twentieth-Century Founding and Twenty-First-Century Prospects." *International Handbook of Semiotics*. Ed. Peter P. Trifonas. Dordrecht: Springer, 2015. 29–113. Print.

Ellis, Kate. *Disabling Diversity: The Social Construction of Disability in 1990s Australian National Cinema*. Saarbrücken: VDM Verlag, 2008. Print.

Faster, Pussycat! Kill! Kill! Dir. Russ Meyer. Perf. Tura Satana, Haji, Lori Williams, Susan Bernard, Dennis Busch, Stuart Lancaster, and Paul Trinka. Eve Productions. 1965. Film.

Flynn, Susan. "New Poetics of the Film Body: Docility, Molecular Fundamentalism and Twenty First Century Destiny." *American, British and Canadian Studies Journal* 24.1 (2015): 5–23. Print.

Fraser, Benjamin, ed. *Cultures of Representation: Disability in World Cinema*. New York, NY: Columbia University Press, 2016. Print.

Garland-Thomson, Rosemarie. *Staring: How We Look*. New York, NY: Oxford University Press, 2009. Print.

Halberstam, Judith. *Skin Shows: Gothic Horror and the Technology of Monsters*. Durham, NC: Duke University Press, 1995. Print.

McDonough, Jimmy. *Big Bosoms and Square Jaws: The Biography of Russ Meyer*. London: Jonathan Cape, 2005. Print.

Mathijs, Ernest, and Jamie Sexton. *Cult Cinema: An Introduction*. Oxford: Wiley-Blackwell, 2011. Print.

Merrell, Floyd. *Peirce, Signs, and Meaning*. Toronto: University of Toronto Press, 1997. Print.

Mitchell, David T., and Sharon L. Snyder. *Narrative Prosthesis: Disability and the Dependencies of Discourse*. Ann Arbor, MI: University of Michigan Press, 2000. Print.

Mitchell, David T., and Sharon L. Snyder. "Representation and Its Discontents: The Uneasy Home of Disability in Literature and Film." *The Handbook of Disability Studies*. Ed. Gary Albrecht, Katherine D. Seelman and Michael Bury. Thousand Oaks, CA: Sage, 2001. 195–218. Print.

Mollow, Anna. "Is Sex Disability? Queer Theory and the Disability Drive." *Sex and Disability*. Ed. Robert McRuer and Anna Mallow. Durham, NC: Duke University Press, 2014. 285–312. Print.

Mudhoney. Dir. Russ Meyer. Perf. Hal Hopper, Antoinette Christiani, John Furlong, Rena Horten, Princess Livingston, Lorna Maitland, Frank Bolger, and Stuart Lancaster. Eve Productions. 1965. Film.

Robocop. Dir. Paul Verhoeven. Perf. Peter Weller, Nancy Allen, Dan O'Herlihy. Orion Pictures. 1989. Film.

Shakespeare, Tom. *Signs of Life: Medicine and Cinema*. London: Wallflower, 2005. Print.

Smith, Angela. *Hideous Progeny: Disability, Eugenics, and Classic Horror Cinema*. New York, NY: Columbia University Press, 2011. Print.

Snyder, Sharon L. and David T. Mitchell. *Cultural Locations of Disability*. Chicago, IL: Chicago University Press, 2006. Print.

Walz, Mitzi. "Fearful Reflections: Representations of Disability in Post-War Dutch Cinema (1973–2011)." *Cultures of Representation: Disability in World Cinema Contexts*. Ed. Benjamin Fraser. New York, NY: Columbia University Press, 2016. 93–109. Print.

Waters, John. "Russ Meyer: Master." *The Very Breast of Russ Meyer*. Ed. Paul A. Woods. London: Plexus, 2004. 42–47. Print.

Whatley, Sarah. "The Spectacle of Difference: Dance and Disability on Screen." *International Journal of Screendance* 1.1 (2010): 41–52. Print.

Žižek, Slavoj. *Agitating the Frame: Five Essays on Economy, Ideology, Sexuality and Cinema*. New Delhi: Navayana, 2014. Print.

CHAPTER 7

"Never the Twain Shall Meet": Myth and Miracles in Jessica Hauser's 2009 Film *Lourdes*

James Casey

When the disabled protagonist Christine (Sylvie Testud) is brought to Lourdes on a pilgrimage, the diegesis exposes the hypocrisy that surrounds ideological myths of impairment. Furthermore, the film takes a satirical look at how the ideologies of ability, gender, and disability are built upon fragile foundations. *Lourdes* (2009) was written and directed by Jessica Hausner and it is the fourth feature film that the Austrian has directed. It was a critical (if not a box office) success, earning four awards at the 2009 Venice Film Festival and was nominated for the Golden Lion award the same year. The film's narrative is situated in contemporary France and it follows Christine, a wheelchair-user with advanced multiple sclerosis who has very limited mobility, as she undergoes an apparent 'miracle' in the Catholic shrine town of Lourdes. Christine is part of a pilgrimage group facilitated by the French Sovereign Military Hospitaller Order of St John of Jerusalem of Rhodes and of Malta, a militaristic religious order whose ethos is to "protect the faith, serve the sick and the poor" (Sovereign Order of Malta).[1] Not a particularly pious character indeed, Christine, just like other disabled characters in the film, does not display much interest in the metaphysical rhetoric that the pilgrimage offers. Thus, she is at once congratulated and scorned for being 'cured.' Looks and comments of derision from the other pilgrims accompany her 'cure,' in addition to scepticism from the hierarchy of the Order of Malta. Christine's predicament and her reactions to it are a cause of dissent in the film, undermining and challenging ableist discourses about disability.

1 The Order of Malta is composed of Knights, Dames (the hierarchy), and various volunteers. Only recently has this organization allowed non-'nobility' to join the higher echelons of the Order and only if these members are suitably pious and have supported the Catholic Church in a significant manner (although it is unclear what this support is composed of exactly). However, membership is still by invitation only (Sovereign Order of Malta). Furthermore, it must be noted that in two particular countries, Ireland and Germany, the Order is still mainly involved in emergency first aid roles and is less hierarchical than is the case in other European countries.

 | DOI:10.1163/9789004424678_009

The film creates beautifully composed visual nuances exposing the ideology of ability and the societal constructs of impairment that impinge upon disabled people and the roles that characters assume under its influence. Tobin Siebers writes that "disability defines the invisible centre around which our contradictory ideology about human ability revolves" (8–9). The ideology of ability has the effect of making us view disability with alarm and dread and, under its dubious auspices, disability is judged "as what we flee in the past and hope to defeat in the future" (Siebers 9). As a society, how can we reconcile the way in which disability is represented in film with our notions of diversity, equality, and acceptance? It is difficult not to predict the justifiable anger that would be palpable if a cinematic text was deemed to be sexist or racist but rarely does society question the images of disability that the media offer us. As Lennard J. Davis argues in his recent monograph, "Disability, seen as a state of abjection or a condition in need of medical repair or cure, is the resistant point in the diversity paradigm" (*The End of Normal* 9). He further writes: "you can't have a statement like 'we are all different, and we celebrate that diversity' without having some suppressed idea of a norm that defines difference in the first place" (Davis, *The End of Normal* 9). While culture and the media are more than willing to display a wide range of traditionally socially scripted, various minorities, these depictions are always "upbeat, happy, touching, proud and above all healthy" (Davis, *The End of Normal* 9). Moreover, such representations of openness and diversity are always an "able, whole one" that portrays difference as "uplifting" (Davis, *The End of Normal* 9). In this chapter I will discuss how a film, such as *Lourdes*, can offer us a complex and nuanced representation of neurological impairment and one that undermines our assumptions about normality and questions our notions of disability. The disabled character of Christine offers us not only an example of the intersectionality of disability, but also illustrates a subtle resistance to the religious and medicalized notions of disability and impairment which Rosemarie Garland-Thomson and Katarzyna Ojrzyńska discuss in their chapter.

1 Robes and Roles

The religious institution of the Order can be perceived as a microcosm of society, as it has a rigid hierarchical structure built upon each member knowing his/her anointed place in the scheme of things, and at its core there is the ideology of ability. Within this hierarchy reside the 'sick' who are exploited as a fulcrum for charitable acts which are designed in a somewhat overly pessimistic view, to increase the status of the Order's members amongst their peers and superiors and, as Kuno (Bruno Todeschini), a suave member of the organization says, to enable them "to atone for [their] sins."

For example, up until the moment of her 'cure' and subsequent pseudo-celebrity status, Christine is rarely seen as anything other than a burden that must be shouldered by the non-disabled members the Order. The distinction between the non-disabled and the disabled (or 'sick') is clearly marked. Within the film, the uniforms of the 'helpers' are in stark contrast to the everyday attire of the pilgrims they serve. The uniformity of the non-disabled members of the organization is more than simply about clothing. It is at the foundation of their ideology that subscribes to the unattainable 'normal' body and equates any difference to otherness. *Lourdes,* in this sense, brings the question of normalcy under the critical eye of the spectator, for it is not the disabled characters who appear to be deviant, morally corrupt, or in need of treatment, but rather it is the normate characters who are represented in a less than favourable manner. Hausner has stated in an interview:

> In Lourdes [the film] we have the uniforms of the Order of Malta. I strive to make the characters less individualistic, conceiving them rather as prototypes which form a religious or social system.
>
> *Lourdes*: Production Booklet 10

The social system they form is strictly divided, each character playing their part within this structure.

As already mentioned, the characters that are in uniform are defined by their place within the hierarchical system. Their uniforms set them apart from the disabled pilgrims. The lines of distinction are clearly marked by the composition in each frame in which the two worlds of the disabled/non-disabled appear – marked not only by physical difference in the form of attire, but also in terms of social etiquette. The Order members' interaction with non-members is extremely formal. The two groups follow a fixed dialogue strategy, the non-disabled institution dictating the flow and content of each interaction. Any transgression of such norms is quickly dealt with by the organization. For example, during the first scene as the collective group dines in the hotel, Cécile (Elina Löwensohn), who is a high ranking member of the Order of Malta, informs the group of the schedule for the next day. Kuno stands beside her as she speaks, ready to make himself useful handing out brochures to the pilgrims, his stance casual and nonchalant when juxtaposed with the strict, upright posture of Cécile. After the short lecture in which Cécile informs everyone that they must "make an effort" for the itinerary to run smoothly and that "the sick shall forget their loneliness" while they are in Lourdes, she finally concludes her oration with the announcement of the competition for "Best Pilgrim" who will receive an award at the end of the tour for their "good deeds."

The shot cuts to Christine and Marie (Léa Seydoux), a young member of the Order, at their table. Marie feeds Christine, for the disabled protagonist has not the use of her arms due to her neurological impairment. The young organization member asks her: "Do you like the trip?" "Yes," Christine answers, "It's a bit touristy, but every pilgrimage is." "Have you been on many?" Marie asks. "Yes. It's the only way I get out," admits Christine, "travelling isn't easy in a wheelchair." Christine's admission is met with a wry smile from Marie, an extremely subtle expression of understanding, as it later emerges that Marie has little interest in the religious or spiritual aspects of the tour.

2 "Never the twain shall meet"

This allusion to a connection between non-disabled and disabled characters is quickly erased when Christine again speaks without adhering to the rhetoric that is expected from her. In a different scene during meal time, two young members of the Order are talking to Marie and another young female attendant. They ask them if they are joining them for a drink later that evening, tempting them with the prospect of Kuno's company, as apparently his presence is desired by the young women. The young attendants ignore Christine and Mr Hruby (Walter Benn), an elderly, embittered wheelchair-user. The event the young members speak of is exclusionary; it is intended as a wholly non-disabled event that is carried out when the "invalids" are put to bed and "duty" has been done. As Kuno, a more seasoned pilgrim veteran, approaches, he greets everyone at the table cordially, but this is the extent of his desire to interact with Christine and Mr Hruby. Christine, however, takes the opportunity to further the brief conversation. She asks with courage, smiling: "We met on the Rome trip … didn't we?" Kuno stares back at her, slightly taken aback. "Yes, of course," he replies, unsure of their previous meeting. "Well, enjoy yourselves," he tells the table and turns his back swiftly to escape the encounter. "In fact," Christine says, making Kuno turn back around, his smile waning, "I rather prefer the cultural trips." Christine's facial expression is sociable and pleasant. Kuno's is not. "Well," he replies, arms opening in a gesture of dismissal, "everywhere is different." He turns and walks away.

Kuno's stare at Christine is not a gaze of desire that he bestows upon the young female order members, but a form of dominance. As Rosemarie Garland-Thomson writes, "When persons in a position that grants them authority to stare take up that power, staring functions as a form of dominance, marking the staree as the exotic, outlaw, alien, or other" (43). The disabled woman has crossed the imaginary boundary laid down by the film. Her actions, minuscule as they are, become a transgression of the social idioms that are laid down by the formal rigidity of the non-disabled Order and therefore she must be censured. Kuno's stare of dominance is accompanied by a derisive verbal acknowledgment of Christine's presence. It is done without pleasure or warmth and it is he who controls the conversation. Her decision to engage with him after an initial greeting fractures the absurd etiquette to which both groups, disabled pilgrims and Order attendants alike, appear to adhere. Therefore, Kuno's subsequent stare, as he turns around, is one of othering. Christine has contravened the rules and is punished for such indiscretion by Kuno's thinly veiled distaste. The non-disabled characters, whom I construe in this example to be members of the Order, are in Lourdes for reasons other than their professed piety. Indeed, many of them, dressed in their quasi-military uniforms, appear uninterested in the whole enterprise. Several, such as the abovementioned Kuno, see the pilgrimage as an opportunity for sexual misadventure, as it is implied that he and Marie have had some variety of sexual liaison. Needless to say, the non-uniformed characters are represented as asexual, that is until Christine undergoes her 'cure.'

The disabled pilgrims have ascribed roles. They all appear to be seeking atonement for their biological misfortunes. This type of discourse is typical of the disabled characters within the text; many seem to play the role of the sorrowful and meek invalid well. Conversely, the non-disabled Order members are more than happy to offer solutions to the problems that the disabled characters face. In fact, as Paul Longmore has written on disability dramas, "They [the non-disabled characters] understand better than the handicapped characters the true nature of the problem" (7–8). The solution that these non-disabled characters provide is usually metaphysical in nature. For example, the body can only be healed when the soul is fully opened. The text frames non-disabled characters' belief in their bombastic advice as dubious, to say the least. However, it also reinforces the parameters of the non-disabled and disabled dichotomy.

3 Excess and Isolation

In the midst of these two opposing echelons, on the one hand, that of disabled, 'sick' pilgrims and, on the other, of non-disabled 'helpers,' is the figure of Christine. In an interview with Karin Schiefer, Hausner said:

> Lourdes also involves the social aspect, in the sense of: "What role do I play in society? Where can I find my place and the recognition that goes

> with it? What do I have to do for that?" Christine, who's in a wheelchair, is an in-between who doesn't belong in either one place or the other.

The disabled protagonist is unsure of her position within the disabled or non-disabled group, her claims to prefer "cultural trips" and her desire to interact with non-disabled characters marking her as dissimilar. She fits into neither group: those of the Order with their traditional view of disability as a tragic predicament to be borne with dignity or the disabled pilgrims who appear to subscribe to the idioms of enforced normalcy. Or, to use Lennard Davis's words to summarize the perspective of impairment from both groups, "the unwhole body is the unholy body" (*Enforcing Normalcy* 134).

Christine's 'miracle cure,' while ambiguous, reinforces her distinction from the two groups and goes some way to expedite her as an example of a dismodernist subject. Davis theorizes that "dismodernism argues for a commonality of bodies within the notion of difference" and supports the idea that "identity is not fixed but malleable" (*Bending Over Backwards* 26–28). Christine's identity is never fully fixed; she is neither one nor the other, neither disabled nor non-disabled. The 'miracle' she undergoes enables her to drift between the two groups, never joining either. However, the 'miracle' itself is not the sole instigator of her fluid identity, but simply the catalyst. Furthermore, there is no revelatory moment within the narrative that leads to this suggestion, rather from the start of the film Christine's character displays little spiritual adherence and is inclined towards a more pragmatic view of her situation, more so than towards the pity that the disabled archetypes wallow in, or appear to wallow in, to fulfil the role they have been assigned by the non-disabled characters. She declares that she goes on the religious tours as it is not easy for her to travel in a wheelchair unaided. She does not shrink from this admission, but rather embraces it.

In addition, as I will discuss further, Christine's acceptance of Kuno's sexual advances, which Kuno instigates after her 'miracle cure,' implies that she will make her own choices rather than those that have been made for her in the past. She has actively courted him from the start of the film and she follows her desires when he responds to her. Another example of her exertion of her own free will without the approval (or concern for approval) of the groups is when one of the first activities she does when she regains some mobility is to go to a café and eat an elaborate ice-cream. She relishes the decadence of the overflowing glass. This is done of her own accord, away from the disapproving eyes of the other pilgrims who cannot understand why she has been 'chosen' to be 'cured.' Christine herself does not understand it. She does not feel any major spiritual awakening and it is others within the text who project their reasons onto her. However, the other characters' projects and reasons are met with disappointment, and indeed dissent, by events within the diegesis and Christine's perceived perfidious behaviour.

Just as Christine's identity is malleable, so too is one of the most strident non-disabled characters – Cécile. Cécile strictly enforces the divide between the 'weak' and the 'strong.' She is quick to reprimand those who show any behaviour that undermines the rule of normalcy that the Order holds as its ideological basis. One evening Cécile is in the dining-room after the evening meal where she is joined by Kuno. Both characters are hanging red balloons emblazoned with the white Maltese cross for the proceeding night's party. Cécile has been growing noticeably paler each day. She collapses in the room violently, and as she falls to the floor, her veil falls from her head, revealing that she has been wearing a wig to hide her baldness. It is unclear what her illness is, but there is little doubt that it is serious. As she is carried from the room on an antiquated stretcher, her illness is fully observed by all who are sitting in the hotel bar. This scene is a stareable sight. It unsettles the onlookers, both disabled and non-disabled, and all eyes are fixed on this unusual occurrence. Cécile's appearance of normalcy has been destroyed, her piety unrewarded by her illness. As Garland-Thomson writes about the visual act of staring, "we stare not just to know ourselves but to know what we will become" (53). Cecile's pious behaviour and selfless acts of charity do not result in her exemption from impairment. Instead, her sickness implies the arbitrary nature of such categories as 'the human' and 'the disabled,' as well as the flexibility of our bodies to develop and degrade, but never stay the same. As Davis writes, "what is universal in life, if there are any universals, is the experience of the limitations of the body" (*Bending Over Backwards* 32).

The filmmaker's decision to represent Christine's impairment as a neurological condition is an important one. The character's disorder, multiple sclerosis (similar to my own impairment of congenital myasthenia gravis) is unpredictable (MS Society of Ireland). If, as several scholars have noted, the non-disabled population may "fear" and misunderstand disability (Siebers 8), then neurological impairments such as MS, myasthenia gravis, muscular dystrophy, and epilepsy, to name but a few, are even more confusing, not only to non-disabled individuals, but to the wider spectrum of disabled people as well. Due to the unstable nature of the impairment and the effects of these long-term disabling conditions, they are not static impairments, but they rather ebb and flow, even on an hourly basis. In the film, Christine's impairment fluctuates from day to day. Indeed, this is used as an explanation for the miracle when she is brought to the medical office in Lourdes by Fr Hartl (Gilette Barbier). The doctors' prognosis, after some physical examination, is that while the rapid regression of her condition is astonishing, it will not last and it is not an uncommon experience for people with her type of disorder. So, in this regard, the diagnosis has the textual effect of casting doubt on the actual spiritual aspect of the miracle, and it also undermines our assumptions about impairments and disability. At the end of the narrative, Christine requires the use of her wheelchair once again, and the miracle is slipping away. This indicates not only the arbitrary and shifting efficacy of many neurological conditions, but how cultural scripts often see disability as a fixed and permanent condition of deficiency and inability as well.

4 Gender and Excess

In the film, the sardonic wit extends not only to our notions of disability (and, indeed, non-disability), but also it offers a critique of the gender roles that are assigned in contemporary society. Similar to disability mythologies, gender roles are culturally scripted notions and the film illustrates the fact that they stem from a prejudicial, and often hypocritical, patriarchal hierarchy. The major members of the Order are predominantly male, and these Maltese 'knights' are rarely engaged in any facilitation of the pilgrims. Rather, it is the female members of the Order that assume the maternal role of caregiver and facilitator. For instance, it is the female characters, such as Cécile and Marie, that are engaged in the day-to-day activities of the pilgrimage. They assist the disabled pilgrims and organize the logistics of the occasion. There is an almost archaic structure to the gender roles of the men and women within the film, the females carrying out the daily tasks, while the males entertain themselves with relaxing.

It is to these male, non-disabled characters that many of the pilgrims look for direction, often receiving hyperbolic answers in return. For instance, when the seasoned (and strictly devout) pilgrim Mrs Spor (Heidi Baratta) asks the accompanying spiritual director Fr Hartl what she needs to do to be healed physically in Lourdes, he informs her, much to the satisfaction of companions, one of whom, Mr Oliveti (Hubert Kramer), delights in seeing the priest challenged on questions of a theological nature, that while he does believe that God can, of course, perform miracles, the pilgrims must first "open their hearts" to God and have their soul healed before their physical ailments can be cured. Mrs Spor accepts Fr Hartl's response, for although it is metaphysical in nature, is he not an ordained man of God? And who better to know the will of God than a man of the cloth? Hausner states that: "My female characters often learn over the course of the film that this masculine authority can't provide them with answers. They are disabled by it" (*Lourdes*: Production Booklet).

Fr Hartl's explanation of, and reasoning for, Christine's cure become less convincing as the narrative progresses when it is suggested that she herself is not the most devout of the group. When Christine recounts the events of her cure to Fr Hartl and Mr Oliveti, she describes the physical and emotional sensations that she experienced, rather than any spiritual awakening. Mr Oliveti asks: "But what about inside yourself? Do you feel a sort of illumination?" "Not really," Christine responds. Hartl and Oliveti slump somewhat in their armchairs, clearly having received the wrong answer and Christine, noticing this, asks if it matters. Fr Hartl again responds with a lesson in catechism in which he informs her that it depends: "let's say it depends on the way you internalize this healing. One may wonder will it reinforce your faith and make your attitude an example for all Christians?" Here Hartl projects the dominant ideological discourse onto Christine's experiences. Like the ideology of ability, this catechism makes assumptions about how one should behave and act. The culturally prescribed roles we are assigned come with responsibilities and protocols as to our behaviour and the film's diegesis suggests the fragile foundations of these restrictive etiquettes. Christine, as I have discussed, is not the most pious of pilgrims, yet she reluctantly plays the role assigned to her by others. Indeed, it is her reluctance and, albeit unconscious, resistance to these culturally scripted roles of gender and disability which suggest a nuanced depiction of impairment which does not rely on archetypical characterization. In several scenes of the film, we can see how Christine offers resistance both to her expected role as a woman and disabled person. A suggestive, nuanced example is when the group travels to the mountains for an excursion on the penultimate day of the pilgrimage.

The afternoon trip to the foothills of the Pyrenees is in itself an exclusionary activity. The previous night at dinner Mrs Oliveti (Helga Illich), one of the few senior female Order members, announces to the gathered group that only those who are non-disabled will be allowed to go on the trip due to the difficult terrain. This may appear to be a logical rationale; however, it further excludes the disabled characters from the non-disabled world. This is a conscious act of isolation and exclusion, for indeed the Order could have chosen a different location for the afternoon trip which was more inclusive, or even hired accessible transport. Instead, it is an act of dominance by the non-disabled hegemony within the diegesis. Film, as David T. Mitchell and Sharon L. Snyder observe, "can produce influential social beliefs about disability" (19), and *Lourdes* subtly illustrates these beliefs with some dose of irony.

The disabled pilgrims are consciously excluded from the leisure activity, since there is no religious purpose to the trip to the mountains. Its aim is that of attaining a pure sense of the environment and satisfaction of the body and the senses, rather than any healing of the soul. The disabled pilgrims are only readily utilized within the religious occasions in Lourdes, and thrust forward to atone for their sins so that, hopefully, their bodies are healed. This is not to abrogate the disabled characters from being complicit in their subordinate position in the film, for in several instances they appear more than willing to fall into easily identifiable stereotypes. For example, one evening in the hotel lobby, a group of mainly disabled characters, nuns and some female Order members stand around in a circle praying and singing. They ask God for what they wish to receive from their journey to the ecclesial town. One young man, leaning on his walker, says: "Lord, my fiancée left me after my motorbike accident. Let me find another fiancée who is better able to handle my disability." Here, as Paul Darke has noted, is an example where "disabled people are as equally socialized into seeing disability as negative as those who are non-disabled" (14). The young disabled man perceives his impairment as a handicap that needs to be "handled." Furthermore, his request to find a new fiancée is perhaps an expression of his masculinity. Russell Shuttleworth, Nikki Wedgewood, and Nathan J. Wilson have noted that being involved in "hegemonic masculine practices... invariably includes an evaluation of one's relative loss/gain in social status" (183). Throughout the text, any display of sexuality or gender by the disabled characters is met by a wall of indifference and dismissive stares by the non-disabled characters. Therefore, we can see how the young man's dialogue suggests that his desire for a long-term relationship may be a conduit to an elevated social position among the non-disabled hegemony for, as the diegesis of the film suggests, the more physically impaired a disabled character is, the greater their distance from non-disabled sexuality.

Christine blurs the boundaries of disabled and non-disabled worlds when she travels to the mountains with the non-disabled members of the pilgrim group. At first, she is denied access to the bus by Marie, who is seemingly jealous of the loss of Kuno's affection that she sees Christine is attracting, even though she has become somewhat more mobile, using only a walking stick for support. However, she is allowed to join the non-disabled group when it is pointed out by Mrs Oliveti that she is taking Cécile's place on the excursion. Evocatively, it is Cécile's removal from the narrative that allows Christine to join the non-disabled activity. Cécile, as I have discussed, is negated from the world of the non-disabled because of her illness and diminished physical state. The dramatic revelation of her infirmity to the staring onlookers is, as Siebers writes, suggestive that "most people do not consider that life's passage will lead them from ability to disability" (60).

Again, within the body of the text, Cécile's disruptive body and her loss of position in the hierarchy undermines the mythical metanarrative of ablebodiedness. Nonetheless, as Siebers writes further, "the human ego does not easily accept the disabled body" (60). Christine is only allowed into the non-disabled world when her impairment is unobtrusive enough not to be a reminder of the fallibility of the human form and, in many cases, the instability of impairments to be a static predicament. Christine takes Cécile's place, not only in the excursion to the Pyrenees, but also metaphorically. She is now the focus of attention within the group. Her apparent cure and unasked for pseudo-celebrity status draw stares of curiosity and looks of derision. Christine becomes almost a physical manifestation of the Virgin Mary after the divisive miracle. This is suggested by subtle visual cues when we see in several scenes that Christine is wearing light blue clothing, similar to the colour that adorns the many statues of the Madonna in the film.

Any resemblance that Christine has to the idealized figure of the Madonna is, however, one which is not only suggested by the camera, but also projected onto her by the other characters. The scene of the bus journey to the mountains, opens with a shot of Christine talking to two middle-aged women in the seats in front of her. She tells them that she wants to start a career as soon as she can and that she believes "great things are in store" for her. One of the women quickly turns around to face the protagonist and says enthusiastically: "Or you could have a family. That's possible, isn't it?" Repeatedly in the narrative, the characters, both disabled and non-disabled, project their wants, needs, fears, and insecurities onto Christine. Christine's role, first as a disabled pilgrim and then as a woman, is being defined by others, not herself. Her decisions appear to be dismissed and, apparently, contingent upon their hegemonic ideological approval. The non-disabled women negate Christine's wish to have a career, a life of her own choosing and, instead, allot her a fixed, culturally scripted role as a mother and caregiver. Of course, before Christine underwent her 'cure' she could not be (and was not) expected, or even considered to fulfil these gendered obligations. As Marian Blackwell-Stratton et al. write,

> Unlike the non-disabled woman, who has socially sanctioned roles as mother and wife (restrictive though they may be), the disabled woman has no adult roles. Neither mother nor wife nor worker shall she be.
>
> BLACKWELL-STRATTON et al. 306

Once more, as the narrative of the film progresses, Christine is faced with a limited interpretation of her identity by the non-disabled hegemony. How she is perceived by the other characters within the text is informed by their restrictive notions of what position she should assume, and again Christine resists their assumptions.

When the group arrives in the mountains, they steadily walk up sharply inclined footpaths to reach flower strewn meadows that look out upon the granite peaks. Graeme Harper and Jonathan Rayner note, on the subject of how landscape can operate in film as a form of pathetic fallacy, that "the metaphoric cinematic landscape is the landscape of suggestion" (20). Here, in the pastures of the Pyrenees, the largely non-disabled group relaxes in their elevated position, not only in terms of their actual physical location high above the town of Lourdes, but also in their position as members of the non-disabled hegemony. And so they sit upon the mountain, like gods of the ideology of ability, refuting (or ignoring) the fragility of their own position. Below them in the town of Lourdes remain the legions of disabled pilgrims with broken bodies in need of treatment and cure. However, on the hillside, the excursionists have left the world of the 'sick' behind. It is here that Christine subverts the expectations once more, not only in terms of her role as a disabled person, but also in relation to the gendered position she is assigned in the text.

Christine approaches Kuno as he sits upon the grass and asks him if he is all alone. After a brief conversation where he tells her that he finds the whole miracle "strange," we see them walking off into the privacy of a wooded area. Marie, staring at the duo, sulks that she is not the focus of Kuno's predatory sexual advances anymore. Significantly, it is Christine that instigates the conversation with Kuno, similar to the scene at dinner where she was censured for violating the rules of disabled and non-disabled communication by Kuno's stare. However, Kuno appears genuinely perplexed and almost vulnerable when Christine approaches him. Importantly, it is Christine that leads him to the privacy of the trees. She has become the predator, the instigator of a romantic and presumably sexual encounter. In doing so, she supplants the gendered and ableist ideological myths that others would project onto her. This may seem like a dubious narrative turn, the predator becoming prey, but Kuno's moral compass is shaky to say the least. In one lingering shot, as he tells Christine he wishes to kiss her, we clearly see he is wearing a wedding ring – an indicator perhaps of his infidelity.

In the last scene of the film, the group gathers for the farewell party where Christine is announced as the winner of the Best Pilgrim award and goes to the makeshift stage to collect the strange honour. Her speech is brief, as she is unsure of what she is required to say. Although Christine did not choose to be cured, the 'miracle' appears to have happened to her and with that come societal expectations from various members of the groups. After her brief speech, the dance floor begins to fill with people. She approaches Kuno and the two of them take to the centre of the floor and slowly move to the music. As he twirls her around slowly, she drops to the floor. The fellow dancers stop and stare as does every other individual in the room. She is assisted to her feet by Kuno and walks unsteadily to the edge of the dance floor. He stands beside her until Mrs Spor, Christine's roommate, pushes Christine's wheelchair up beside her. "I don't need it," Christine tells the older woman.

A few seconds pass and Kuno says sheepishly: "I'll be back in a second." He walks away from the two women (and the wheelchair) and after a few moments Christine, with a slight hint of acceptance that he may not be back, sits back into the wheelchair, much to Mrs Spor's pleasure, as she has enjoyed the significance of being Christine's unofficial carer. She leans down and whispers something into Christine's ear and the protagonist nods smiling. The two leave the frame and the film ends. Christine does not appear embittered by the apparent rejection from Kuno, nor does she look significantly perturbed by resuming her position in the wheelchair after two days of walking independently. Kuno's rejection is a dismissal by the non-disabled echelon and, due to her 'cure,' she has already been excluded from the disabled group. Now she no longer truly fits into the narrow ideologies of either faction, her identity with either group is flexible and changing, moving between each and adhering to none and in that flexibility lies her complexity and, as is implied by the character's appearance at the end of the film, contentment with her own identity rather than one laid down by others.

5 Conclusion

The rationale for this chapter, and what I hope I have illustrated even a little, is that impairment is not always the defining characteristic of a disabled character and that the disability narrative can communicate this in a subtle way rather than act as a metaphor for the insistence on the ideology of ability or even some other disability metanarrative which may, for instance, suggest that all disabled people have a strong disabled identity. Impairment is a part of disability, but not as significant a part as the negative societal perceptions of it. Moreover, these negative societal perceptions have flowed over into contemporary cinema with its fascination with returning the disabled character to an acceptable state. However, there exist certain examples of films, as the evidence has suggested, that do not insist on a return to a mythical normalcy for its disabled characters. Christine may not be the most likeable or politically aware of disabled characters. She does not resist the rule of oppression by embracing their disabled identity wholeheartedly, but nonetheless she may give us an alternative to the mainstay of disability stereotypes that saturate modern cinema.

The disabled protagonist in *Lourdes* does not wholly conform to stereotypes of disabled characterization. Christine is never fully integrated, or allowed to integrate, into either of the strata of the pilgrimage social classes. Instead, she partially inhabits both worlds and never fully knows the role that she is expected to play by either party. She is not defined, nor does she allow herself to be fully defined by either group. In her liminality she refutes the metanarratives that they represent. The difference between the two groups, disabled and non-disabled, is clearly defined and reinforced by dialogue and diegesis. However, this difference and the irrationality of the characters and the roles these characters take (with the exception of the protagonist) are dealt with in a humorous fashion. This humour is not of the crass kind that has so frequently been the mainstay of Hollywood cinema and it does not regress to constant biological difference and the effects of impairment as a source of puerile hilarity. Instead, the film makes us question our attitudes to impairment and how we consider a disabled character should operate within a story and its narrative. It does not mark the different body as abnormal – rather only our attitudes towards physical differences and the constant desire to 'fix' them permanently come across as odd.

Identity and diversity have become central issues of debate in our contemporary society. We would be led to believe that identities are no longer prescribed, but rather freely chosen. Nevertheless, when it comes to impairment and physical disability, often there is no choice for individuals, but rather there is a narrow set of cultural scripts that are projected on to them. Disabled people do not see themselves as objects of pity or needing to 'overcome' their perceived misfortune but, equally, not all disabled people see themselves solely as victims of a disabling society, but rather continue their fight for equality in their own diverse ways. Individuals are as complex and varied as their impairments. As Tom Shakespeare notes, "[m]any disabled people will prefer to seek out what they have in common with non-disabled people, promoting inclusion and equal status, not separatism" (82). In this context, Shakespeare acknowledges that the various disability rights' movements may not be the only paradigms of disability, although such a social constructionist perspective is essential to ensuing issues of human rights and equality, but argues rather that sometimes disability is not the defining characteristic of an individual with an impairment. Instead, it is a more subtle and more complex predicament one finds oneself in where one may regard oneself as neither a hostage to fortune nor a victim of an overwhelming disabling society. *Lourdes* offers us such a perspective.

Furthermore, diversity is the dominant ideological zeitgeist of our contemporary moment. Differences in gender, sex, race, religious affiliation, age, and nationality are no longer regarded as being the opposite of 'normality.' Rather difference is celebrated and embraced as a reflection of the true nature of humanity itself. While racism, sexism, xenophobia, and homophobia are no longer acceptable, although they are still very much present, there remains one category of humanness that is not considered within the wider canon of diversity. Disability continues to be regarded as in need of cure, eradication, and almost exclusively as being outside 'the norm' and in the realm of medicalization. Michael Davidson writes that

> disabled people do not think of themselves as "variants" from some norm, yet they live surrounded by triumphalist narratives of athletes or public figures who have conquered their "handicaps" to live "normal" lives.
>
> DAVIDSON 233

The analysis of prescribed notions of disability, such as the one carried out in this chapter, foregrounds that these paradigms of 'overcoming' are precisely what the cinema and mass media and wider society are obsessed with.

Disability and impairment violate the paradigm of diversity by being designated as outside 'the norm,' outside the acceptable. As I have hoped to illustrate, culture is central to the construction of disability as a contravention of the healthy, non-disabled body. Often film achieves this by excessive representation and construction of disability as a predicament in need of fixing. This suggests, as Davis has noted, that disability represents the last remnant of that which is deemed to be not 'normal' in an era that purports to claim there is no such thing as 'normal.' It is perceived as less as the non-disabled, healthy body. In cinema this healthiness takes various, subtle forms, such as emotional maturity, psychological balance, and the selfless behaviour of the non-disabled characters. This paradigm is almost reversed in *Lourdes,* however. The nuances and subtleties are amplified to suggest the fragility of the cultural notions of non-disabled and, indeed, disabled bodies. It is in this representation where, perhaps, the true phenomenon occurs.

Works Cited

Blackwell-Stratton, Marian, et al. "Smashing Icons: Disabled Women and the Disability and Women's Movements." *Women with Disability: Essays in Psychology, Culture and Politics*. Ed. Michelle Fine and Adrienne Asch. Philadelphia, PA: Temple University Press. 1992. 306–32. Print.

Darke, Paul. "Everywhere: Disability on Film." *Framed: Interrogating Disability in the Media*. Ed. Ann Pointon and Chris Davis. London: BFI, 1997. 10–15. Print.

Davidson, Michael. *Concerto for the Left-Handed: Disability and the Defamiliar Body*. Ann Arbor, MI: University of Michigan Press, 2008. Print.

Davis, Lennard J. *Bending Over Backwards: Disability, Dismodernism and Other Difficult Positions*. New York, NY: New York University Press, 2002. Print.

Davis, Lennard J. *The End of Normal: Identity in a Biocultural Era*. Ann Arbor, MI: University of Michigan Press, 2014. Print.

Davis, Lennard J. *Enforcing Normalcy: Disability, Deafness and the Body*, London: Verso, 1995. Print.

Garland-Thomson, Rosemarie. *Staring: How We Look*. Oxford: Oxford University Press, 2009. Print.

Harper, Graeme, and Jonathan Rayner. Introduction. *Cinema and Landscape*. Ed. Graeme Harper and Jonathan Rayner. Chicago, IL: University of Chicago Press, 2010. 13–28. Print.

Hausner, Jessica. Interview by Karin Schiefer. *Austrian Film Commission*, Sept. 2009, http://www.austrianfilms.com/news/en/jessica_hausner_talks_about_lourdes. Accessed 9 May 2019.

Longmore, Paul K. "Screening Stereotypes: Images of Disabled People." *Screening Disability: Essays on Cinema and Disability*. Ed. Anthony Enns and Christopher R. Smit. Lanham, MA: University Press of America, 2001. 1–18. Print.

Lourdes. Dir. Jessica Hausner. Perf. Sylvie Testud, and Bruno Todeschini, Coop 99, 2009. DVD.

Lourdes: Production Booklet. Venezia 2009, https://coproductionoffice.eu/assets/films/lourdes/presskit/HAULOU-Pressbook.pdf. Accessed 9 Jul. 2019.

Mitchell, David T., and Sharon L. Snyder. *Cultural Locations of Disability*. Chicago, IL: University of Chicago Press, 2006. Print.

Multiple Sclerosis Society of Ireland. "Living with MS," https://www.ms-society.ie/pages/living-with-ms. Accessed 9 May 2019.

Shakespeare, Tom. *Disability Rights and Wrongs*. Routledge: London, 2006. Print.

Shuttleworth, Russell, Wedgewood, Nikki, and Nathan J. Wilson. "The Dilemma of Disabled Masculinity." *Men and Masculinities*. 15.2 (2012): 174–94. Print.

Siebers, Tobin. *Disability Theory*. Ann Arbor, MI: University of Michigan Press, 2008. Print.

Sovereign Order of Malta. FAQs, https://www.orderofmalta.int/sovereign-order-of-malta/faq/. Accessed 9 May 2019.

PART 4

Bodies that Matter: Representing and Experiencing Non-standard Physiques

∴

CHAPTER 8

A Dwarf – A Metaphor and a Body in Words and Images

Agnieszka Izdebska

The chapter focuses on the representations of dwarfs in selected twentieth-century literary works. The changing images of people of short stature – perceived as a group of people with disability who in the past had a rare professional status in European culture (especially at the Spanish court of the Habsburgs from the sixteenth to the beginning of the eighteenth century) – are seen here as examples of a general shift in the depictions of disability and disabled people. The works I refer to are representative of the evolution that has taken place. They illustrate a departure from using dwarfism as a metaphor towards showing non-normative bodies just as bodies, which define us as human beings and which are sometimes freakish, sometimes quite common, or both at the same time. This "major paradigm shifts in recent critical thought and practice" (29), which Garland-Thomson and Ojrzyńska discuss in their chapter and which finds a reflection in the new politics of representation, is an offshoot of the changes in the discourses that define the position of various minorities in Western culture (Adelson xvi) and the way the human body is perceived today. In the twentieth century many underprivileged groups successfully fought to have their subjectivity recognized and make themselves heard. Nowadays their new status is acknowledged, but the details of the evolution of cultural representations of dwarfism are intriguing enough to warrant exploration.

Dwarfs used to have a unique position at the Spanish courts of the Habsburgs and Bourbons. They were seen as a perfect embodiment of the idea of *barocco* – irregularity of shapes and forms – and precious gifts offered to royal children or nobles (e.g. Charles V sent two dwarfs to the Polish king Sigmund Augustus). Some of them obtained relatively high positions, becoming court officials or ladies-in-waiting. But most of the court dwarfs merely had the status of pets or slaves (Tuan 2). They were jesters; they were served in pies during parties (as a form of entertainment, of course) (Tuan 155); they performed as pawns in "The Courtier's Philosophy" – a "Monopoly"-like game which Phillip II loved to play. Their position is a perfect illustration of a remark given by an infant princess in a well-known fairy tale by Oscar Wilde, entitled "The Birthday of the Infanta."

 | DOI:10.1163/9789004424678_010

Looking at a dwarf in a state of despair brought about by the sight of his own reflection in a mirror, the Spanish princess says: "Indeed he is almost as good as the puppets, only of course not quite so natural" (Wilde 201).

Not all of these people have been forgotten, though – there are many paintings presenting Spanish rulers with the smallest court members and most of us are familiar with Diego Velazquez's canonical portraits of dwarfs. The painter had a unique attitude towards the people that he depicted. Jonathan Brown and Carmen Garrido, writing about Velazquez's portraits, acknowledge that

> by dedicating the same artistry to the dwarf as to the prince, Velazquez reverses the flow of energy in the conventional contrast between the perfect and the deformed, forcing us to contemplate the dwarf as a person and not merely as a pretext to glorify the beauty of the prince.
>
> BROWN 146

These depictions adhered to the popular convention of presenting jesters' services and followed the same pattern: a master holds his or her hand on a dwarf's head. This gesture reflects the relationship between them: the overpowering domination, dependency, and the sense of being another's property, but at the same time a kind of symbiosis, an intimacy between the dwarf and the master.

Thus, dwarfs have long been visible in European culture – and they were not exclusively represented as 'crippled' or 'disabled.' Their depictions show traces of the ambiguous social and aesthetic legacy I have outlined above. It is not my intention to present all aspects of the historical evolution of the status of people of short stature in European culture. Obviously the topic is far too broad for a single chapter. Furthermore, some research on this topic has already been published, such as Betty M. Adelson's 2005 book *The Lives of Dwarfs: Their Journey from Social Curiosity to Public Liberation*, the subtitle of which aptly summarizes the change that has taken place. Instead, the chapter offers a general reflection upon the representations of people of short stature in Western culture and provides a historical framework to build upon. It traces their subjectification and increased social visibility in the cultural texts which seek to challenge the pervasive use of non-normative bodies as metaphors, a phenomenon that fits in well with David T. Mitchell and Sharon L. Snyder's concept of "narrative prosthesis," defined as "a crutch upon which literary narratives lean for their representational power, disruptive potentiality, and analytical insight" and "a potent symbolic sight of literary investment" (49).[1]

1 For more on narrative prosthesis, see Goodley and Mackiewicz's chapter in this volume.

The chapter focuses on a few novels. The first literary work to be discussed is *The Dwarf* (1944), a well-known novel by Nobel Prize winner Pär Lagerkvist. The next one is *Drabina Jakubowa albo podróż* (*Jacob's Ladder or the Journey*, 1988) by Władysław L. Terlecki, a Polish novelist. The three other literary texts to be analyzed are: *Geek Love* (1989) by Katherin Dunn, *Mendel's Dwarf* (1998) by Simon Mawer and, finally, a series of fantasy novels *A Song of Ice and Fire* (1996–2011) by George R.R. Martin. The above-mentioned texts are very different from one another: their authors use various genres and aesthetic conventions, and they were created in different times. Yet, all of them have a common denominator: they feature dwarfs as important characters. Furthermore, all of these texts refer to the ambivalent 'courtly heritage' of people of short stature: in each of them the position of the dwarf protagonist is strongly determined by the historical status of people of short stature, who were seen as curious and entertaining humanoid creatures and who were relegated to the margins of the world of power. Nevertheless, these characters are often desperately eager to gain the power to influence the course of events.

The narrative of *The Dwarf* by Pär Lagerkvist is based on the diaries of a fictional dwarf, written at the court of an Italian Renaissance prince. The events are thus described from the perspective of a person of short stature. Although it is not a historical novel, the plot is set in a place modelled upon a sixteenth-century Italian duchy. The character of the Prince, the protagonist's master, is patterned after two real figures: Ludovico Sforza and Cesare Borgia.

The eponymous character of the novel presents himself on the first page of his manuscript: "I am a dwarf and nothing but a dwarf" (Lagerkvist 5). He perceives himself as a creature belonging to a breed older than the human race. He writes: "We dwarfs have no homeland, no parents; we allow ourselves to be born of strangers, anywhere, in secret, among the poorest and most wretched, so that our race should not die out" (Lagerkvist 15). He feels an alien among the people around him and he is a merciless observer of their behaviour. Their acts seem to him reckless and dictated by emotional impulses, thus rendering human beings worthy of contempt. He is proud to be the only one who does not pretend to be something or somebody: "Only I *am*" (Lagerkvist 20).

Surprisingly, the only person whom he does not despise is the Prince. The dwarf writes about him with admiration: "He is very treacherous" (Lagerkvist 7) and adds: "I will not deny that he is a great man; but nobody is great to his dwarf" (Lagerkvist 7). The main character sees the relationship between his master and himself as very complex. He feels that he symbolically represents the Prince in his absence: he wears the same clothes and behaves like him, but he is aware of the fact that nobody notices him in the Prince's presence. The protagonist is like his master's shadow, and he follows him constantly – visible and invisible at the same time. He writes:

> Even the ignorant mob understands that the master's dwarf is really the master himself, just as the castle is he ... and the court with all this pomp and splendour ... all that is *He*. They have no notion of the power I really represent. And it fills me with satisfaction to see that I am hated!
>
> LAGERKVIST 17–18

But the role of the dwarf is not limited to representing his master. When during a huge feast that ends the war the protagonist is ordered to assassinate a number of enemies of the Prince, using poisoned wine, he takes this opportunity to kill a lover of his master's wife, simply because the dwarf dislikes him and, what is more important, because he 'can' do that. While he is pouring wine into don Ricardo's goblet, he meets the Prince's eyes:

> Human eyes are sometimes like that – a dwarf's never. It was as though everything in his soul had floated to the surface and was watching me and my actions with mingled fear, anxiety, and desire; as though strange monsters had emerged from the depths.... I know what he wants.
>
> LAGERKVIST 148

The dwarf is aware of the fact that he acts in a way in which his master would not dare to act. Being watched by the Prince, he feels like a tool in the hands of fate. He has power, which he loves so much, and he decides about life and death. The protagonist explains: "I felt how the world had, through me, been filled with terror and doom, and transformed from a brilliant feast to a place of fear and destruction" (Lagerkvist 153). At the end of the novel, the dwarf, imprisoned in the dungeon of the castle, waits for his master to send for him. He is quite certain that soon the Prince will need his dwarf again.

It is rather obvious that Lagerkvist's novel is constructed like a parable: the disabled protagonist is more of a literary device or, to use Snyder and Mitchell's words, a crutch that the novel leans on, than a round, well-developed, psychologically credible character. He does not evolve, while almost all other characters change. At some point in the novel, we realize that the dwarf could be an embodiment of the dark side of the Prince himself, his Jungian shadow, not a real, autonomous person. The dwarf suggests this in a fairly straight-forward manner: "I was a viper and the evil genius of his Most Princely Grace, and it was his expressed wish.... Human beings are too feeble and exalted to shape their own destiny" (Lagerkvist 216). The protagonist comments on people's admiration for art: "Human beings like to see themselves reflected in clouded mirrors" (Lagerkvist 225) and he offers them himself as a sharp clear mirror. That is why he claims that he scares people, who are in fact afraid of "the dwarf within them, the ape-faced manlike being who sticks up its head from the depths of their souls" (Lagerkvist 29–30). Finally, the dwarf's atypical body is just a screen onto which people's inner, invisible monstrosity is projected.

On the one hand, Lagerkvist uses the ages-old stereotype which is deeply rooted in the symbolic model of disability, described by Garland-Thomson and Ojrzyńska in their chapter. According to this ableist, stereotypical view, a deformed body denotes a deformation of the soul, and thus Lagerkvist's protagonist looks like a monster, acts like a monster, and 'is' a monster. In this respect the dwarf bears close resemblance to Richard III. As David T. Mitchell and Sharon L. Snyder comment on his portrayal in Shakespeare's play, "Difference demands display, display demands difference" (55). They elaborate on this cultural rule in the following way:

> Either the "deviant" body deforms subjectivity, or "deviant" subjectivity violently erupts upon the surface of its bodily container. In either instance the corporeal body of disability is represented as manifesting its own internal symptoms.
>
> MITCHELL and SNYDER 58

But at the same time, Lagerkvist's dwarf is not a person at all. He is not 'a body' either. He is almost a pure metaphor of monstrosity which is integral to the human condition.

In Lagerkvist's novel, the story is told from the perspective of an outsider. A similar narrative strategy was used in *Drabina Jakubowa* (*Jacob's Ladder*) by Władysław Terlecki. Both Lagerkvist's and Terlecki's characters directly illustrate Mitchell and Snyder's suggestion that "to represent disability is to engage oneself in an encounter with that which is believed to be off the map of 'recognizable' human experiences" (5).

Terlecki, considered to be one of the most eminent founders of the modern Polish historical novel, published *Drabina Jakubowa* in 1988. The novel is a narrative about a journey around Russia at the end of the eighteenth century. Its protagonist, Alexander, is an employee of a Polish count, who has a secret mission to deliver an important letter from the king of Poland to Catherine the Great. The novel is an example of philosophical fiction, typical of the eighteenth-century early European novel, and also serves as a parable of the Polish fears of its powerful neighbour. At the end of the story, the Polish dwarf is absorbed by the monstrous tsarina in a sexual act.

Although, to some extent, the text presents the protagonist as a flesh-and-blood character, his main role in *Drabina Jakubowa* is metaphorical. As regards the realistic aspect of the novel, the author was inspired by a historical figure – count Józef Boruwłaski, a famous Polish dwarf who was a social sensation at the turn of the eighteenth and the nineteenth centuries (Adelson 19–20). Alexander – like Boruwłaski in his own published memoirs – shows a lot of self-awareness and offers valuable insights into the social perception of people of short stature. He feels like a toy or a kind of talking parrot, curious and funny. He is also depicted as a sage who, because of his physical otherness, observes from a distanced perspective people's suspicious and pathetic actions that he considers unworthy of intelligent beings. But, in a more general sense, Terlecki uses the figure of the dwarf to lay bare human powerlessness when confronted with mechanisms of history that mercilessly crush them.

This conflict between the small and powerless individual and those who represent the social and historical forces that control the world is most conspicuous in the fragment which shows that Alexander, like Jonathan Swift's Gulliver in the land of giants, is a person whose senses are heightened. He perceives reality as a place where the intense sensory presence of "big people" can be felt: the fragrances of their bodies, sounds of their voices, and touches of their palms. These violent experiences cause trauma:

> He was taken to balls. He compelled admiration of giant, noisy men. Squeals of women, just as coarse and huge as them, accompanied his every appearance. They took him in their arms. They lifted him up. Their breaths were saturated with the smell of liquor. They gaped. He was pressed against ample, heaving breasts of women, which moved up and down. He then felt the smell of their sweat and the blusher rubbed into their skin. The powder from their wigs cascaded onto his face. But the earth still rotated on its axis at the very same time and beyond it.[2]

Alexander can do nothing to protect himself against that massive and noisy assault of those giants and their world.

The two novels are obviously very different in terms of their narrative structure and possible interpretations, but they are also similar in much more sophisticated ways. They present the world from a dwarf's points of view, giving the reader precious critical glimpses of the typically sized society and its members' perceptions of those who do not fit the bodily norm. Both characters

---

2 "Prowadzono go na bale. Wzbudzał podziw ogromnych, hałaśliwych mężczyzn. Piski kobiet, tak samo ordynarnych i wielkich, towarzyszyły każdemu jego pojawieniu się. Brali go na ręce. Podnosili do góry. Wydmuchiwali przesiąknięte zapachem trunków powietrze. Wybałuszali oczy. Wielkie piersi kobiet, do których go przyciskały, podnosiły się i opadały. Czuł wtedy zapach roztartego różu i zapach potu. Osypywał mu się na twarz puder z ich peruk. A ziemia obracała się nadal na swojej osi w tym samym czasie i poza jego miarami" (Terlecki 279). Trans. A.I.

have the same attitude towards others, whom they call "big people": their corporeality fills them with disgust. The shape and the size of their bodies determine their position in the world completely and render the boundary separating them from "the normate"[3] impassable. Nevertheless, both characters are, above all, metaphorical figures that serve the function of narrative prostheses, rather than psychologically credible portrayals of people with non-normative bodies.

The protagonists are used instrumentally both by the novelists and by other characters in the texts. Alexander as well as Lagerkvist's character are located both in the middle and on the periphery of the dynamic world of power and manipulation. They influence the course of events, but mostly serve as other people's tools and thus the scope of their decisions is rather limited. They both desperately want to be part of history, politics, and philosophical debates of their times. But they are excluded from all of that because of the shapes of their bodies which define their position in the social hierarchy of the "big people's" world. Thus, both texts offer a powerful commentary on the social position of people of short stature and yet in a sense render them largely invisible as humans.

Published in 1989, Katherine Dunn's novel *Geek Love* definitely has a special position among the twentieth-century works of literature featuring dwarf protagonists. Its story is told by Olympia, a hunchbacked albino dwarf, who, in a flashback narrative, reveals the history of her family. Her parents were the second generation of the owners of a freak show and they experimented with chemical substances in order to produce offspring with atypical bodies who would become new members of their troupe, "The Fabulous Biniewskis." Olympia tells the readers about her siblings, parents, and their life on the road, but the real central figure of the story is her demonic brother, Arturo, who performed as Aqua Boy since "his hands and feet were in the form of flippers that sprouted directly from his torso without intervening arms or legs" (Dunn 7–8). Arty also purported to be a prophet. During his performances, he gave his audience what he called "testifying." As Olympia explains,

> What Arty wanted the crowds to hear was that they were all hormone-driven insects and probably deserved to be miserable but that he, the Aqua Boy, could really feel for them because he was in much better shape.
>
> DUNN 115

3 As Garland-Thomson and Ojrzyńska have reminded us in their chapter, the normate is "the veiled subject position of cultural self, the figure outlined by the array of deviant others whose marked bodies shore up the normate's boundaries" (Garland-Thomson 8).

He founded a kind of a sect, described by one of the characters as "*a quasi-religious cult making no representations of a god or gods, and having nothing to say about life after death*" (Dunn 227). "Arturism" offered "Peace, Isolation, Purity" (Dunn 227) to its followers, which could be attained by subsequent amputations reducing their bodies to the ideal shape: head and torso. Arturo created a subversive quasi-religion out of freakishness and disability. He was a dictator who, in fact, controlled both the family and the sect, and who easily manipulated people, including Olympia, who loved him blindly. She was completely subordinated to her brother, but, at the same time, she was afraid of him. After she delivered his child, she was determined to protect her daughter from Arturo's power.

Dunn's novel is a parable written in the convention of the grotesque. It could be interpreted as a statement about the status of physical otherness in contemporary culture, as it scrutinizes such concepts as: beauty, ugliness, normality, oddity, sanctity, and obscenity. But the whole carnivalesque story is told by a person who is constructed as a round, psychologically well-developed character. Olympia quotes Arty's words:

> We have this advantage, that the norms expect us to be wise. Even a rat's-ass dwarf jester got credit for terrible canniness disguised in his foolery. Freaks are like owls, mythed into blinking, bloodless objectivity.
>
> DUNN 114

She is a complex human being and a self-aware individual. She lives in a fragile balance between memories of the former terrible bittersweet phantasmagorical life of "The Fabulous Biniewskis" and the everyday life of an aging hunchbacked albino dwarf working for the radio. She constantly analyzes her relationships with others, fully aware of the fact that she perfectly matches the popular image of 'a freak.' She writes:

> People talk easily to me. They think a bald albino can't hide anything. My worst is all out in the open. It makes it necessary to tell about themselves … so they try to set me at ease by revealing our equality, by dragging out their own less-transparent deformities.
>
> DUNN 156

Yet, Olympia also has a lot to hide: her past, complex emotions, murderous plans, and love for her daughter, who is not supposed to learn who her mother is until the end of the novel, when Olympia reveals this herself in a letter to her daughter. Earlier in her life, the freakish Olympia was also a medium through which Arty's demonic voice could be heard. As the main narrator in the novel, she highlights the arbitrariness of the notion of 'normalcy.' Catherine Spooner brings out this aspect of the novel in the following way:

> Dunn's narrative demands the abandonment of normality on the part of the reader, complete immersion into Olympia's topsy-turvy world. While the pleasure it provides is partially dependent on the perception of the difference of that world and its shocking nature, there is also a sense in which Olympia invites the reader to share that world, to become, in the words of Browning's freaks, "One of us."
>
> SPOONER 73

Olympia is constructed as a complex person – a woman and a mother. No matter how strange and hermetic the world of "The Fabulous Biniewskis" from which she emerged is, her motives are clear and credible. What determines her actions both in the freak show reality and in the non-disabled world of "the norms" and makes her develop as a character is love for her family, be it her parents, Arturo, or later her daughter.

The protagonist and narrator of *Mendel's Dwarf* by Simon Mawer is Benedict Lambert, a dwarf who is a geneticist. He also believes that he is the famous scientist Gregor Mendel's ancestor, probably his great-grandchild. The protagonist constantly analyzes his own situation in the normate world. His research is focused on discovering the gene that determined the shape of his body which so strongly defines him. The plot of the novel is constructed around Benedict's love affair with a married woman, Jean Miller. He tries to protect his lover against domestic violence and her powerful husband, and offers her shelter in his own flat. Benedict has difficulties in fully grasping the complex relationship between Jean and her husband: when his beloved decides to return to her oppressor's house, he feels confused. The situation is even more perplexing when Benedict, as a geneticist, helps the Millers become parents in a fertility clinic. Only Jean knows that Benedict is the sperm donor and that he has used all his professional skills to choose the right embryo. As Mawer describes it,

> Benedict Lambert is sitting in his laboratory playing God. He has eight embryos in eight little tubes. Four of the embryos are proto-Benedicts, proto-dwarfs; the other four are, for want of a better word, normal. How should he choose?
>
> MAWER 250

At the end of the novel, after a regular-sized boy is born, Jean's husband discovers who the father of the child really is and decides to kill the baby.

The narrative of the novel is constructed as a dramatic monologue. Benedict, as the narrator of the story, assumes the role of an entertainer and a master of ceremonies. Like in a circus, he remains in the middle of the performance and explains to the audience what is going on. He often refers to himself in the third person, which increases the reader's emotional distance to the story and to Benedict as a character, also underscoring his role as a showman in the performance. In the last, dramatic scene of the novel, Benedict uses a different grammatical form:

> Hugo Miller set to work. From Mendel to the future: the tenuous chain of descent, the passage of DNA down the generation, was soon broken. I suppose that at that moment I was struggling out the forecourt of the Institute. It was pouring with rain. Watch: a dwarf, panicking through puddles.
>
> MAWER 309

He speaks in the first person, without self-distance, but still remains in his role of the storyteller.

Benedict directly addresses the implied reader, using question tags, such as: "I got a first class degree. You expected that, didn't you?" (Mawer 57) or "I know you don't really need this; you're already up there with me, aren't you?" (Mawer 250), which gives the narrative a conversation-like tone. Benedict defines his position as a storyteller, a character, and a master of ceremonies very clearly, being aware of the fact that the reader may condemn his deeds:

> Unforgivable? Have I forfeited all sympathy? But you must understand I have never looked for your sympathy.... Sympathy is an unctuous, slimy emotion.... I have never asked for it. Never so much as once have I played the poor, sad dwarf, smiling through his tears.
>
> MAWER 257–58

Mawer is obviously playing here with the reader's emotional responses: Benedict's actions, motives, and views provoke ambivalent reactions. What contributes to this strong feeling of ambivalence is the fact that the novel combines lectures on eugenics with a scandalous romance and thriller. Edgy and provocative, this strategy locates *Mendel's Dwarf* dangerously on the verge of kitsch.

However, Mawer's novel addresses many issues that are crucial to the place of disability "on the map of identity and marginality" (Mitchell and Snyder x) in contemporary Western culture. Mawer's protagonist explains how his protagonist's atypical body automatically defines him:

> *A problem you have to live with.* That's a good one, isn't it? It isn't something I *live with*, as I might live with a birthmark or a stammer, or flat feet. It is not an *addition*, like a mole on my face, nor a *subtraction*, like premature baldness: it *is me*. There is no other.
>
> MAWER 22–23

His non-normative corporeality completely determines his life and the way he perceives the surrounding world. Although many people who meet him repeat how brave he is establishing his scientific career and giving public lectures, his response is simple: "In order to be brave, you've got to have a choice" (Mawer 5) and the choices available to him are limited because of his atypical body.

Benedict perceives himself as a result of a pure coincidence:

> "You're special," my mother would insist as she dragged me off to one or another of those specialists – pediatricians, orthopedists, neurologists, orthodontists – who could never do anything at all. "You are special, that's why you have all these people looking after you." For a while I was fooled by her assertions … but soon enough I learned the truth: I am exactly what I seem – an aberration, a mutant, the product of pure, malign chance.
>
> MAWER 11–12

As a geneticist, Benedict challenges the medical model of disability which is deeply rooted in the binary able-bodied versus disabled, ill versus healthy, and normal versus abnormal dichotomies and which determines the way he is perceived by society.[4] He is aware of the fact that: "A reasonable estimate is that on average every one of us carries about four harmful recessive mutations. Sometimes, if you are unlucky like me, you carry a dominant one" (Mawer 264). He knows that everybody around is – in terms of genetics – a hybrid (like his friend Jean who has eyes of different colours) or a mutant, but he is the special one. And he knows exactly the price of this uniqueness.

The main theme in *Mendel's Dwarf* is eugenics. That is why the plot of the novel is doubled in a way: the protagonist of the background story is Gregor

4 To learn more about the medical model, see Garland-Thomson and Ojrzyńska's chapter in this volume.

Mendel – the father of genetics. Eugenics, depicted as an ideological sister of biology, is deeply grounded in the belief that human body and society can be improved to reach 'excellence.' As we learn from the novel, the climax of this strife for perfection was Auschwitz, the ultimate symbol of the extermination of those labelled as 'the Other' as part of the 'Final Solution.' Yet Benedict is certain that people have not drawn conclusions from this horrible lesson. They are still not ready to accept the diversity, 'imperfection,' and the innate hybridity of human beings. He accuses humankind of participating in a ceaseless, completely immoral chase, rather than a quest, after an illusion of perfect bodies:

> At least the old eugenics was governed by some kind of theory, however dreadful it may have been. The new eugenics, *our* eugenics, is governed only by the laws of the marketplace. You get what you can pay for.... Are we really such intellectual dwarfs ... as to imagine that the laws of supply and demand can be elevated to the level of philosophy? Because that is what we have done. We have within our grasp the future of mankind, and as things are going the future will choose silicone breast implants and liposuction and hair transplants. It will be eugenics by consumer choice, the eugenics of the marketplace. All masquerading as freedom.
>
> MAWER 286

While giving his lecture, Benedict does not even suspect that he is directly involved in the processes he describes. At the end of the novel, Jean's husband, using both personal and ideological reasons, decides about the death of Benedict's son. There are many characters in the novel who have a tendency to elevate themselves to a God-like position. And Benedict is no exception. Thus, he is not an innocent critic of contemporary civilization and its vicious desire to manipulate nature.

Mawer plays with almost all cultural clichés of dwarfism. Benedict is a jester, a performer in a freak show, and a representative of a gnomic, primitive tribe of dwarfs who have been living in caves for ages, as the dark, ancient deities of the earth. But, at the same time, he is a warrior. He describes his interactions with the outside world in military metaphors: "I am inured to hurt. You build bastions around you, Maginot lines of defences, iron curtains of barbed wire and razor wire, minefields, and free-fire zones" (Mawer 188). Benedict is also a man and a sexual being who is sensitive to the carnal aspects of life.

Benedict values the order of the world, its madness, and stupidity. He has a very similar position in the world to the one occupied by Olympia, the protagonist of Dunn's novel. His status of an outsider helps him provide a satirical image of contemporary culture, perceived as an enormous, immoral, and thoughtless marketplace.

Tyrion Lannister is one of many characters of George R.R. Martin's popular epic fantasy *A Song of Fire and Ice*, which has been adapted into a cult TV series entitled *A Game of Thrones*. Tyrion, a dwarf and a son of Lord Tywin, is a very complex person and one of the most fully developed characters in the novel. His sister, Cersei, sees him as a monster and accuses him of killing their mother who died giving birth to him and she is also certain that he poisoned her son. His father thinks that his existence is an insult to the family and would gladly kill him if he were not one of the Lannisters. This becomes evident when Tyrion is put on trial for allegedly poisoning Cersei's son, Joffrey. When asked whether he admits his guilt, he responds:

> Of Joffrey's death I am innocent. I am guilty of a far monstrous crime.... I was born. I lived. I am guilty of being a dwarf, I confess it.... I have been on trial for being a dwarf all my life.
>
> MARTIN, *A Storm of Swords* 1995–96

His words clearly foreground the fact that he is being accused of the crime that he did not commit, simply because of his impairment which is seen here through the prism of the symbolic model of disability in that it is equated with moral corruption. In a sense, the characters' readiness to adopt such a reductive perspective and blame their relative of a crime on the grounds of his non-standard embodiment allows the readers to question who the real monster is. At the very least, the protagonist's speech draws attention to the Rancierian inegalitarian distribution of the sensible, which Ojrzyńska and Wieczorek discuss in their introductory chapter, and the stigmatization that he is subjected to. But all of this is absolutely ordinary in the world of *A Song of Fire and Ice*. Even if Tyrion is seen as a monster capable of evil deeds, he is just one of the entire host of monstrous characters, and his actions pale in comparison with those of his beautiful sister.

On the one hand, he is a person who, in a sense, ostensibly accepts his own corporeality (e.g. he is a strongly sexual man), but, on the other, he is absolutely aware of the fact that the shape of his body defines him. When asked why he reads so much, he answers:

> Had I been born a peasant, I might have been left to die or sold to some slaver's grotesquerie. Alas, I was born a Lannister of Casterly Rock.... I must do my part for the honor of my House.... Well, my legs may be too small for my body, but my head is too large, although I prefer to think it is

> just large enough for my mind.... My mind is my weapon.... That is why I read so much.
>
> MARTIN, *A Game of Thrones* 123

But this weapon is neither worse nor better than those that others have. In the world of the novel, a world dense with intrigues, treachery, and bloody, inconsiderate violence, where no one can be sure if they have any impact on the course of events, Tyrion is a coherent protagonist. He loves, hates, struggles to survive, and murders, like everyone around him. There are a lot of characters who have some form of impairment or disability in that cruel reality: Tyrion is just one of them. He wants to survive like everyone around him and, like everyone else in this brutal world, he is driven by his passions. Revenge on his father is more important to him than the survival prospects. Constructing the character, Martin broke most of the stereotypes associated with dwarfism as if they had never existed. We do not know the end of the complicated plot of Martin's novels yet, so we can only speculate who Tyrion Lannister will ultimately prove to be in the story.

Paradoxically, when juxtaposed with the above-mentioned literary characters, the dwarf from Martin's novel is the only one who is just who he is. He is not used instrumentally as a literary tool to convey some message. The difference between *The Dwarf* by Lagerkvist and *A Song of Fire and Ice* is obvious and evident. Both novels depict worlds which are highly stylized and their characters are dressed in historical costumes inspired by medieval and Renaissance fashions. But their two dwarf protagonists are constructed differently: one is just a metaphor and the other is a fully-developed, round character. This is partly because of the aesthetic convention of *A Song of Fire and Ice*: Martin's world is in a way free from realistic circumstances – it ignores all possible historical contexts (the novel, when compared with, for instance, the story of the Plantagenets, is a fairy tale for naïve teenagers) – and Tyrion is part of a fantasy narrative – not a realistic one. That is why he, as a character, is not a vehicle for any social, moral, or philosophical message apart from one: a person who is deemed powerless by his or her stature should be extremely clever and lucky to survive in this world of pure, cruel, shameless, and unmasked power. Moreover, *A Song of Fire and Ice* belongs to popular literature. It is based on a complex plot and is not informed by any specific ideological agenda. Still, we can treat popular culture as a barometer of social change: dwarf characters can be part of a freak show or an epic game of thrones as well. They are just part of global entertainment: it is the aesthetic context that defines them rather than the shapes of their bodies.

Dwarfs used to have a very peculiar position in European culture, but the evolution of their cultural portrayals is symptomatic of a general change in constructing human disability. In the twentieth-century literature, dwarf characters underwent a remarkable metamorphosis: initially defined solely through the shape of their visible and, at the same time, invisible bodies, they changed from a metaphor or a literary tool into complex characters and paradoxically regained their corporeality and completeness as human beings. This process of subjectification has also helped reverse the non-disabled gaze and look critically at the 'normal' society and the exclusionary, arbitrary ways in which it constructs 'the disabled Other' and at contemporary models of bodily perfection. The recent novels that I have discussed show that the bodies of dwarfs can be as much as bodies, sexual and sensual, male and female. Rather than being seen as extraordinary or abnormal, they have become part of the spectrum of human variety.

Works Cited

Adelson, Betty M. *The Lives of Dwarfs. Their Journey from Social Curiosity to Public Liberation*. New Brunswick, NJ: Rutgers University Press, 2005. Print.

Brown, Jonathan, and Carmen Garrido. *Velazquez. The Technique of Genius*. New Haven, CT: Yale University Press, 1998. Print.

Dunn, Katherine. *Geek Love*. New York, NY: Warner, 1990. Print.

Garland-Thomson, Rosemarie. *Extraordinary Bodies: Figuring Physical Disability in American Culture and Literature*. New York, NY: Columbia University Press, 1997. Print.

Lagerkvist, Pär. *The Dwarf*. Trans. Alexandra Dick. New York, NY: Hill and Wang, 1958. Print.

Martin, George R.R. *A Game of Thrones*. New York, NY: Bantam, 1996. Print.

Martin, George R.R. *A Storm of Swords*. New York, NY: Bantam, 2000. Epub.

Mawer, Simon. *Mendel's Dwarf*. London: Abacus, 2011. Print.

Mitchell, David T., and Snyder, Sharon L. *Narrative Prosthesis: Disability and the Dependencies of Discourse*. Ann Arbor, MI: Michigan University Press, 2000. Print.

Spooner, Catherine. *Contemporary Gothic*. London: Reaktion, 2006. Print.

Terlecki, Władysław. *Drabina Jakubowa albo podróż*. Warszawa: Czytelnik, 1988. Print.

Tuan, Yi-Fu. *Dominance and Affection: The Making of Pets*. New Haven, CT: Yale University Press, 1984. Print.

Wilde, Oscar. "The Birthday of the Infanta." *Complete Short Fiction*. Oxford: Oxford University Press 1979. 185–202. Print.

CHAPTER 9

Disability and Its Doubles: The Conflicting Discourses of Disability in Susan Nussbaum's *No One as Nasty*

Edyta Lorek-Jezińska

The fascination with the 'abnormal' and suffering body noticeable in some twentieth-century and more recent theatre has placed disability among the features of transgressive corporeality. In theatrical terms the so-called 'deviant' body has been a means of reaching the periphery and exploring otherness, as well as conducting an experiment in the limits and possibilities of the human body. In the work of DV8 Physical Theatre, for instance, a disabled dancer in the 2003 performance and 2004 film entitled *The Cost of Living*[1] opens new spaces for exploration. His impairments form the tensions along which experimental dance develops, in a similar way to which the bodies of non-disabled dancers struggle against gravity in other projects realized by the same company. We can consider the other dancers' movements on the horizontal plane close to the floor as a way of trying to understand and experience the space and motion from the perspective of their disabled partner, or as a technique characteristic of modern dance, breaking with the dominant vertical movement of traditional choreography (cf. Brown 64).

Similar tensions occur in the experience of performing a play in complete darkness to children with vision loss and to audiences with no vision impairment in *Ukryte* (*The Hidden*) by the Polish theatre company Mouth to Mouth Republic.[2] This experimental project operates on two levels simultaneously: as a project whose primary aim is to integrate audiences with impaired and standard vision, and as a form of radical experimentation with conceptual visual minimalism. The 'disabled' perspective radically changes a performance and its reception, as well as negotiating the public space for the representation of disability. In terms of aesthetics, such performances can be classified as conceptual experiments in transgressing ordinary experiences, sensibilities, and preconceptions. In a highly dissensual fashion, they open up the space for a radical redefinition of performative arts, the performer's body, or theatrical

1 The film can be watched at: https://vimeo.com/74966965.

2 To learn more about the play, visit the company's website: http://www.ustausta.pl/ (available in Polish).

 | DOI:10.1163/9789004424678_011

imagination. In a sense, such experiments are in line with Tobin Siebers's arguments about the importance of the disability perspective for the development of modern art:

> If modern art has had such enormous success, it is because of its embrace of disability as a distinct version of the beautiful. No object has a greater capacity to be accepted at the present moment as an aesthetic representation than the disabled body,
>
> "The Art of Disability"

and thus give rise to a disability aesthetics that facilitates a change in the Rancierian distribution of the sensible.[3]

However, the conceptual use of the highly trained and 'abled' body of a double amputee, or the experimental reduction of visual stimuli, and many other projects of a similar kind (e.g. Robert Wilson's performances or Samuel Beckett's drama), account for only a portion of the presence of people with disabilities on the stage. Much of the drama and theatre created by disabled artists aims at negotiating a more realistic space for disability. Such a tendency can be seen in the case of seven American plays collected in the anthology *Beyond Victims and Villains: Contemporary Plays by Disabled Playwrights* (2006) edited by Victoria Ann Lewis. What the collected plays have in common, according to the editor, is their rejection of the traditional and problematic discourses of disability. These discourses are organized along the dichotomy contained in the title of the collection, according to which, in a majority of cultural representations, a disabled person embodies either a villain or a victim. Moving 'beyond victims and villains' largely means establishing radical or alternative perspectives on disability in order to go beyond or move away from the stereotypes and clichés surrounding it.

This is most conspicuous in *No One as Nasty* by Susan Nussbaum, the last play in the anthology *Beyond Victims and Villains*, written in 1995 (premiered in 2000) from the post-Independent Living Movement perspective, where – in institutional terms – Janet, the main character, enjoys the full rights of an independent citizen, aided by personal assistants and drivers in order to realize the ideals of independence. The protagonist is a white woman in her thirties or forties, living alone in a flat and using a power wheelchair. The play focuses on Janet's relation to her personal assistants, Lucy and Lois, and explores a number of real and imagined situations, following no traditional linear plot development. The protagonist is accompanied onstage by the imaginary character

3 The editors of this volume discuss the Rancierian concept of the distribution of the sensible in detail in their preface.

of Janet 2, who can switch between her disabled and nondisabled selves. Janet sometimes participates in the stage events but in many scenes she adopts a metadramatic perspective, commenting on the parts enacted by Janet 2. The play creates no clear sense of what is real and what is dreamed or imagined, while the episodic scenes often happen simultaneously between different pairs of characters and smoothly move into the next ones happening in unrelated imaginary locations. Nussbaum's heroine oscillates between the absolute denial of disability and its difference, and an attempt at mapping it against other forms of social, cultural, racial, and sexual disabilities, represented in the complex relationships between doubles, alter-egos, and the mental projections of the disabled self. My main objective is to investigate the contradictions involved in making sense of disability both in opposition to and within the dominant discourses of disability.

Although all the plays included in the collection have been said to reject these stereotypes, Nussbaum's drama seems to come very close to embracing them as important points for the discovery and definition of one's identity. Through a complicated multidimensional structure mixing reality, dream, and projection, the play presents the paradoxical nature of disability expressed in the reversals of power relations and the redefinition of social stereotypes. The play's distancing effects achieved by metacritical commentaries, the main character's self-criticism, and the characters' fluidity encourage constant negotiation of meanings and a search for identity which consists of fragmented and projected selves, both disabled and non-disabled, similar to a double or ostentatiously different from each other in terms of race or gender. The play's major concerns are: the subversive uses of clichés and the dominant discourses of disability, the strategies for confronting disability with other forms of social and cultural marginalization and exclusion, as well as the exploration of the problematic relation with a personal assistant and the understanding of the boundaries of one's own corporeality. All of this helps problematize the ableist, one-dimensional types of representation mentioned in the very title of Lewis's collections.

The two categories of victims and villains breed rejection mixed with pity and fear, respectively, and correspond to the exclusionary moral and medical models of disability, also discussed by Rosemarie Garland-Thomson and Katarzyna Ojrzyńska in Chapter 1. The category of villains refers to the tradition of marking evil characters by some form of physical 'deformation' or impairment. In this way, disability has been associated with immorality, evil, and punishment, and realized in the concepts of the monstrous and the uncanny (cf. Davis 175). The perception of a disabled individual as a victim emphasizes the ableist perspective in which the healthy/'normal' person offers help and pity to the disabled Other, who accepts it with gratitude. Lewis comments on the problematic nature of the so-called "charitable gesture" contained in the concept of pity (Introduction xiv-xv), while Joseph P. Shapiro shows how pity can be oppressive to disabled people because – viewed in this perspective – people with disabilities are seen as "childlike, dependent, and in need of charity or pity" (14). The concept of the victim is directly linked to other clichés and dominant discourses of disability which Simi Linton addresses in her book *Claiming Disability: Knowledge and Identity*. One of the significant concepts related to pity is that of loss and deficit, which defines disability as an "atypical" experience (Linton 5). This perspective is perpetuated by most of the definitions of disability that Linton examines, which refer to "incapacity, a disadvantage, deficiency" (11). It is also strongly rooted in the consequences of the medicalization of disability, which in some ways improved the living conditions and life expectancy of many people with disabilities, but had a negative effect on the way disability has been conceptualized and understood (Linton 11). The medical discourse, which will be discussed below, as Linton argues, "casts human variation as deviance from the norm, as pathological condition, as deficit, and, significantly, as an individual burden and personal tragedy" (11) and presents the "victims" of impairment as passive, miserable, unhappy, confined, and afflicted (25–27).[4]

However, both the medical discourse and the moral narrative that are often present in the cultural representations of disability can take apparently positive and active forms. Lewis claims that both of these discourses can be very attractive in a dramaturgical sense:

> "moral" and "medical" models of disability continue to dominate theatrical depiction, not only because they fill a deep human need to define ourselves as "normal" against some standard of abnormality, but also, in terms of theatrical practice, because they are dramaturgically useful.
>
> Introduction xxii

Both discourses have a strong transformative and tragic potential, since they insist on internal conflict, struggle, and often a form of victory over weaknesses. Moreover, they feature dramatically powerful symbols and organize knowledge

4 Interestingly, the transition from the freak show, in which disability represented a curiosity or variation, to the medical discourse, where oddities were treated as a disease to be cured (Shapiro 32) also meant seeing disability as the condition of a victim, or a charity case. Robert Bogdan suggests that with the domination of the medical paradigm, the freak show exhibits began to be seen as "'humble and unfortunate' 'pathological rarities'" that were to function primarily as doctors' patients and identified as "sick" and "to be pitied" (64).

of the world around seemingly crucial dichotomies. Since medical discourse approaches disability as an illness which should be eliminated, this has given rise to two popular motifs: a disabled person as 'a heroic overcomer' who manages to overcome illness and get reintegrated into the so-called 'healthy' society and 'a heroic suicide' who chooses death over disabled life and is brave enough to put this choice into action. The moral or religious discourse, by contrast, treats disability as a punishment for a sin or some other form of transgression. The focus in the narrative falls upon moral improvement rather than physical ability (Lewis, Introduction xxi-xxii). In both cases disability often functions as a metaphor or sometimes a hyperbole of the general struggle of human beings against the imposed limitations. In such cases disability narratives serve the purposes of the so-called 'normal' members of society. The overcoming rhetoric has been severely criticized by Simi Linton, who sees it as a story of "personal triumph over a personal condition" (18). Such a perspective demands from a disabled person an adjustment to the social environment, while disregarding his or her needs and abilities. The internalization of society's expectation of the disabled people to "overcome" "rather than demand social change" is, according to Linton, as "exhausting and self-defeating" as the demands of "Super Mom" for women (Linton 18). Some of these considerations of the ambivalent presences of characters with disabilities and their stories are embraced by the concept of narrative prosthesis, developed by David T. Mitchell and Sharon L. Snyder. The authors examine multiple instances of using disability as a literary 'supplement,' or, as Dan Goodley and Marek Mackiewicz-Ziccardi put it in their chapter, "a crutch: a prop on which to hang a myriad of stereotypes" (39). Disability sometimes functions as a convenient tool of characterization or an element of a plot that provides a means of categorization and is based on recognizable narrative patterns, but, more importantly, it can also operate as a disruptive category, bringing about the crisis of identity and order (cf. Mitchell and Snyder 47–49).

My main concern is to investigate how drama and theatre deliberately address the established narratives and discourses of disability, trying to bring them into crisis. These processes often involve the difficult act of negotiating constructionist and essentialist approaches to disabled corporeality (cf. Garland-Thomson), mediating between the tensions imposed by cultural and social boundaries, as well as the limitations and tensions within the disabled body itself, often projected upon its various – both human and non-human – prostheses.

Susan Nussbaum is a writer who, as Lewis argues, tries to challenge the stereotypes concerning disability with laughter and comedy (Introduction xxxvii). In the Author's Statement published with the play text, Nussbaum playfully relocates the topic of disability from the margins by making it become the central and most interesting subject for drama:

> There have been times when I've been urged to "stretch" and write about something other than disability. I have no interest in anything other than disability, however. What could be more interesting than disability?
> NUSSBAUM 345

The dramatists whose works were selected for the anthology are connected, as Lewis claims, by "a desire to turn the official story upside down, to break open the clichés and seriousness of the common images of disability," challenging the images that often "infantiliz[e]" and "invalidat[e]" disabled people (Introduction xxxvii). They also in a sense take advantage of the "natural" humour deriving from the potential incongruity between the experience of disability and conventional social expectations (cf. Walters 272). It is quite obvious that these works are likely to offend some of their audiences because, instead of avoiding the negative stereotypes, they openly address or seemingly perpetuate them (Lewis, Introduction xxxvii).

The opening monologue in Nussbaum's *No One as Nasty*, as some critics have already pointed out (Lewis, "The Dramaturgy" 97), rejects the victim and villain stereotypes, and the moral and medical narratives of disability. It presents disability as an accident, and only an accident, rather than as a lesson to be learned or a punishment for sins or part of some divine agenda. Having stated that, the play confronts and subversively activates the previously rejected narratives because they form the social constructions of disability that the main character encounters or reflects upon. The very title *No One as Nasty* plays with the villain stereotype, since it is the name given to the main character – a quadriplegic woman using a power wheelchair – by her personal assistant, who is often verbally and psychologically abused by her. A villainess – a serial murderess – is also one of several alter egos with which the protagonist identifies. In one of her macabre and comic projections, she creates the character of a Mystery Woman, who is performed by her alter ego Janet 2. The Mystery Woman is a serial killer of men, the ultimate villainess who sucks the life out of the men whom she seduces with her attractive body. While discussing the dream/projection, Janet comes to think that she projects herself into this figure because of the power and physical attractiveness that the villainess possesses, yet, at the same time, she becomes aware of another compensatory aspect of the dream. The first victim of the Mystery Woman is a driver, the one who caused Janet's disability. The projection of herself as the villain gives her an imaginary power to take revenge on the perpetrator of the accident. The mixture of the comic and the macabre – associated with the Mystery Woman and sometimes with the main character – revalorizes the villain's function, playing, through contrast and analogy, with the cultural constructions of evil disabled characters and the common distribution of virtue along the beauty line, also discussed by Goodley and Mackiewicz-Ziccardi in their chapter with reference to kalokagathia.

One of the essential sites where discourses and experiences of disability have been negotiated in cultural texts is the body. In *Extraordinary Bodies*, Rosemarie Garland-Thomson discusses two strategic positions in relation to the body – constructionism and essentialism (23), the tension between which has given rise to the interactional model of disability, mentioned earlier by Garland-Thomson and Ojrzyńska in their chapter (29). Lewis sees both of these stances as aiming at "liberating disability from its status as absolute and unchangeable catastrophe" ("The Dramaturgy" 102). While constructionism questions the concepts of difference and normalcy and shows them as relative constructs, essentialism emphasizes individual experience as the site on which the disabled identity can be formed:

> Strategic constructionism destigmatizes the disabled body, makes difference relative, denaturalizes so-called normalcy, and challenges appearance hierarchies. Strategic essentialism, by contrast, validates individual experience and consciousness, imagines community, authorizes history, and facilitates self-naming.
>
> GARLAND-THOMSON 23

In its tendency to integrate disability into social structures, constructionism is, according to Garland-Thomson, running the risk of rejecting the bodily differences – of "eras[ing] the materiality of the body" (145). Nussbaum's play uses both strategies in often contradictory ways, emphasizing difference particularly through exposing the body's materiality, while drawing significant analogies between disability and other forms of otherness subject to similar processes of rejection, exclusion, and stigmatization. The main character often defines the identity of the disabled person as a struggle with the body – a small detail in its anatomy or clothes differentiates the normal body from the disabled one. And this small detail – like a pair of uneven pant legs – ironically and hyperbolically represents a disabled person's life: "That's the whole story of crip life" (Nussbaum 371).

Through various ironic references, the play shows attempts at reclaiming the traditional derogative terms such as "cripple" or "crip," a strategy also discussed by Goodley and Mackiewicz-Ziccardi in relation to grassroots disability activism and Robert McRuer's crip theory. One of the contradictions of the main character is manifested in her pride of being a "cripple" and the feeling of extreme insecurity concerning her own status. In some scenes, she uses the words "cripple" or "crip" as terms that people with disabilities have reclaimed and re-appropriated provocatively to set their own identity against other groups "with militant self-pride" (Shapiro 34). To use the word "cripple" to describe one's own identity and group belonging is actually, as Shapiro argues, to choose the element that "scares the outside world the most" (34). In fact, the whole "nastiness" of the main character is a provocative and sometimes also aggressive use of what terrifies the non-disabled members of society, but also empowers people with disabilities. Yet it seems that in this case, despite all the heritage and conveniences of the Disability Rights and Independent Living Movements, such an attitude is an almost hysterical reaction to the perpetual crisis of identity and status that the main character experiences.

Both constructionist and essentialist definitions of disability rely to some degree on its comparisons to other forms of social and cultural marginalization and exclusion. "Parallel constructions" of disability, race, and gender form one of the five strategies employed by playwrights to create "the new paradigm of the social model of disability," according to Lewis ("The Dramaturgy" 95, 97). The strategy of parallel construction is part of a wider trend in Critical Disability Studies, discussed by Garland-Thomson and Ojrzyńska in their chapter, including the intersections between various approaches to the concept of the Other in postcolonial and feminist theory as well as in relatively new branches of the humanities, including ecocriticism and posthumanism. In this context, one of the most interesting conceptual aspects of Nussbaum's play is building the subversive analogies and tensions between disabled people and other underprivileged groups. *No One as Nasty* self-consciously addresses the problems of disability's "entanglement" with other forms of social oppression and marginalization of sexual, gender, ethnic and racial minorities, also mentioned by Goodley and Mackiewicz-Ziccardi in their chapter. Experimenting with the balancing of powers, the play enters the forbidden territories of racism and colonial exploitation, and refers to the acts of discrimination against sexual minorities. While the main character finds her lesbian identity almost totally unproblematic, interpreting people's gaze as directed at her physical condition rather than sexual orientation, she focuses her attention on making sense of her racial position as a white woman. This reflection on the difference and similarity between being black and disabled, shared by Janet and her black personal assistant, moves between the various experiences of exclusion associated with the segregation of black people and the erasure of people with disabilities from public life. The bitterness of their memories is summed up in an ironic commentary about Christopher Reeve, an actor famous for his Superman role and disability activism after his horse-riding accident which rendered him quadriplegic:

> *Lois*: Look at it this way. At least you belong to a minority where famous stars can suddenly be members and join your movement. It's not like Christopher Reeve is gonna fall off a horse and be black.
> *Janet* 2: Although I bet Chris sure wishes he could choose, you know? Between being treated with hatred or pity?
> *Lois*: What would you choose?
> *Janet* 2: Hatred.
> *Lois*: Shows what you know.
> NUSSBAUM 366

The corporeal definitions of identity are here constructed by the social reactions to otherness – pity and hatred.

The analogy developed between disability and blackness is also highlighted in the relation between the white disabled person and her black assistant. In another configuration Janet and Lois are on opposite sides representing, according to the former, "a racial dynamic" – "acting out the end result of society's racist drama" (Nussbaum 370). The complex power relationship between the disabled person and the assistant is here reduced to the master and slave pattern. In a scene following the presentation of little incidents illustrating Janet's seemingly irrational demands on the assistants, the former seems to self-consciously overemphasize her own power as a white woman, in this way downplaying her own dependence on others. It is also a reaction to how her own commentary on the sexual abuse of her disabled acquaintance by his assistant has been ignored by other characters participating in the scene. In this respect the master and slave pattern seems to compensate for abuse and violence involved in the rape case:

> *Janet* It's the contemporary version of picking cotton. We come from different worlds, but here we are, acting out the end result of society's racist drama.
> *Lois*: You act like you invented slavery. Why don't you just concentrate on being a human being? Maybe everything's not about race.
> *Janet*: You don't think there's racial dynamic here?
> *Lois*: Yeah, if you put it there.
> *Janet*: Wait, I don't put it there, it's *there*. It's been there for hundreds of years, and it's here now, in my life, in my head. I'm trying to deal with it.
> *Lois*: But you make everything into a racial thing.

> *Janet*: That's not true. There's also class, sexism, homophobia, ableism. Together with race, those are my Big Five.
>
> NUSSBAUM 370

The constant and repetitive bombarding of the personal assistant with what sometimes seems to a non-disabled person a trivial detail copies the relation between the white master and the black slave. But Lois refuses to see their relation in those terms, trying to go beyond socially inherited categories and approach each other simply as human beings. The insistence with which Janet chooses to see racism and slavery in their relationship is, on the one hand, a way of empowering herself socially, identifying with the more powerful and dominant part of society. On the other hand, she seems to be intrigued by the fact that a member of a minority group might wish to see the world beyond categorizations, to see herself not as a black person but simply a human being. Trying to understand racism, she also tries to comprehend her social position and construction of disability, because to her, social life seems to consist of her Big Five: racism, "class, sexism, homophobia and ableism" (Nussbaum 370).

In the context of the social divisions that cut across Janet's world, it is quite ironic that she should entertain the thoughts of sharing the same hero with non-disabled people – Superman – Christopher Reeve. In a sense, Superman represents the same fantasy to non-disabled people as to people with disabilities. In one of the several comic scenes featuring Reeve as Superman, Janet projects herself as drinking martini in a restaurant together with Christopher and trying to reassure him that he will manage as a disabled person, that in fact the life of people with disabilities is an adventure and it is "really funny" (Nussbaum 378). Janet and Janet 2 manage well up to the point where words start to mean different things when referring to a disabled person – e.g. saying that people will look at him in a new condition means staring at him, while stating that he will be invisible is a commentary on the invisibility of disabled people in society. In a showering scene Christopher Reeve is called a traitor and a coward, and he is criticized for announcing publicly that he will walk, thus abandoning the disabled community and, above all, inscribing his own story into the overcomer narrative (Nussbaum 366). However, the insistence with which the image or thoughts of Christopher Reeve return to Janet throughout the play indicates the potential he holds as a member of the disabled community, who can help change the surrounding world to accommodate and welcome disabled people. He also represents the dream of discarding disability – having just "one week off … disability per year" (Nussbaum 371), the thought that Janet considers in her monologue, but which she tries to suppress.

In all the projected and realistic scenes, the central relation is developed not between Janet and her alternative selves and doubles, but between herself and her personal assistant. The play presents the repetitive acts of counteracting the non-docility of the disabled body with the meticulous process of making bodily attributes controllable and completely definable. It exposes the futility of such measures through irony and reversed power relationships. The uncontrollability of the body is translated into control over the personal assistant, who becomes a prosthesis of physical functions. It seems that the whole process of negotiating power and submission, control and docility, which, according to Michel Feher, operates as a tension within the body – not outside it – is here externalized into the control and resistance to, and of, the personal assistant, since the body itself resists the personal and social demands impressed upon it. In the case of people with disabilities the self-disciplining or "self-styling" (Feher qtd. in McLarren 155–56) processes within the body are externalized through power exerted upon the prosthesis in an attempt to match the expectations of 'normal' corporeality. The aggression and frustration transferred upon the assistants derive from the tensions between the demands on the body to yield to the expectations and routines of everyday life and the impossibility of fulfilling them without the help of an assistant.

According to Peter Freund, the "discomfort or pain" experienced by disabled people could be seen as a consequence of "an incompatibility between social-material arrangements and the body" (185). In one of the scenes Janet insists on having her trousers pulled up and the pants legs arranged symmetrically, asking her personal assistant to repeat the act of rearranging them. The scene is then developed into a surrealistic sequence of several personal assistants performing the same activity of pulling the trousers up and then arranging them in turns, and commenting on the difficulty and futility of these acts. Since Janet's disabled body cannot be re-modelled, she insists on having control over her garments – an act that seems inconsequential to her assistant, but shows to her that she can have some influence on reality and on her own body. It seems that the personal assistant's body becomes a site of tensions and negotiations of the so-called "complex embodiment" (Siebers, *Disability Theory* 25), which embraces both social and physical factors conditioning the lives of people with disabilities.

The scene juxtaposes two perspectives – the disabled and the non-disabled one – in multiple exchanges between the characters conducted on several levels. What seems neurotic and inconsiderate to Janet's assistants is explained in an earlier conversation with the imaginary self as simply demanding the same standards for herself as for non-disabled people. When she insists on having her pants arranged properly, the protagonist refuses to accept that the dress codes might be different for disabled people, and that the ones that she demands to respect might be simply internalized from the dominant culture (Nussbaum 371). This attempt at controlling the uncontrollable by exerting power on the assistants is juxtaposed with the scenes in which without another person's help Janet cannot perform the simplest of actions, and she is forced to wait for hours for the late assistant to come and relieve her. While Janet starts the play with an important statement that disability is an accident not a punishment for being a bad person, thus rejecting the moral model of disability, she refuses to accept the fact that an accident can also affect a non-disabled person. To her, being late because of an accident is an act of ill will. In the relation between the disabled person and her assistant the body's needs are externalized and partly performed by another person. Although Janet justifies to herself that she has the right to survive, she admits that she feels ashamed because of her "needing" things (Nussbaum 367). This shame reappears in various contexts, underlying her often violent and bitter responses to the assistant's silence.

Another attempt at defining her own identity in a conversation with her alter ego represents a confrontation between the radical and moderate approaches to disability and normalcy. When Janet complains that her life can be reduced to being "someone's job," Janet 2 tries to persuade her that everyone is dependent on others and that is often defined through the work they perform. Having argued that everything is different for disabled people because they are on the wrong side of the divide, Janet is asked: "Do you want everyone to run out and get disabled so you won't be misunderstood?" (Nussbaum 386). She responds:

> *Janet*: Yes. I want everyone to be disabled. I want everyone to be really, really disabled. Then no one will be disabled 'cause disabled will be normal, and there will be a small minority of able-bodied people who will comprise a slave underclass.
>
> NUSSBAUM 386

The effectiveness of such a projection lies in its simultaneous affinity to utopia and dystopia. A world without disabilities is a utopian and ideal dream, but the way it is created also makes it a dystopian vision. On the personal level, it comes from bitterness and a sense of injustice, yet in social terms, the vision reverses the commonly accepted social structure. It is a travesty of the ideology of ability (Siebers, *Disability Theory* 8), whose extreme form is the utopian/dystopian vision of perfect and healthy human beings. The striking element is the function ascribed to able-bodied people as a slave underclass, which paradoxically seems to be another expression of Janet's inability to embrace and accept the relation she needs to enter into with her assistant. Slavery would be a system in which using somebody else's non-disabled body will be socially imposed and institutionally justified. Janet's vision in a sense also radically comments on the significance of disability as the ultimate symbol of discrimination and marginalization. The tendency to use the disability rhetoric to justify other forms of discrimination such as racism or sexism, discussed among others by Tobin Siebers, derives from its presumed objectivity:

> Disability marks the last frontier of unquestioned inferiority because the preference for able-bodiedness makes it extremely difficult to embrace disabled people and to recognize their unnecessary and violent exclusion from society.
>
> SIEBERS, *Disability Theory* 6

Janet's utopia exposes the violence of such exclusion by using an equivalent criterion for social discrimination against nondisabled people.

To conclude, *No One as Nasty* gives no final answers to the multiple questions it asks and the problems it raises on both personal and social levels. It ends on a personal note, showing uncertainty, but also openness to learn about the perspectives of others. By both constructing and deconstructing dominant discourses and images of disability, acting out fictional scenes and projections of power, failure, or discrimination, multiplying events and characters, exaggerating and touching upon difficult questions, and offending and laughing at cultural clichés, Nussbaum's play presents the complexity of the disabled people's experience and the often contradictory conceptualizations of disability that they have to face and make sense of. In this multiplicity and openness, *No One as Nasty*, does what, according to Garland-Thomson and Ojrzyńska, Critical Disability Studies is fundamentally engaged in – it primarily "interrogates disability" (32). According to Lewis, "transforming the theatrical landscape of disability" depends on

> whether the space is transformed by being inhabited by a radically material disabled/impaired body(ies). And not just *any* habitation but one in which the social status of the disabled participant is equal to others using the space.
>
> "The Theatrical Landscape"

Nussbaum's play exposes the tensions that operate in such a space and the cost of maintaining an equal status within it, since they affect the disabled character and the one that assists him or her in this process.

While *No One as Nasty* can certainly be classified as experimental because of its epic theatre techniques, structural fragmentation, and surrealist imagery, its major innovative contribution is its psychological complexity. By staging the intricacies of the living experience of disabled people, the play exposes the impossibility of sealing the concept of self and individual corporeality in one physical body. The multiplication of characters presents unstable and provisional selves none of which form a solid identity. The ambivalent relations between a person with physical disabilities and her or his personal assistant problematize the questions of independence and dependence as well as of the limits of one's self. The dependencies between one's ego, alter-ego, and prostheses expose the extent to which people are being constructed by others and objectify other people in their personal scenarios. The tensions involved in commanding non-docile bodies illustrate the complex processes of customizing external reality and 'de-normalizing' the space these bodies live in.

Finally, Nussbaum's play addresses the question of social and cultural exclusion and marginalization. It provocatively confuses and humorously juxtaposes various cases of discrimination. By subversively asking questions of which social 'disability' is easier to live with, the play exposes the mechanisms behind victimization and abuse of power. It shows various forms of disempowerment as a network in which disability is placed as sometimes a privileged place in relation to some forms of exclusion and sometimes as the ultimate form of social isolation and helplessness, exposing the constructedness of seemingly natural categories and norms.

Works Cited

Bogdan, Robert. *Freak Show: Presenting Human Oddities for Amusement and Profit*. Chicago, IL: University of Chicago Press, 1990. Print.

Brown, Carol. "Making Space, Speaking Spaces." *The Routledge Dance Studies Reader*. Ed. Alexandra Carter and Janet O'Shea. London: Routledge, 2010. 58–72. Print.

Davis, Lennard J. "Visualising the Disabled Body: The Classical Nude and the Fragmented Torso." 1997. *The Body: A Reader*. Ed. Mariam Fraser and Monica Greco. London: Routledge, 2005. 167–81. Print.

Freund, Peter. "Bodies, Disability and Spaces: The Social Model and Disabling Spatial Organisations." 2001. *The Body: A Reader*. Ed. Mariam Fraser and Monica Greco. London: Routledge, 2005. 182–86. Print.

Garland-Thomson, Rosemarie. *Extraordinary Bodies: Figuring Physical Disability in American Culture and Literature*. New York, NY: Columbia University Press, 1996. Print.

Lewis, Victoria Ann, ed. *Beyond Victims and Villains: Contemporary Plays by Disabled Playwrights*. New York, NY: Theatre Communications Group, 2006. Print.

Lewis, Victoria Ann. "The Dramaturgy of Disability." *Points of Contact: Disability, Art and Culture*. Ed. Susan Crutchfield and Mercy Epstein. Ann Arbor, MI: University of Michigan Press, 2000. 93–108. Print.

Lewis, Victoria Ann. Introduction. *Beyond Victims and Villains: Contemporary Plays by Disabled Playwrights*. New York, NY: Theatre Communications Group, 2006. xiii–xlv. Print.

Lewis, Victoria Ann. "The Theatrical Landscape of Disability." *Disability Studies Quarterly* 24.3 (2004): n. pag., http://dsq-sds.org/article/view/511. Accessed 9 May 2019.

Linton, Simi. *Claiming Disability: Knowledge and Identity*. New York, NY: New York University Press. 1998. Print.

McLarren, Peter, L. "Schooling the Postmodern Body: Critical Pedagogy and the Politics of Enfleshment." *Postmodernism, Feminism, and Cultural Politics: Redrawing Educational Boundaries*. Ed. Henry A. Giroux. New York, NY: State University of New York Press, 1991. 144–73. Print.

Mitchell, David T., and Sharon L. Snyder. *Narrative Prosthesis: Disability and the Dependencies of Discourse*. Ann Arbor, MI: University of Michigan Press, 2000. Print.

Nussbaum, Susan. *No One as Nasty*. *Beyond Victims and Villains: Contemporary Plays by Disabled Playwrights*. New York, NY: Theatre Communications Group, 2006. 343–92. Print.

Shapiro, Joseph P. *No Pity: People with Disabilities Forging a New Civil Rights Movement*. New York, NY: Three Rivers, 1994. Print.

Siebers, Tobin. Interview by Mike Levin. "The Art of Disability." *Disability Studies Quarterly* 30.2 (2010): n. pag., http://dsq-sds.org/article/view/1263/1272. Accessed 20 July 2016.

Siebers, Tobin. *Disability Theory*. Ann Arbor, MI: University of Michigan Press, 2008. Print.

Walters, Shannon. "Cool Aspie Humor: Cognitive Difference and Kenneth Burke's Comic Corrective in The Big Bang Theory and Community." *Journal of Literary & Cultural Disability Studies* 7.3 (2013): 271–88, https://www.academia.edu/9254414/Cool_Aspie_Humor_Cognitive_Difference_and_Ksenneth_Burke_s_Comic_Corrective_in_The_Big_Bang_Theory_and_Community. Accessed 9 May 2019.

PART 5

Beyond Therapy

CHAPTER 10

Between Therapy and Art: Borderline Space in Polish Theatre of People with Intellectual (Dis) Ability

Dorota Krzemińska and Jolanta Rzeźnicka-Krupa

1 Introduction

The chapter examines the process of creating a personal, social, and cultural space that allows the form of human diversity that has been labelled as intellectual disability to emerge as a phenomenon defined in terms of socio-cultural potency and ability, and not as a deviation from an arbitrary norm (i.e. as disability). The analysis will focus on selected aspects of the artistic work of several theatre companies from Tricity,[1] which consist of adults who were clinically diagnosed with low-functioning intellectual disabilities. Each of the ensembles has been running for approximately fifteen years. For quite a while now, we have been following their work, attending their performances, and talking with the actors, instructors, directors, and associates. Each of these companies has staged at least a few plays and all of them have taken part in various disability arts festivals.

Our analyses of their theatrical work will be illustrated with the empirical data collected during open in-depth interviews which provide examples that are firmly rooted in the social experience of the companies' members and their collaborators. Adopting a perspective that centres on empirical social phenomena helps examine the transformation of the meanings that construct the theatrical practice and output of people with disabilities. Their artistic work was initially deeply embedded in a clinical approach to disability, which is characteristic of the medical model, but it gradually evolved towards the social and cultural models, which allowed for different ways of approaching disability and living with it.

---

1 Tricity is an area which consists of three administratively separate cities that function alongside one another: Gdańsk, Gdynia, and Sopot, all of which lie in the north of Poland on the edge of Gdańsk Bay and the Baltic Sea.

 | DOI:10.1163/9789004424678_012

In this chapter we want to focus primarily on the process of gradual departure from the model of theatrical activities viewed as a form of therapy and rooted in the medical model towards theatre as an art form, which comes closer to the social and cultural models of disability, all of which have already been described in the chapter by Rosemarie Garland-Thomson and Katarzyna Ojrzyńska. This evolution has created a space in which boundaries could be crossed, and the meanings that have been attributed to people with intellectual disabilities, to the ways they function, to their place in society, and to their creative output could be negotiated and altered. In other words, it has created a possibility to establish a space that allows for Rancierian dissensus as described by the Editors, i.e. a space in which those who have been deprived of voice acquire the right to speak and be heard, thus making it possible to reconfigure the inegalitarian distribution of the sensible.

This chapter employs a selection of contemporary theories of the humanities, developed in various fields. Our general point of departure is the value-laden concept of Otherness which creates a dividing line between the self and the Other. As has already been explained in the first two chapters of this book, this division involves an asymmetry of power and builds a rigid hierarchy in which the Other is relegated to a position of inferiority. This applies to a whole range of binary oppositions that dominate our thinking and perception of reality. Examples include the Self/Other, the Occident/Orient, and, importantly, the non-disabled/disabled. Since one of the aims of our chapter is to find the meanings that construct the space between the far ends of the spectrum that represent clear and stable categorizations, we also focus on the concepts that question conventional boundaries. One of such concepts is Mikhail Bakhtin's idea of "the borderline between oneself and the other" ("Discourse" 293) and crossing generic boundaries, which allows for an intermingling of cultural phenomena, increases one's creative potential, as well as prompts one to create new linguistic forms to describe reality. Other concepts employed in the chapter include the categories of hybridity and

> the Third Space of enunciation, which makes the structure of meaning and reference an ambivalent process, [and] destroys this mirror of representation in which cultural knowledge is customarily revealed as integrated, open, expanding code,
>
> BHABHA 37

as defined by Homi Bhabha. What interests us, however, is not so much the postcolonial thrust of Bhabha's theory, but its emphasis on allowing other positions to emerge, on renegotiating the binary thinking. We argue that the work of the theatrical companies discussed in this chapter creates the borderline/ third space and allows for the emergence of Rancierian dissensus.

2 Locating the Polish Theatre Companies in the Social and Institutional Contexts

When discussing the work of Polish theatre companies that operate at facilities providing support for adults with intellectual disabilities, one has to present at least a brief overview of the socio-institutional context in which they run. For years, people with intellectual disabilities who have reached the age of maturity have been neglected and left without support. While as adolescents they had access to mostly segregated special education, once they grew up, they had no educational or rehabilitative opportunities that would guarantee a proper quality of life. This resulted in the fact that adults with disabilities were effectively confined to the domestic sphere which, although important, should not be a substitute for full participation in the community. They were thus deprived of the chance to experience new things, acquire new skills, and develop interpersonal relationships. Despite the best efforts of the families, they were forced to stay at home. This most common scenario for adults with disabilities has often led to their infantilization to the point of them never being allowed to live independently.

A significant change occurred towards the end of the 1980s. The system transformation that began in 1989 redefined the political, social, and cultural landscape of Poland. The collapse of the old order in Eastern Europe paved new paths for people with disabilities. In the early 1990s, they were recognized as a group that remained under the greatest threat of marginalization and exclusion. Occupying a space on the margins of society, they were viewed as victims and, as such, became the focus of public attention. Antonina Ostrowska, Joanna Sikorska, and Barbara Gąciarz describe this in the following way: "at the time, both in the media and in political addresses, people with disabilities were one of the most frequently featured groups who paid most dearly for the transformation" (9). While it seemed that the changes would have a negative bearing on their quality of life, it soon turned out that their situation would actually improve:

> systemic and individual mechanisms that helped counter marginalization began to appear.… Since 1991, regulations that laid the foundation for new policies towards people with disabilities have been introduced. Organizations of people with disabilities have also been established with a

> view to forming pressure groups and protecting their interests in the emerging social order.
>
> OSTROWSKA, SIKORSKA, and GĄCIARZ 9–10

The people who benefited the most as a result of these changes were adults with intellectual disabilities who began to leave the space on the margins and move towards the centre. This was largely possible because of the promotion of integration, social inclusion, and actions aimed at countering marginalization, and the subsequent attempts to improve the social environment in line with the social and relational models of disability (Goodley 11–12, 15–17). These trends led to a proliferation of adult day care facilities, many of which opened at the beginning of the 1990s. They provided the much-needed support for people with disabilities, allowing for further social and professional rehabilitation after completing secondary education. Such institutions were initially called occupational therapy workshops and adaptive centres, but they were soon renamed to community centres for people with disabilities, or vocational development and training centres. Their place in the system of support for people with disabilities was cemented by normative and legislatives acts (e.g. the Act on Employment and Vocational Rehabilitation of Persons with Disabilities, Journal of Laws of 1991, No. 46, item 201 and its 1997 amendment: the Act on Vocational and Social Rehabilitation and Employment of Persons with Disabilities, Journal of Laws of 1997, No. 123, item 776). The rise of these institutions is also connected to the proliferation of groups offering theatre activities as an important alternative to other forms of therapy.

The approach to theatre of people with intellectual disability has changed drastically over the last twenty years. It gradually evolved from a form of therapy rooted in the medical model to far more complex activities that defy the traditional understanding of intellectual disability, instead adopting the perspectives promoted by the social and cultural models. Inevitably, this process is tied not only with the evolution of the meanings ascribed to intellectual disability, but also, and perhaps more importantly, with the attempts to negotiate and change the perceptions of the skills and abilities of people with ID, their potential for being active and creative, and, in short, to their very position in society and culture. In a sense, this evolution also corresponds to the transition from the representative regime of the arts to the dissensual aesthetic regime of the arts, as defined by Jacques Rancière. While the former relies on

> forms of normativity that define the conditions according to which imitations can be recognized as exclusively belonging to an art and assessed, within this framework, as good or bad, adequate or inadequate,
>
> RANCIÈRE 17

the aesthetic regime of the arts is much more liberating and free from strict conventions as it "revokes the representative tradition's scales of grandeur" (Rancière 30).

The roots of the theatre workshops, however, were clearly therapeutic and their principles were laid out by the medical model. The publications explaining the basic precepts of group therapy portray people with disabilities as having physical, psychological, or intellectual impairments, and thus being in need of reparative intervention that would restore them to 'normalcy' (e.g. Kozaczuk; Lorenc). Ultimately, the patient or the care-receiver is supposed to be 'healed by working' and participating in therapy, which is seen as a 'curative measure.' The problem with such statements is not only that they are deeply rooted in the medical model, but also that they shape the perception of people with disabilities and their rehabilitation through art therapy. It also implies that people with disabilities should be treated differently than those non-disabled. Disability is thus seen as a medicalized, personal deficit, and a 'personal tragedy.' Defined in such a way, it has to be corrected or repaired through rehabilitation founded upon "the ideology of 'normality'" (Oliver 55). Such an attitude forces people to aspire to the homogenous norm and to hide otherness. Importantly, art therapy, too, is based on an essentially asymmetrical relationship between the two parties involved in the process, i.e. the able-bodied therapist who has vast professional knowledge, and the person with ID who is supposed to be improved and 'repaired,' and is ultimately expected to overcome his or her disability.

This short discussion of the context in which the Polish theatre companies of people with intellectual disabilities were established and in which they are still functioning points to the fact that the outcomes that they desired to produce were not artistic. Currently, the vast majority of Polish organizations offering support to people with ID rely on theatre activities, but only a few of them have developed their own methods of work and tried to make their performances more and more professional. We are particularly interested in the work of theatre groups that have experienced the dissonance resulting from occupying the space between art and therapy. This dissonance may largely be caused by various forms of interaction with(in) the group: forming a community, learning about other people and their skills, talents, limitations, and needs, as well as getting to know their preferences as far as the choice of plays and roles is concerned. The question of how to define what they do has become especially relevant in the light of the new ideas and concepts that paved the way for recent ways of defining and approaching disability. Since the 1990s, disability in Poland has increasingly been seen as a multifaceted and complex phenomenon that is determined by culture and society. This has made the carers and some of the actors realize that their work has transcended therapy and moved closer to theatre.

The groups we are referring to have gone through a similar process. The theatre companies of people with disabilities based in Tricity have participated in various festivals, both national and regional, which stimulated the emergence of a common idea rooted in their shared experience and outlook on their own work. Some of the therapists/theatre instructors/directors recognized the creative potential of the people they worked with and refused to be confined to the oppressive and exclusionary context of institutional therapy and rehabilitation. Instead, they decided to create an informal association – IM+.[2] Their decision was facilitated by the positive feedback that they received from theatre professionals. Their main goals were set out in the manifesto which also voiced their objections against viewing both people with intellectual disabilities and the art they create as Other, different, lesser, and determined by therapeutic principles. In a way, it also stressed the need for dissensus, as defined in the chapter by Katarzyna Ojrzyńska and Maciej Wieczorek, i.e. the need to reconfigure the existing power relations in such a way as to allow marginalized groups to partake in the life of society on equal terms.

These practitioners' experience helped them develop a more integrated, communal approach based on mutual support and collective search for new forms of artistic expression and a new place for theatre companies of people with disabilities within the mainstream. IM+ aims to promote, popularize, and deinstitutionalize the art created by people with ID, and, thus, to remove the stigma of lack of professionalism that was attached to it. This is best summarized in their manifesto, where they claim that

> we believe that performances created by theatre companies and musical ensembles of people with disabilites, albeit amateur, CAN BE and ARE an important part of culture. We would like to change the public awareness as well as the image of people with disabilities, and, in consequence, improve the conditions of their life. To make this happen, we want to engage in specific artistic and social activities.
>
> SPICA et al.

All of the companies that this chapter focuses on have been affiliated with institutions supporting people with intellectual disabilities in Tricity. IM+ is an informal association, and it consists of five theatre companies and one instrumental ensemble, affiliated with six different institutions: the musical ensem-

2 The association has a Facebook profile: https://www.facebook.com/pg/grupaimplus/about/?ref=page_internal.

ble Remont Pomp[3] (Pumps Refit – it is made up of both people with intellectual disabilities and non-disabled pupils, students, as well as volunteers from Poland and other countries) and the theatre companies: Mimoto,[4] Kasablanka,[5] Teatr Ubogi Relacji (Scanty Theatre of Relations),[6] Razem (Together – an integrated company consisting of actors with disabilities and non-disabled performers),[7] and Biuro Rzeczy Osobistych (Personal Property Office).[8] The performances they create only employ spoken language to a very small degree, since verbal communication poses a challenge for a number of actors with ID. The plays are often adaptations of canonical texts, but some of the productions are also based on the personal experience and ideas of the actors. The performances they create usually rely on movement, sound, visual imagery, props, and pantomime to communicate their message. Each of the ensembles has staged at least five plays. Teatr Ubogi Relacji and Kasablanka have been active for the longest time – they have been running for over twenty years, and they were founded when the first institutions supporting people with disabilities, i.e. community centres for people with disabilities, were established.

3 The Empirical Context

To avoid indulging in what Doris Bachmann-Medick calls "metaphysical speculations" (cf. 271–72), we have decided to ground our analyses in the empirical data gathered during field research on Polish theatre companies of people with intellectual disabilities. We have used quotations taken from transcripts of open in-depth interviews and field notes to support our claims.[9] Our analysis

3 Some information about the company is available at: http://psoni.gda.pl/remont-pomp/.

4 The company has a Facebook profile: https://www.facebook.com/pg/teatrmimoto/about/?ref=page_internal.

5 A short history of the company (in Polish) can be found at: https://gfitmw.pl/teatr-kasablanka/. Some excerpts from their performances are available on Youtube (e.g. a trailer of their performance inspired by Shakespeare and entitled *Mr H* is available at: https://www.youtube.com/watch?v=WB4FULKYptc).

6 At present, the theatre does not have a website.

7 A short history of the company (in Polish) can be found at: http://psoni.gda.pl/teatr-razem/. The company also has a Facebook profile: https://www.facebook.com/teatrazem/.

8 More information about the company can be found at: http://www.tbro.psonigdynia.pl/or/and the company's Facebook profile: https://www.facebook.com/pages/category/Community/Teatr-spo%C5%82eczny-biuro-rzeczy-osobistych-593677267390127/.

9 The interviews quoted in the present chapter have been conducted by both of us and the students of the University of Gdańsk whose research we supervised. The individual and

of the source material focuses on the following categories: art, therapy, theatre, disability, and the process of creating performances (Gibbs; Miles and Hubermann). They will be examined from two perspectives: that of the therapists or instructors working at the institutions where the theatre companies operate, and that of the actors.

The fragments provided below are only a small part of the material that we have gathered. Nevertheless, we feel that they are perfect illustrations of the analytical categories and theoretical concepts introduced in the chapter. We took the liberty of adding our commentary and highlighting the parts that are most relevant to the idea of going beyond the boundaries of a theatre that is excluded, based on the therapeutic model, and that presents 'the inferior Other' – people with intellectual disabilities.

4 Between Therapy and Art

In the following fragments the therapists who run the theatre workshops talk about their experiences and their own perception of and approach towards what they do and the art they create. Barbara talks, for instance, about discovering the actors' skills, using drama to teach them "to perform a role and to identify themselves with it" and creating longer and more elaborate performances. She states: "we started combining socio-therapy and drama with music and saw the opportunities that this offers … that we can create something more than drama." Both Barbara and Adam underscore the fact that their work aims at challenging the unequal relationship between the disabled actor and non-disabled audience:

> **Adam:** We don't do this work only for therapeutic reasons – we go further than that. Of course, we have socio-therapeutic aims. However, it's not that we interfere with the lives of disabled people in order to integrate

group interviews, and their transcripts have been prepared by: Janina Wróblewska (who used them in her unpublished M.A. thesis "O grupie Kasablanka: Zajęcia teatralne w życiu dorosłych osób z niepełnosprawnością intelektualną" ["On Casablanca: Theatre Activities in the Lives of Adults with Intellectual Disability"], Gdańsk, 2008), Grzegorz Bartecki, Damian Michnowski, and Patrycja Makiła (who used them in their unpublished term paper entitled "Twórczość osób niepełnosprawnych intelektualnie w perspektywie terapeutów ŚDS Nowiny" ["The Art of People with Intellectual Disabilities from the Perspective of the Therapists of the Nowiny Centre for People with Disabilities"]). One of the group interviews was recorded by Jacek Spica, a therapist who works with one of the companies and the organizer of MASSKA Festival.

them with the open environment, as is often the case. Rather, we change the attitude of the environment by showing that a disabled person is a normal human being! ... Our work is a form of therapy for society.

Barbara: The spectator shouldn't see a disabled person, but rather his or her own emotions, something that he or she also experiences. The fact that the play is performed by a disabled actor shouldn't be brought to the foreground.

Adam also discusses the role of theatre of people with disabilities and explains whether he sees it as a form of therapy or primarily as an artistic endeavour.

> **Adam:** The art of disabled people? Should we situate it in therapeutic or artistic contexts? I think that creative work is a form of therapy for every artist. I don't mean to say that every artist is mad, but they experience different feelings than ordinary people because they, for instance, paint or perform roles, and, in a sense, heal themselves by doing that. In my opinion, art belongs to both of these contexts.

Adam thus goes beyond the conventional binary opposition between therapy and art, demedicalizing the latter and presenting it as a universal and necessary aspect of the creative process.

5 Enabling Theatre

The therapists frequently talk about the actors' disabilities and the meanings that are ascribed to them in theatre. Adam mentions the sense of being "normal" and "non-disabled" that is often experienced by the actors

> **Adam:** If they feel non-disabled on the stage, then there is no need to inform everyone after the performance that they are learning disabled. Because there are many people who are ashamed of the fact that they have some intellectual disability.... They are also aware of the fact that they are disabled and thus they want to hide it. For instance, Daniel – when he enters the stage and turns on the light, his main desire is that no one should realize that he is disabled. *He becomes a totally different person there, a person without intellectual disability*. [emphasis added]

The fact that the therapists who run the workshops repeatedly talk about the disabilities of their actors renders the phenomenon of disability all the more ambivalent; on the one hand, one cannot avoid talking about it, but, on the other hand, it is in certain aspects unimportant and irrelevant. In a sense, it disappears. Dealing with the actors' impairments is inevitably a part of the process of creating a performance. It is especially true as far as the assigning of roles is concerned, since one has to take the performers' individual limitations and difficulties into consideration, be they linguistic, motor, mnemonic, etc. However, as their work progresses, when they rehearse and identify or familiarize themselves with their characters, disability gradually disappears – it ceases to be relevant. Even the impairments that initially appeared to be a major hindrance might become a fascinating means of artistic expression. The people who run the companies play a crucial role in this respect, as they know the strengths and weaknesses of individual actors and are capable of devising roles and constructing performances in such a way that they are perceived and experienced as art per se, and not through the prism of the performers' otherness. This is reflected in the fragment provided below:

> **Adam**: We have many actors like, for instance, Gienio, who is not even able to perform a certain physical script on the stage and he is not able to understand that he is supposed to raise his right arm three times and thump his left foot three times. He is unable to coordinate these movements. Thus, it is important that we give him a role that will not accentuate the fact that he cannot do this. He needs to be given tasks that he will be able to perform.... The last performance was very difficult to memorize – it had many parts with which we – non-disabled people – would not be able to cope with, but they did well because they spend all their time on the stage. They always have to do something: one specific action after another, and this helps them memorize the script – *they are totally invaluable in this respect! At this very moment, they are in no way disabled, because they do this better than an ordinary person or they can do this with one gesture, because they have so much experience.* [emphasis added]

These words may well be analyzed in the context of Homi Bhabha's idea of an encounter in the third/hybrid space, an encounter that is based on an asymmetrical power relationship between the non-disabled spectators and actors with intellectual disabilities. Defined by Bhabha as a place where meanings are deconstructed and a new model of cohabitation is negotiated, the category makes it clear that, as will later be shown, it is possible to look at people with disabilities and their skills and natural abilities in a new light. The traditional attitude towards people with intellectual disabilities is thus contested. While they are often viewed as incapacitated, infirm, unintelligent, passive, and helpless, in contrast to their able-bodied counterparts, who are seen as creative, active, and resourceful, the encounters that take place during the theatre workshops and in the theatre itself challenge the negative perception of people with intellectual disabilities and problematize their otherness. These encounters make it possible to look at the actors through the prism of the meanings that have, heretofore, been reserved for the non-disabled people. The biggest paradox is that when one looks at disability from such a perspective, certain aspects that appeared to be stable and unchangeable become irrelevant. The actor with disability, whose identity has been defined in negative terms and who has been viewed as the Other, is seen in a new light and his or her identity needs to be seen in a new light as well.

Such theatre workshops, rehearsals, and performances can be seen as encounters in the third space. As the supposedly 'inferior' actors share the same experience with the allegedly 'superior' able-bodied spectators, the meanings ascribed to people with disabilities gradually change and the traditional binary oppositions are unsettled. A shift from defect to effect takes place and the person who was earlier seen as weak, disabled, and uncreative suddenly becomes strong, enabled, and creative. The borderline third/hybrid space reveals and foregrounds differences – they become visible, but, at the same time, they are called into question and erased as a result of the change of perspective. This is not to say that impairments cease to exist, but, rather, that they are seen in a different light. Theatre can be such a borderline space, a safe place where actors with intellectual disabilities are not under any pressure to adapt to normative standards, a space where freedom of expression is of utmost importance and disability is not denigrated. It has the potential to become a dissensual space that allows for the full subjectification of people with disabilities who are given the chance to express themselves on equal terms with the rest of society and be appreciated for who they are.

Arkadiusz describes theatre of people with intellectual disability in a similar way. In the interview, he talks about how the initial difficulties and obstacles eventually translated into an idiosyncratic style of acting, a familiarity with the theatrical conventions, and the ability to adapt to unexpected situations:

> **Arkadiusz:** It's a different theatre genre – the so-called theatre of movement, visual theatre, in which movement and bodily expression have replaced words.... Here it is more difficult because communication with disabled people should be more concrete. However, I don't think it is

> really so, because some things are universal, because we've all been raised in the same culture. This concerns them as well! Thus, if we're not operating with some sophisticated symbols or signs, it can be easier than we thought.... But what were the results? Various, for various reasons: we couldn't convey everything through signs ... I couldn't create a sign that would be legible, and the actors could not make up for this with their pantomime.

The therapist is very forthright about the problems they have been facing. In another fragment of the interview, he recalls a situation in which he was supposed to place two chairs in the backstage area, but forgot to do so, leaving the actors no choice but to improvise. The actors were able to do just that, and they simply sat back to back. The effect that this created was arguably more powerful than the one achieved in the original staging. For Arkadiusz, this clearly challenged the conventional idea that people with intellectual disabilities lack flexibility.

This mishap became an important experience for the actors who were put in a very difficult position, especially since they had to improvise quickly as they had to go on stage and could not afford any delay. This is what one of them had to say:

> **Magda:** Yes, and Arek forgot about the chairs. It went as follows: when we were entering the stage, when we were to perform with those chairs, which were supposed to be in the wings, there were no chairs because Arek had forgot to bring them. So we thought that we need to quickly ... come up with our improvs. And so: I came up with something different and Marek came up with something else, we both did, right? And then we performed. There was no reason to be nervous. We pretended that the chairs were there and we performed!

In the interview, the therapist and the actors question the way of describing and approaching people with disabilities that is peculiar to the medical model. Their ability to cope with the mishap, which indeed required a great amount of flexibility, clearly points to the fact that they should not be defined through the prism of the seemingly objective 'impairments,' and thus reveals the arbitrariness and absurdity of conventional assumptions. Their ability to solve the problem that quickly in a stressful situation is, indeed, at complete odds with what is believed to be typical of people with ID, who are described in medical texts mainly in terms of deficits and inabilities (e.g. lack of abstract thinking and flexibility, formulaic cognition, inability to live and act independently, etc.) which have an immense, wholly negative impact on their identity.

6 Preparing the Performances

The next issue addressed by the interviewees was how the companies prepared the performances and worked on their self-development. They did not answer the question about their long and difficult work directly, but they nevertheless shed some light on the complexities of the process:

> **Arkadiusz:** At the beginning we did two or three performances which were a combination of the scenes that we improvised during rehearsals. Well, this is our method when we explore a topic. The topic is chosen by me or another person from the group – it does not really matter. Most often the topic is one word or a sentence which is supposed to start a process which may, but does not have to take place – it may be performed on the stage in the process of improvisation. Such a process begins with pure improvisation and then we try to select something from it, we filter some things out, some aspects – for instance, this sounds good, let's have it!

Arkadiusz's perspective is complemented by an interview with one of the actors, who describes what they do during the workshops, how they familiarize themselves with theatrical conventions, and how they approach certain activities, exercises, or short pieces:

> **Magda:** We improvise. We, for instance, show an improvisation: when there's a chair and we simply try to improvise … with this chair, that it is on fire! And when the chair was on fire, we ran, we were scared and this is what improvisation is all about. I've learned to improvise.

Arkadiusz also talks about the casting process and about how the actors prepare for their roles. He stresses that before performing a dramatic piece, they all create individual roles by focusing on the character's psychological profile, their interpersonal relations with other characters, and their strong and weak sides. He then explains that he makes the decisions regarding casting on his own as certain roles that are central to a given performance have to be performed properly. The actors with disabilities are nevertheless important in the entire process and it is obvious that they are very invested in it. They are still reliving this experience – they remember and talk about the characters and dissect the story they staged:

> **Sylwia:** Then we performed *Macbeth* … Krzysiu was Macbeth and I was Lady Macbeth. Lady Macbeth was a strict queen and she wanted to kill king Duncan. She kept looking through the window to see if Macbeth was or wasn't coming … And there were the witches: "All hail, Macbeth, that shalt be king hereafter" and so on … these witches stirred the brew in their cauldron. It was all fake, a kind of fiction. Lady Macbeth was cruel and she only looked in this direction and in that direction to see if Macbeth was or wasn't coming. Macbeth had a friend Banquo.… Banquo was played by Janek. I had this dagger which I gave to Macbeth to kill king Duncan. I mean Lady Macbeth gave the order. She was a beautiful woman, but she had a character that did not match her beauty and she gave the order. Macbeth arrived on horseback …, "Look Macbeth, you need to kill king Duncan." He went quietly, and first killed Banquo and then king Duncan. Then the witches stir their brew … and again: "All hail, Macbeth, that shalt be king hereafter" and they stir and stir.… After some time Macbeth is killed …
>
> **Marek:** … and then Banquo, my friend, and I met him … Banquo in *Macbeth* … he was a dead man, a dead man … I was afraid and my head was hurting …
>
> **Sylwia:** *Macbeth* was a very difficult play, but we did well .… people liked it, it was interesting. We were performing Shakespeare.… It was difficult to play. It was difficult when Lady Macbeth had to at that moment look whether he was or wasn't coming … Banquo, Macbeth rode a horse, as I said, and the witches then say: "All hail, Macbeth, that shalt be king hereafter," well, it was difficult, we had to rehearse .…

The most interesting moment, the one when what Bhabha would call the third space is created, is the time when the performance is ready and it is presented to an audience. This is how the actors with ID and the therapists describe it:

> **Arkadiusz:** They're nervous, or rather anxious and agitated. You can feel some emotional tension and you can see that after the performance there is a huge "phew." … Honestly speaking, it all depends on the importance of the performance.… Everyone feels its importance.… Of course, if they weren't nervous, this would mean that they weren't aware of it.

Magda: I think that when we're on the stage or when we enter ... then every one of us sitting here for sure feels a bit stressed. It's impossible not to have stage-fright! There is always some stage-fright. After some time the stage-fright disappears, I don't know how to put it ... it disappears later. And we perform and it's no longer there. It's not easy, the audience, but stage-fright is always there and will be, but with time it disappears!

Marek: I'm only stressed when there is a cameraman who is filming us, this gives me stage-fright! ... I have stage-fright before the performance.

When the disabled actors perform in front of a non-disabled audience who have fixed ideas of what to expect from the Other, the preconception that a person with an intellectual disability 'cannot do anything good' inevitably comes into play, resulting in an encounter that is based on a significantly asymmetrical power relationship. Barbara and Adam both talk about this:

Adam: When we don't know something, we're often afraid of it. It is most often the case that you come to see a theatre performance and you learn that the actors are learning disabled, and you instantly take a step back and you develop a negative approach. You think: what can they possibly show?! *This leads to a stigma, based on a preconception that if a person has an intellectual disability, he or she cannot do anything good.* [emphasis added]

Barbara: I've heard many times that I'm exaggerating, that I'm trying to make disabled people able-bodied and that I'm only pretending that they are not disabled. In fact, to make people watch it, I do everything possible to hide their disability. There are two different approaches: one of them is that people think that disabled people are like "animals" and whatever you tell them, they say that therapists are exaggerating and trying to hide disability.

The aim of the theatre they create, however, leads to a transformation of meanings, to their displacement and reorientation.

The latter part of the interview with Adam also deals with attempts to challenge stereotypes, to empower the actors, and to adopt a dialogical position associated with Bakhtin's borderline. Both Bakhtin and Bhabha believe that liminal spaces make it possible for us to alter the meanings ascribed to Otherness and to collectively devise new norms of coexistence. For Bhabha, this occurs as a result of negotiation, while for Bakhtin, the Otherness of the borderline is not to be discarded or denigrated, but understood. The fragment cited below points to such an interpretation:

> **Adam**: When we arrived in Szczecin, where we received an award, we were the only company of disabled people and we were surrounded by students.... They didn't know how to treat us. Did we come here to trigger some response, like "oh, you poor things"? Did we want pity? They were also probably curious to find out if disabled people can do something really good.... They weren't dumbfounded, because it took them a while to figure out that something's wrong. This sounds awkward, but what I mean is that something is different, that these actors on the stage are not able-bodied, but ... Because you can see that Ania has the Down syndrome, she wore a mask and in the end she took it off – *it was a moment when everyone saw that she has slanting eyes and that she looks a bit different from everyone else* [emphasis added]. Well, you could also tell it by Gabrysia's looks ... or they may have thought that she came from the Sakha Republic .... So the people gathered in the auditorium who professionally work in theatre or who are theatregoers and did not find themselves in the theatre by pure chance – *they saw that disabled actors can show something good and they gave us a standing ovation for ten minutes!* [emphasis added]

When analyzed in the context of Bhabha's theory, the spectators clearly occupy a superior position. This fact may be attributed to their able-bodiedness and perceived creativity which render them talented enough to create meaningful texts of culture that serve to reinforce and perpetuate their socio-cultural dominance, or, as Rancière would have it, the existing, highly inegalitarian distribution of the sensible. The actor with ID is then seen as a domesticated Other who is only capable of imitating real artists and performers, as someone who is defective and inferior. The asymmetrical encounter in the third, theatrical space confronts the able-bodied spectators with unexpected qualities of people with disabilities, qualities that have theretofore been reserved for the non-disabled. They are thus forced to recognize the new status of the Other, and the meanings ascribed to people with disabilities are radically altered. As Adam puts it, "they saw that disabled actors can show something good and they gave us a standing ovation for ten minutes."

The relationship between the non-disabled and people with disabilities is essentially asymmetrical and it leads to objectification. The non-disabled spectators arrogate, at least initially, the right to form authoritative judgements on the creative output of people with ID. They reify and objectify the disabled actors, and do not expect them to produce "something good." From this perspective, which Bakhtin labels as monologic,

> *another person* remains wholly and merely an *object* of consciousness, and not another consciousness. No response is expected from it that could change everything in the world of my consciousness.
>
> "Toward a Reworking" 293

Embodying strong categories and thus occupying a privileged position, the spectator shows certain domineering tendencies, claims to have "the *ultimate word*" ("Toward a Reworking" 293), and, as a consequence, produces what Bakhtin terms as a monologue. Ultimately, the dissensual third space (the hybrid space, the borderline) brings the non-disabled and people with disabilities into direct confrontation, granting the latter the right to express themselves. Theatre becomes the place where the fusion of horizons of non-disabled spectators and disabled actors takes place. It is a space where the "highly intense struggle of *I* and *other*" elaborated by Bakhtin becomes visible "in every external manifestation of a person" ("Toward a Reworking" 295). The struggle is, for instance, embodied by spectators' momentary inability to answer the question that they pose themselves. As Adam puts it, "you instantly take a step back and you develop a negative approach. You think: what can they possibly show?!" It is the moment which Bakhtin describes in terms of

> [t]he exceptionally keen sense of *one's own* and *the other* in the word, in style, in the most subtle nuances and twists of style, in intonation, in the speech gesture, in the body (mimic) gesture, in the expression of the eyes, the face, the hands, the entire external appearance, in the very way the body is carried.
>
> "Toward a Reworking" 294–95

Paradoxically, as a space of an encounter between non-disabled audience and disabled performers, theatre becomes the borderline where the 'Self' and the 'Other' interact and confront each other.

A theatre in which non-disabled members of the audience encounter disabled actors becomes a borderline space in which a conflict between the Self and the Other arises. A spectator who goes to the theatre to see a performance has certain preconceptions and expectations which are put to the test when he or she is confronted with disability. Analyzing Jérôme Bel's *Disabled Theatre*, Gerald Siegmund notes that when the audience is faced with disabled actors on stage, their expectations are disrupted. What we see cannot be classified as good or bad art, or good or bad acting (13). At the same time, in the spectator's monologic attitude, which is based on his or her own presumptions, one can find some cracks caused by the presence of the Other. This creates a mental space in which the audience can attribute new meanings to the Other and enter a dialogic relationship with the previously assigned meanings. It opens up a space in which the Other can freely express himself or herself. Furthermore, Siegmund claims that disabled theatre creates new possibilities. He states: "When theatre is disabled, it seems that our implicit and tacit value judgements and the ideas and attitudes they rely on are made explicit again. They are once again open for discussion" (Siegmund 13).

The actors describe the moment when the performance is over in the following words:

> **Marek:** After the performance I felt very good, I was happy. The light was the reward, the floodlight.
>
> **Magda:** And I also think the applause, the appreciation, that there is appreciation when the actors finish the performance and the leader or the director [the jury?] enters and gives thanks.
>
> **Karol:** I like it when people applaud in the end. When the performance is over, people clap their hands loudly. I like it. In the end we all hug!
>
> **Sylwia:** People are happy, they clap their hands, we laugh, great! We're happy we're done, we've given a performance! We've won the Grand Prix! Two years ago we played *Romeo and Juliet* at Wybrzeże Theatre. We received a big lamp – it was the Grand Prix for the performance.

During the curtain call, the actors with disabilities become the beneficiaries of the encounter in the third space. As the audience recognize the quality of the performance and reward the actors with applause, the latter are filled with pride and their identity is affirmed. This atmosphere of mutual happiness and satisfaction leads to a Bakhtinian unfinished dialogue which conquers the monologic perspective in a Bhabhan hybrid space. The actors are no longer seen as objectified, disabled artists, but, rather, as what Bakhtin calls "the human being[s]-personalit[ies]" ("Toward a Reworking" 291). Such theatrical performances clearly lead to a reconfiguration of the distribution of the sensible and, in consequence, allow for the subjectification of people with disabilities who are no longer seen as inferior. The egalitarian principle is realized, and the actors are no longer seen as those on the margins of society, but are, instead, embraced as its valued element. Their work exceeds the non-disabled spectators' low expectations and becomes liberated from the existing conventions according to which it would be seen as 'inferior' and, possibly, non-artistic. As the performance is recognized and appreciated as art, a transition from the representative regime of the arts to the aesthetic regime of the arts takes place.

7 Why Am I in the Theatre?

The interviewees with intellectual disabilities also answered questions about the reasons why they became actors and what theatre means for them. All the interviews point to the fact that their success is largely possible due to their hard work, commitment, and ability to transcend their own limitations.

> **Magda:** I first came here to see what the theatre workshop with the director Arek looks like and I didn't like it at first. Then I entered and sat with them and then something tempted me.... I sat with them longer, and then I was tempted to join in.... And so I entered the room but it was only later that I got involved; I saw them perform. I came there a few times and I stayed for good and so now I'm in the company. I simply do it for pleasure and I also learn to act; you don't speak your role, but you do it – I mean, you simply perform it! ... Well, the first performance in a play was my success.... When I performed in *Romeo and*..., I thought I would really be stressed out. I didn't expect that it would turn out this way, that it would be a success!
>
> **Sylwia:** The workshop is fun; we simply come here. You can relax; you stop thinking about your problems, you only think about the play! You, for instance, invent a home, a family, you watch a film.... You can come up with a play, for instance, there is a film – say, a film drama – you watch a film and then talk and on the basis of the film you can do ... a lot.... It's great; you can achieve a lot. A success... You can learn a lot.... You can think!
>
> **Marek:** I've been with the company for a while ... because I need to come here to make a performance for people. I really like this acting, because I like it when there are people, because I play wonderful roles.... I like performing for people.... People watch it and then they applaud five or seven times. I'm happy and I like it.

One of the theatre companies whose work we have been analyzing, Teatr Biuro Rzeczy Osobistych (Personal Items Office), finds itself in a very special place now. The company has managed to change the perception of the art of people with disabilities and has come close to achieving the goal they set before them – turning professional. Not only would this be the crowning of their achievements, but also the final step of their departure from the therapeutic context determined by the medical model of disability. In the fragments provided below, Zbigniew Biegajło, the founder and director of BRO, Iwona Siekierzyńska, a mainstream theatre director, and Aleksandra Nieśpielak, a professional actress, talk about their latest project, *Moja Sprawa* (*My Business*).

Zbigniew: During the 17 years of BRO's existence, its work was hermetic. After some time, however, I realized that we're facing a wall and that if our work is supposed to reach outside and if we want to create a new quality, we need to invite people who will show us how to do this from another perspective, who will teach us (and me) something. And it's an experiment for me.... Those whom I had in mind were experienced practitioners who work in theatre, who have some training and education in this field, who share a certain approach to their artistic work. And now I see the difference, after I've been watching Iwona's work for the last few months. I see that this way of thinking is different. I see all the nuances and details.

Iwona: For us, for me, for the actors of Biuro Rzeczy Osobistych, and for professional actors whom we invited, it was an interesting encounter, which immediately caused a lot of agitation. *Most of these people said that they have never had such a thing before. Such an encounter. Professional actors met with amateur actors who additionally have intellectual disabilities. This triggered a lot of emotions* [emphasis added]. Some said that it was difficult, but they were also curious how that experience would change them.... But from the very beginning I was aware of the fact that these two worlds aren't very distant from one another. Both parties work with the same medium – they perform roles on the stage. We had actors on both sides. The only difference was their professional status.

Aleksandra: We have to be authentic enough to perform with them on the same stage, because the only thing that can be successful on the stage is truth. I also think that the text we have been working on also serves as a pretext for us to experiment. In terms of acting, every play is an experiment.... And what's attractive about this project is ... I'd call it differently. *I wouldn't say that we are professional actors, and they aren't, because they have such a level of concentration that I would certainly call them professional actors. They've been performing for so many years that they really know what they're doing. For me it was a surprise* [emphasis added].... I see that they've been doing this for so long that they know how to feel the character's emotions, how to be in the role, how to be on the stage. For me this was very professional. It was something I didn't expect. I also think that the text is so different from the previous texts I worked with that it merges these two worlds. On the one hand, it sets disabled people in a certain context, showing that they also have families and that these families experience certain things because of their disability. We've got two perspectives that clash here: our world and their world. I sometimes wonder which one is better. The one in which they express their emotions

> and themselves and speak all these nice things in such a sincere and open way, or perhaps our world in which we experience some limitations due to our upbringing and education, because there are things that you should or shouldn't do. We wear masks. And so I wonder which world is more real.

At another point she said that:

> **Aleksandra:** Popular beliefs cherished by society have little to do with the reality. I was totally surprised that they are so intelligent and that they can be so ironic. *They can laugh at the same things, they feel the same emotions, and the only problem that they have is to communicate these emotions to us* [emphasis added]. Because they understand each other perfectly well. They feel and experience things in the same way. *The way they perform, create scenes, experience their roles.... It's all incredible to me! It's no different from our feelings!* [emphasis added] We experience emotions in the same way.

In the therapeutic model of theatre, the Other is markedly different, believed to be worse than the Self, and perceived as someone who should aspire to the norm, someone we can objectify. Seeing this Otherness in the third space of the theatre makes it possible to look at it differently, to interpret it in a new way, and to assign new meanings to it. Bakhtin claimed that Otherness is not to be rejected, but understood. The uneven power relationship is transformed as the actors with ID are no longer seen as inferior since their Otherness (their disability) is mediated through art and is no longer subject to the hegemonic processes of interpretation.

8 Conclusion

Prior to writing this chapter, we asked ourselves the question of how to define the theatrical work of people who are seen by Polish society as intellectually disabled. Is their work more of an art form or should it be classified as a form of therapy? What is the role of the theatre of people with intellectual disability in Polish culture and society?

In her book *Więcej niż teatr* [*More than Theatre*] which focuses on the Polish student theatre movement, renowned Polish sociologist Aldona Jawłowska describes the work of student theatre companies that operated in communist Poland from the mid-1950s to the 1980s. She explains:

> My intention is to present student theatre as a multidimensional phenomenon which cannot be contained within the frameworks of social activity or art. It is more than a social movement and more than theatre. It is also an institution, a place to live in, a form of entertainment, and a peculiar sanctuary for misfits. However, above all, it is an attempt to challenge the existing culture with an alternative cultural entity. It is not about verbal description … but about taking action in order to find one's own way of living and form of creativity.
>
> JAWŁOWSKA 5[10]

Jawłowska's way of understanding theatre and art bears much in common with our reflections on the theatre companies of people with intellectual disability based in Tricity (and also other Polish theatre companies) which we have been observing for some time now. Such theatres have formed a social movement whose visibility is increasing and which defies contemporary artistic standards, questioning what deserves to be called art and why. They thus foster emancipatory goals and challenge the position assigned to people with cognitive

---

10 Having examined disability theatre in Poland and the evolution of the tenets, ideas, and goals of the theatre companies in the last twenty years, one may find some similarities in their ways of thinking. This affinity is mostly reflected in their search for 'cultural islands' which enable participation in culture and social inclusion of people who are at risk of social exclusion, through artistic activity. This way of thinking, which bears close resemblance to Jawłowska's ideas about the Polish student theatre movement, informed the project entitled "Więcej niż teatr" ("More than Theatre") which has been run since 2015 by the Grotowski Institute as part of the European Capital of Culture Wrocław 2016. One of the authors of this article, Jolanta Rzeźnicka-Krupa, participated in this project. Its major goal was closely connected with the functioning of people with disabilities in arts. As the curators of the project: Jana Pilatova, Justyna Sobczyk, Magdalena Hasiuk, and Anna Zubrzycki explain,

> Examining the field of performing arts and in particular theatre, visual arts, and film, we wish to analyze the ways in which the subjective presence of people seen as disabled verifies widely accepted beliefs. It appears that the categories, tools, and language that we have so far used require redefinition. Our aim is to draw public attention to the art of people with disabilities which has been developing in Poland in the last twenty years and to approach it from a broad perspective. We wish to create a common space which will enable an encounter between non-disabled people and people with disabilities, a space in which numerous questions will be posed in order to start a discussion. We hope that this will help us develop our work with actors/people with disabilities. The activities scheduled as part of the project are supposed to inspire their participants to go beyond their specialization, to transgress their limitations, to meet other people who also work in the field of theatre, brut art, film, and music.
>
> "Więcej niż teatr"

impairments in culture and society. Their work is essentially dissensual – they move from the representative regime of the arts to the Rancierian aesthetic regime and subjectify people with intellectual disability, giving them a platform through which they can speak and be heard.

Trying to define the current situation of the theatre of people with ID in Poland and its evolving identity, one may compare it to the metaphor of a "non-place," understood as a product of supermodernity, which Marc Auge describes in the following way: "If a place can be defined as relational, historical, and concerned with identity, then a space which cannot be defined as relational, or historical, or concerned with identity will be a non-place" (77–78). He adds that

> [p]lace and non-place are rather like opposite polarities: the first is never completely erased, the second never totally completed; they are like palimpsests on which the scramble game of identity and relations is ceaselessly rewritten.
>
> AUGE 79

Polish theatre of people with intellectual disability is presently trying to find its own place. It seems uncertain of its own identity and thus remains suspended in a peculiar non-place. A question should therefore be asked: what are the products of the so-called DisArt which is commonly seen as disabled, dysfunctional, dissatisfying, unintellectual, unwanted, unknown, unprofessional, unappreciated, and marginal? We do not define this art with such prefixes as dis- or un-. We see it as an art which does not strive to meet the demands of normalcy, but rather seeks and sets new standards. It liberates itself from arbitrary conventions and becomes an expression of the Rancierian aesthetic regime of the arts. The traditional clinically oriented approach to disability, which gave rise to art therapy (including drama therapy) and which still has some bearing on the everyday practice of the institutions supporting people with ID, seems to be insufficient and inadequate.

Disabled theatre confronts us with the stage as a place of emancipation and subjectification, and disability as a social and political problem. Benjamin Wihstutz writes that

> to do theater … means to present something to an audience, to make something visible and audible, to put oneself in the limelight. The question of who in society has a stage at their disposal and, hence, the chance to perform publicly, and who is being denied this chance, is therefore an eminently political question.
>
> WIHSTUTZ 35

The stories presented in this chapter show that the ideas informing the social perceptions of disability in Poland, which define normalcy and the value of art as well as the margins and areas of exclusion, are no longer valid. They also foreground the need to search for a third, dissensual space, a borderline in which disability art and disability itself can be renegotiated and new meanings, identities, cultural narratives, and texts of culture can emerge, thus helping reconfigure the inegalitarian distribution of the sensible.

Translated by Katarzyna Ojrzyńska and Maciej Wieczorek

Works Cited

Auge, Marc. *Non-Places: Introduction to an Anthropology of Supermodernity*. Trans. John Howe. London: Verso, 1995. Print.

Bachmann-Medick, Doris. *Cultural Turns: Nowe kierunki w naukach o kulturze*. Trans. Krystyna Krzemieniowa. Warszawa: Oficyna Naukowa, 2012. Print.

Bakhtin, Mikhail M. "Discourse in the Novel." *The Dialogic Imagination: Four Essays*. Ed. Michael Holquist. Trans. Caryl Emerson and Michael Holquist. Austin, TX: University of Texas Press, 1981. 259–422. Print.

Bakhtin, Mikhail M. "Toward a Reworking of the Dostoevsky Book (1961)." *Problems of Dostoevsky's Poetics*. Ed. and trans. Caryl Emerson. Minneapolis, MI: University of Minnesota Press, 1984. 283–302. Print.

Bhabha, Homi K. *The Location of Culture*. London: Routledge, 1994. Print.

Gibbs, Graham. *Analyzing Qualitative Data*. London: Sage, 2007. Print.

Goodley, Dan. *Disability Studies: An Interdisciplinary Introduction*. London: Sage, 2011.

Jawłowska, Aldona. *Więcej niż teatr* [*More than Theatre*]. Warszawa: PIW, 1988. Print.

Kozaczuk, Lucyna. *Terapia zajęciowa w domach pomocy społecznej* [*Occupational Therapy in Nursing Homes*]. Toruń: Interart, 1995. Print.

Lorenc, Anna. "Założenia i cele terapii zajęciowej" ["Tenets and Goals of Occupational Therapy"]. *Postępy Rehabilitacji* 10.1 (1996): 73–80. Print.

Miles, Mathew B., and A. Michael Huberman. *An Expanded Sourcebook Qualitative Data Analysis*. London: Sage, 1994. Print.

Oliver, Mike. *The Politics of Disablement*. London: Macmillan, 1990. Print.

Ostrowska, Antonina, Sikorska, Joanna, and Barbara Gąciarz. *Osoby niepełnosprawne w Polsce w latach dziewięćdziesiątych* [*Disabled People in Poland in the 1990s*]. Warszawa: Instytut Spraw Publicznych, 2001. Print.

Rancière, Jacques. *The Politics of Aesthetics*. Ed. and trans. Gabriel Rockhill. London: Bloomsbury Academic, 2013. Print.

Siegmund, Gerald. "What Difference Does it Make? Or: From Difference to In-Difference. Disabled Theatre in the Context of Jérôme Bel's Work." *Disabled Theatre.* Ed. Sandra Umathum and Benjamin Wihstutz. Berlin: Diaphanes, 2015. 13–30. Print.

Spica, Jacek, et al. "Manifest IMPlus" ["The IMPlus Manifesto"]. *R.U.D.A. Rozwój. Uczestnictwo. Doskonalenie artystyczne* 2 (2012): n. pag. Print.

"Więcej niż Teatr" ["More than Theatre"]. *Instytut im. Jerzego Grotowskiego*, n.d., http://grotowski-institute.art.pl/projekty/wiecej-niz-teatr/. Accessed 12 May 2019.

Wihstutz, Benjamin. "'… And I am an Actor': On Emancipation in Disabled Theater." *Disabled Theatre.* Ed. Sandra Umathum and Benjamin Wihstutz. Berlin: Diaphanes, 2015. Print.

CHAPTER 11

"…and we all": The Phenomenon of Theatre 21

Wiktoria Siedlecka-Dorosz

In 2016, Justyna Sobczyk, a theatre educator and the founder of the Warsaw-based Theatre 21 (T21),[1] the first professional Polish theatre company of people with intellectual disabilities, won the prestigious Kamyk Puzyny (Konstanty Puzyna's Stone). The prize was awarded to Sobczyk by *Dialog*, one of the oldest theatre magazines in Poland, and the Polish Book Institute for her "theatrical activity which combines art with life and unique creativity with social engagement" ("Kamyk" 23). This was followed by a series of interviews with Sobczyk and her actors, which appeared in the Polish press, radio, and television. Yet, it was not the first time T21, with which I have been collaborating as a theatre scholar and instructor since 2012,[2] had been shown in the Polish mainstream media. In 2014, the company attracted the attention of one of the largest Polish commercial broadcasters. A short feature appeared in the news programme called "Fakty" ("The Facts"), which is watched by an average audience of 2.5 million people. The members of T21 presented themselves naturally, without affectation, showing how much they enjoy life. This is what they are like – they share their positive energy with others and they are incredibly charismatic actors. In Poland we call such people 'stage beasts.' They were simply born to perform.

The short feature focused on the educational project "O!swój" which was launched in recent years and was addressed to teachers and students of middle and secondary schools. The word 'oswój' is a second-person singular imperative of the verb 'oswoić,' which means 'to familiarize somebody with something.' The verb also means 'to tame.' As such, it relates not so much to the actors – 'the stage beasts' – but rather to the audience or, more specifically, to their conscious and subconscious fears of disability and the unknown that need to be allayed, tamed. The actors underscore the fact that they treat theatre as a medium that helps them communicate their personal experience. Yet, the

---

1 The theatre company has a Polish website http://teatr21.pl/. Short descriptions of most of the performances given to date by 21, photographs, and trailers are available in the 'Repertuar'-' Spektakle archiwalne' section.

2 Fascinated with the work done by T21, I participated in the rehearsals and travelled with the company to various festivals. I also co-organized a series of workshops for schools as part of the educational project "O!swój" (which have always been run by a theatre pedagogue and an actor of the company). At present I collaborate with Fundacja Teatr 21 (Theatre 21 Foundation), supporting their work in the field of disability theatre and education.

 | DOI:10.1163/9789004424678_013

aim is not so much to exorcize the actors' emotions in a therapeutic fashion, but to educate the viewers and offer them some food for thought. As the actress Barbara Lityńska posits,

> It is normal that an actor speaks about himself. But we do not perform to feel good. We do this so that the viewer may take something out of the performance. We – actors – have the right to communicate something to others.
>
> *21 myśli* 78

Thus, Theatre 21 also serves the role which another of its actors, Piotr Swend, defines as the major aim of theatre in general, when he asks "Why do people need theatre?" and responds "to be open to other people" (*21 myśli* 165). In a more general sense, the performances that they create perfectly fit in the Rancierian art of dissensus, which the editors of this volume define in their introductory chapter define as the form of art that

> allows for the emergence of the egalitarian principle, giving voice to those who have traditionally been deprived of it and placing their problems in the spotlight, thus leading to the subjectification of people with disabilities.

The actors of T21 shed light on the situation of people with intellectual disability in Poland, speaking in their own name and from their own perspective.

At the same time, the title of the project may also be read as an exclamation 'O! swój!,' which people sometimes use when they see a familiar person, someone they know, who is close to them, and who is not a stranger. The teachers involved in the project participated in a theatre workshop which centred on playwriting, directing, and working with one's body and voice. It was also concerned with theatre pedagogy. At the same time, the students watched performances by Theatre 21. The results of the project were published online on the website of the theatre company in the form of a guidebook with descriptions and scenarios of workshops to be used by anyone interested in this topic. Unfortunately, at present it is only available in Polish.

This guidebook opens with the following words describing T21, which currently consists of sixteen actors, most of whom have the Down syndrome:

> Otherness is the source of our identity. It is an uplifting experience which also creates numerous challenges not only for us, but also for our audiences, without whom our work would be meaningless. After all, we address universal topics: we tell stories about dreams being confronted with

> reality, about aspirations, about work, or rather unemployment, about love, desire, friendship, family, and about tradition and its social framework. In all of these areas, mechanisms of stigmatization and exclusion can be found. And this is not just because we are the ones who talk about these issues. When we talk about our struggle with reality, we also talk about you – our audience – and about your experience. We address our common issues and reveal the boundaries of "the norm." Our performances are open to your expectations as well as to your fear. We are not afraid of your fear.
>
> Theatre 21, "O!Swój: Podręcznik"

These words accurately define the work of T21. The company challenges the cultural stereotypes of intellectual disability, the fixed images of the intellectually disabled Other which are strongly rooted in the medical and the charity models. Alluding to Robert McRuer's theory, one could say that they crip[3] Polish culture, in which disability arts have long been labelled as a form of therapy. The actors reimagine their 'otherness' as a source of crip pride and creativity, and a valuable aspect of human variety.

T21 celebrated its tenth anniversary in 2015. This was when the idea for the first book about the company was born. Published in 2016 under the title *21 myśli o teatrze* (*21 Thoughts on Theatre*), it owes its unique, artistic design to Radek Staniec and Maria Szczodrowska. The book opens with an essay by two Polish scholars Justyna Lipko-Konieczna and Ewelina Godlewska-Byliniak, which offers a comprehensive introduction to the company's aesthetics and achievement. The main part of the album consists of a series of photographs by the award-winning Grzegorz Press, which are accompanied by twenty-one quotes from the conversations about theatre that the actors of T21 had with Justyna Sobczyk. Press spent a few months documenting T21's work on *Klauni, czyli o rodzinie. Odcinek 3* (*Clowns, or about a Family. Episode 3*), but the album also includes his photos of other rehearsals and performances as well. These photographs depict the actors in and outside their stage roles – they combine the private and the theatrical. As Lipko-Konieczna and Godlewska-Byliniak argue,

> This tension conspicuous in the representation of things happening on the stage, of the process of artistic creation and of being together helps see through the socially imposed mask of disability and discover the individual faces of the actors of T21.
>
> LIPKO-KONIECZNA and GODLEWSKA-BYLINIAK 29

3 In Robert McRuer's words, cripping can be defined as "radically revisioning, from committed anti-ableist positions, the taken-for granted systems in which we are located" (22).

It is in the theatre that the actors can show their real selves, thus challenging the harmful stereotypes that are present in the social imaginary and that have been giving shape to the masks that people notice when they see them outside the stage.

All of this shows that the phenomenon of T21 is durable and durability equals constant development. Ten years is plenty of time, especially in the lives of young people and children who have over these years entered adulthood. It makes an enormous difference whether one is fifteen or twenty-five years old. Let me thus briefly present the history of the company.

The founder of the company, Justyna Sobczyk, studied theatre and pedagogy in Poland. She later moved to Germany, where she continued her studies in the area of theatre pedagogy at Universität der Künste. During her stay in Berlin, she saw the performances of RambaZamba[4] – a theatre company (founded in 1991), which consists of actors with intellectual disabilities. She discovered that this was something that she wanted to do in life. Justyna was fascinated with RambaZamba and therefore decided that she was going to work with adults with the Down syndrome.

Justyna returned to Warsaw and started looking for individuals who would like to work with her. But people were very sceptical about her ideas. No one wanted to talk to Justyna and she was not even allowed to meet with her future actors. Largely by accident, Justyna came across a conference that was organized at the Community Special School "Dać Szansę" ("Give a Chance").[5] She finally met people who wanted to talk to her and was allowed to organize a theatre workshop for their students. This was not really what she dreamed of – the oldest students were sixteen and seventeen years old. She was quite disappointed. On the other hand, she was happy to have this job. Still, things were not the way she had earlier imagined. The rehearsals were held in a small, cramped gym. At first, they staged some traditional Polish Christmas plays, but they did that in a non-traditional, innovative way. Parents and teachers greatly appreciated these performances. Justyna challenged the conventional idea of what a school performance should be like and created a totally new formula. This was when the name of the company was invented. The genetic aberration that is commonly known as the Down syndrome is often referred to as trisomy 21.

In 2005 they made their first performance which was staged in the local park, outside the school – *Orfeusz + Eurydyka = WNM* (*Orpheus + Eurydice = Great Never-ending Love*, 2005). The actors were growing up, and two members of the company fell in love with each other. Justyna knew that this feeling would never be fully verbalized and so they decided to use the story of two

4 The theatre company has a German website: https://rambazamba-theater.de/.

5 The Polish website of the school: http://www.dacszanse.edu.pl/.

mythological lovers to express it. The performance was attended by the well-known Polish actress Stanisława Celińska, who told Justyna that she resembled the famous theatre practitioner Tadeusz Kantor. She said: "You are a real Kantor in a skirt," to which Justyna responded: "I hope not…"

Today Justyna says that she simply cannot believe it that at the very beginning she was on her own and now so many people support her – including professionals who collaborate with T21 on a regular basis. A half of her collaborators are actors. The others are professional theatre practitioners who create music and multimedia projections for the performances, dramaturgs, choreographers, costume designers, and light technicians.

The company is a constant work-in-progress. Regardless of whether they get the money for their projects or not – the idea is that 'the show must go on.' The rehearsals always take place twice a week: on Mondays and Wednesdays. It has become a kind of habit which no one wants to change.

Most members of T21 are also a group of friends who attended the same school. We all know that such bonds of friendship can be very strong. Importantly, the school that the actors attended covered all the levels of education, so they spent many years in the same place with the same people. Although they left school, they still meet in the theatre. There are several things that motivate them to continue their work:

- first of all, they simply like it;
- they are happy that they can visit different places together. They performed at many important festivals: Normal Fest in Prague, Menteatrál in the Czech Republic, No Limits Festival in Berlin, and the biggest international theatre events in Poland: Malta Theatre Festival in Poznań, Brave Festival in Wrocław, and All About Freedom Festival held at the European Solidarity Centre in Gdańsk. In 2016 T21 for the first time participated in a theatre festival that was not a disability theatre festival – Stage Festival in Helsinki;
- they love performing in front of an audience;
- they always anxiously wait to be given a role in a new performance;
- in 2014 they started earning money for their performances.

The first time they received money for their work was a very important moment. Justyna says that their bodies suddenly changed. They were very happy and spent all the money that they earned on the very same evening.

Justyna is aware of the fact that her company operates in Warsaw – a city which has more and more to offer to her actors – workshops, internship, and sometimes employment – and this poses a challenge. She has to give them something really important to make them stay. Otherwise, they will leave – because they are wonderful and talented people. They play important roles in other places and participate in numerous occupational therapy programmes. This motivates Justyna to transform T21 into their work place.

Initially T21 was a school theatre, but they moved out of their school environment, first to the park and then onto the stages of various theatres in Warsaw: Studio Theatre, Dramatic Theatre, Popular Theatre, Baj Theatre, and New Theatre. They used to dream of having their own stage, but Justyna thinks that such dreams are impractical because the city does not need another theatre. What she would like to do instead is create a new public institution in collaboration with another party. She would like to try something unusual and see what will come out of a collaboration between T21 and another organization. The company has developed thanks to the support that they received from various institutions – Warsaw theatres and the Theatre Institute in Warsaw. Justyna sees a potential in such collaboration. T21 has a lot to offer not only in the field of theatre and art, but also in the area of education.

What makes T21 a professional theatre company? And why did they decide to turn professional? It is not really about the professionals who support T21 in what they do. Of course, those people play an important part, but it is more about the actors. Many people, including myself, are impressed by their professional skills, since they are able to stage three different performances in two days, and they have no problems with the text, nor do they confuse the themes.

The amount of money they receive for their work is still symbolic. At present they do not have to earn their living, and they do not need money to survive. It is rather a struggle to keep the theatre going and to reinforce its position in the cultural landscape of Warsaw. This is how T21 understands turning professional: the actors give performances and they want to be appreciated. T21 also stages plays for children, educates, and collaborates with teachers.

As regards their method of work, Justyna finds it difficult to give it a name. She says that she is like a tailor, who each time takes measurements, cuts the cloth, and tries the new garment on. She does not use any particular method or formula. However, there must always be a reason why both she and her actors need and want to make a performance. And it has to be a strong reason which will motivate them to start a long period of artistic research and production. The process usually lasts a year, though the time they spent on one of the more recent performances *Upadki* (*Downfalls*, 2015) was much shorter and much more dramatic. As Justyna describes it,

> Imagine that our team is hiking in the mountains, we are wandering around, together but well off the track. We give up! I give up, the dramaturgs give up, the composer gives up – at the moment of crisis, we do not

> know what to do next, but the actors continue their work – the don't give up. They want to do everything. They improvise!

They are masters of improvisation. You say something, and they enter the stage and do it. They have no problem with anything. When one of them is ill, all the others want to take his or her place. Everyone wants to perform and they constantly put forward their own ideas.

If something is too difficult, Justyna has to simplify the message. Sometimes you need to explain some ideas. But this rarely happens. Recently, for instance, it has turned out that the actors do not know what a paradise is. Justyna decided to solve this problem in a creative way. She asked Teresa, who speaks a language that only she can understand, to explain the meaning of the word. The members of the company sat in a circle. Teresa started to talk and no one could understand her. The actors were confused. Yet, in this way Teresa showed that no one really knows what a paradise looks like. Justyna takes a lot of inspiration from her actors, which can be seen as a very post-dramatic method, a form of collaborative devising. They create the script together, they write down improvised dialogues, they focus on themselves, and they talk about their own problems. This is what makes their performances so powerful.

After many years, Justyna joined her actors on the stage in *Upadki* (*Downfalls*, 2015), but this was not because they needed her help. It was the decision of the dramaturg, who said:

> you're the one who motivates them and who promises to create a theatre company and to make them earn money – so you are a part of it. And together you need to verify whether these promises are real. Who believes in these promises more?

Because the actors may say it is all a lie. Even when they made a performance about money, commissioned by the National Bank of Poland, the money that they used on the stage was fake, and they still do not have a permanent place where they could put on their plays. Like most performances of T21, *Upadki* is closely related to everyday experiences of the actors. In this case, their economic exclusion was brought to the fore.

It may be useful to briefly present all the performances by T21 (till 2016) in a chronological order:

- *Orfeusz + Eurydyka = WNM* (*Orpheus + Eurydice = Great Never-ending Love*, 2005);
- *Lot nad Panamą* (*A Flight over Panama*, 2006) – based on Donald Haase Janosch's fairy tale *The Trip to Panama,* it poses the question: What does the place where you would like to live look like?

- *Alicja* (*Alice, 2008*) – inspired by Lewis Carroll's novel and the autistic actress Marta Stańczyk. When compared with the outgoing, charismatic actors with the Down syndrome, Marta seemed invisible in the earlier productions. The idea was to put her in the foreground and to present autism as a wonderland;
- the happening *Miasto, Manifest* (*The City, a Manifesto*, 2009), which critically approached the absence of people with disabilities in the city;
- *Portret* (*Portrait*, 2010) – an unconventional journey into one's mind inspired by Michele Lemieux's award-winning *Stormy Night*, which received a German literary award in the category of children's and young adult literature;
- *Uwaga, Purim!* (*Attention, Purim!*, 2011) commissioned by the POLIN Museum of the History of Polish Jews and presented at Studio Theatre in Warsaw. The performance was playful and transgressive; it also involved elements of crossdressing;
- *Ja jestem ja* (*I-Am-Me*) addressed to children at the age 3–7. Premiered in 2011 at Baj Theatre in Warsaw, it was based on an interesting book about a search for one's identity – Mira Lobe's *Das kleine Ich bin Ich* (*Little I-Am-Me*). Justyna made a performance for children because adults too often cry when they see disability and she wanted her young audience to react differently. Her aim was to familiarize the children with people with the Down syndrome and autism;
- *I my wszyscy. Odcinek 0* (*And We All. Episode 0*, 2012) was the first of a series of performances inspired by the actors' idea to create a theatre soap opera. The concept derived from the fact that one of the members of T21, Piotr Swend, has a role in a popular Polish soap opera *Klan* (*The Clan*), and is among the very few people with intellectual disability who have been employed in Polish television, which was the source of jealousy for his colleagues;
- *Śmiertelnie trudna gra* (*A Deadly Serious Game*, 2013), inspired by Wolf Erlbruch's *The Goose, Death, and Tulip*;
- *Statek miłości. Odcinek 1* (*Love Boat. Episode 1*, 2013) – the second episode of the series;
- *Upadki. Odcinek 2* (*Downfalls. Episode 2*, 2015), which was commissioned by the National Bank of Poland;
- *Tisza be-Aw* (*Tisha B`Aw, 2015*) – a performative action commissioned by the POLIN Museum of the History of Polish Jews and presented in the museum gallery. Dressed up like athletes, the actors and other practitioners involved in the creative process performed well-known playground games which are based on rivalry and elimination. Described in greater detail further in this chapter, the performance alluded to Action T4 – the programme of the

involuntary euthanasia of mentally ill and intellectually disabled people in Nazi Germany and in German-occupied territories;
- *Klauni, czyli o rodzinie. Odcinek 3* (*Clowns, or about a Family. Episode 3*, 2015) – the last episode of the series, which alludes to the aesthetics of circus and freak shows;
- *Pesach* (*Passover*, 2016) – a performative action commissioned by the POLIN Museum of the History of Polish Jews. Presented in the museum, it was organized to celebrate the Jewish festival that commemorates the liberation of Jewish people by God from slavery in Egypt, which paved the way to their freedom as a nation under the leadership of Moses.
- *Hamlet V* (2016) – a performance commissioned by the Helena Modrzejewska National Stary Theatre in Kraków. The whole, 24-hour-long event included ten different art installations and performances. The performance given by T21 alluded to Andrzej Wajda's film *Hamlet IV*, featuring the famous Polish actress Teresa Budzisz-Krzyżanowska in the main role, which has a strong message about social exclusion and the underrepresentation of some people in certain professions. The female members of T21 invited the audience to the female dressing-room only to remind them that disabled actors, such as themselves, have for centuries been mostly excluded from theatre industry.
- *Indianie* (*The Native Americans*, 2016) – a performance made in collaboration with the New Theatre in Warsaw.

The performance that deserves special attention is *Tisha B'Av* (2015). There are two main reasons why T21 got interested in the Jewish day of mourning. First of all, one of the company's members is a Jew and secondly, Theatre 21 received an invitation from the POLIN Museum of the History of Polish Jews (and the sponsor of the museum, Boeing, wanted to support Theatre 21).

After Purim and Tu Bi Shvat comes a very sad, special day in the Jewish calendar. Tisha B'Av commemorates the destruction of two Jewish temples. All that has been left of these holy places is the Western Wall (the so-called 'Place of Weeping'). On Tisha B'Av, Jewish people meet together in order to read Torah and talk, and thus find a way to recover from the loss. They also pray and fast. Religious Jews could not imagine how this sad celebration, which is more like a funeral, could be turned into a performance.

It all started with looking for a theme. Justyna knew from the very beginning that it would be about the war. On Tisha B'Av Jewish people keep going back to their greatest tragedies, including the Holocaust. What served as a prelude to the Holocaust was Action T4. It was a programme of the extermination of first children and later adults with disabilities and epilepsy, as well as mentally ill people. Action T4 was not only motivated by the Nazi struggle for racial purity, but also by economic factors. Preparing for the war, Hitler knew that he will need hospitals and medical staff for his soldiers.

The whole campaign of 'life unworthy of life' was carried out in such a way that some people even asked the authorities to euthanize members of their families and their closest people, believing that this was the best they could do for them. The Reich Committee for the Scientific Registering of Hereditary and Congenital Illnesses was established. It was a secret organization which decided whether a given child was worthy or unworthy of life. Already before the outbreak of the Second World War, in September 1939 the Ministry of Internal Affairs required that all doctors and nurses should report every birth of a child with a disability such as: the Down syndrome, underdeveloped limbs, or cerebral palsy. The Nazis wanted to develop methods of exterminating people on a large scale and in a supposedly 'humanitarian way,' and thus invited doctors to take part in their project. They exterminated those deemed as 'useless eaters' with carbon monoxide, which was later used in concentration camps.

The Nazis knew that thousands of people would be euthanized. So they found a large building where medical files could be stored and later studied. Their headquarters were located at 4 Tiergartenstrasse in Berlin in a tenement house confiscated from a Jewish family. The name of Action T4 is an abbreviation of this address. Within two years, seventy thousand people were officially killed. Afterwards, Hitler officially announced the end of Action T4, because it was no longer possible to keep these murders a secret. Germans started to panic. They were afraid of hospitals.

This in a way connects with the history of the company, since it was in Berlin that Justyna Sobczyk came up with the idea of founding a theatre of people with the Down syndrome, which she later called T21. This was a moment of illumination – when put together, all these facts merged into one long story.

When the actors started their work, they knew that Tisha B'Av is a sad day and they asked if they were going to cry. Justyna made a joke: "Oh, yeah, you won't have to do anything – you'll just stand and cry. You can cry out all your sorrows." They talked about the fact that a tragedy may happen, but one has to go on. When asked about their personal tragedies, the actors mentioned: the death of the father or mother, the father's interment after the martial law was introduced in Poland in the 1980s, or two strokes suffered by another actor's father. They have experienced a lot in their lives.

The performance was simple. It consisted of gymnastics, which was very popular in Nazi Germany, and which was closely connected with the cult of healthy, ideal body.[6] It also included a series of games, which all aimed at

6 Excellent examples of the promotion of a perfectly shaped, healthy Aryan body may be Leni Riefenstahl's famous documentary *Olympia* (1938), or the collection of nude photographs by Hans Surén entitled *Mensch und Sonne*. First released in 1924, the latter was allowed "to be [re]published in 1936, and by 1940 it reached its tenth printing" (Lewy 90). Discussing the way

excluding the weakest member of the group (e.g. dodgeball). The weakest one – the one who was hit with a ball – was called names (The Dumb, Rat, Stupid Johnny, etc.). Then, the person was to leave the room and he or she would never return on the stage (even for the applause). On the surface level, it seemed like great fun, but not all of the players enjoyed the games. Those who won were the only ones who were satisfied.

Justyna returned to the conversations that she had with the mothers of her actors a few years earlier, because this was how she learnt the stories of the destruction of their private temples… The actors knew that the audience could hear the voices of their mothers in their headphones. They knew that there were two parties that contributed to one performance – they and their mothers who in their stories went back to the moments when their children had been born. These were stories of social exclusion, and the lack of support from the family, friends, and medical staff, but also of love and acceptance. The members of T21 knew that their mothers were the 'silent heroines' who gave them their lives. The actors were very happy about their mother's contribution to the performance, and they did not even want to listen to what they said to the audience.

The actors asked why they were not supposed to show themselves to the applauding audience. They really love this moment. Still, they were also aware of the fact that many people with disabilities lost their lives as part of Action T4. Justyna explained: "We do not return, because they didn't return either" and they accepted it. They wanted people to remember this story so that it would never happen again.

Let me finish with the words of Edwin Bendyk – a journalist who collaborates with the Polish weekly *Polityka* (*Politics*). After seeing *Tisha B'Av*, he wrote the following words on his blog:

---

in which the book promoted an Aryan-Olympian bodily ideal, Johann Chapoutot argues, "Sport was certainly aimed in part at cultivating health and beauty. It thus performed a vital function for both the individual and the race. But it also served the people and the state" (182). He goes on to quote from Surén who stated in his *Mensch und Sonne* that

> After the National Socialist seizure of power, we live in an era of action. Action demands that each National Socialist must work on their body according to the precepts of the Aryan-Olympic spirit. The great legislator Solon elevated gymnastic training to the rank of state education. Gymnastics became the duty of the citizen – today, it must become the duty of the people. It is on gymnastics that performance is built, not only that of the athlete but also that of the soldier.
>
> qtd. in CHAPOUTOT 183

For a nuanced discussion of the role and representations of the healthy, athletic, and productive male body in the Nazi Germany, see also Hoberman.

> The performance is not about history or the past. It shows that the willingness to relegate and eliminate those who are labelled as "the other" from society, including their extermination, is deeply rooted in our culture. The seemingly innocent kindergarten games frequently contain a large dose of cruelty. Selection and exclusion take place every day at every moment – because fate willed it, or because the shape of your nose is different, because you have a different skin colour, or because you have an impairment that makes you different. The memories of the mothers of children with the Down syndrome are shocking. They recall that doctors treated them in an inhumane way, simply because they did not know how to cope with the otherness of the newborn baby. They were abandoned by friends or by their own families. The mother was also stigmatized – if she had given birth to such a thing, it means that it must have been her fault.… The message is clear and hard to digest, as hard as the lives of T21 actors off the stage, when instead of friendly audience, they face indifference (at best) but usually mindless cruelty of their brethren who cannot accept their otherness.

To change this, Theatre 21 creates a space in which a new form of encounter between the actors and the audience is possible, where the exclusionary normate logic, which renders disposable all those who do not fit in the bodily or mental norm, is replaced with acceptance and admiration, and where 'the other' becomes familiar.

A Postscript

In 2018 T21 devised and staged another important performance entitled *Rewolucja, której nie było* (*Revolution that Was*), which was a response to the first major sit-in at the Polish parliament, staged by people with disabilities, their parents, and carers. Lasting from 18 April to 27 May 2018, the sit-in did not bring the expected results. The demands of the protesters, the major one concerning the increase of the modest state benefits that people with disabilities receive in Poland, were not met. Having spent forty days in the corridor of the Polish parliament, having been cut off from shower facilities and having access to only one bathroom, the people engaged in the sit-in, feeling humiliated and disappointed, 'suspended' the protest. Using the material mementoes of the sit-in: original posters with slogans in Polish and English (e.g. "Polish people with disabilities have the right to live in dignity," "Disabled people in Poland receive terribly low benefits: – social pension 174 EUR per month, – care allowance 36 EUR per month"), letters and postcards received and written by the protesters, bedsheets, and whistles, *Rewolucja, której nie było* reconstructs and examines the events that took place at the Polish parliament only a few months earlier as well as their social reception. It also offers a space for the actors to manifest their subjecthood, express their reflections on the protest, and voice their desires and political postulates, all of which in one way or another relate to different aspects of freedom, autonomy, and self-determination. In a sense, the performance continues the legacy of the protest. As Justyna Lipko-Konieczna, who acted as a dramaturg and script-writer in the process of devising the performance, explains, the second part of the performance symbolically announces the opening of the Downtown Centre of Inclusive Art, a space where T21 will "prepare the ground for the revolution, understood as a change in the perception of people with disabilities and their right to have rights" (97).

This change can only be possible in a space where people with disabilities speak with their own voice. In the performance, this voice is heard most vehemently in the monologue composed by one of the actresses, Barbara Lityńska, during the rehearsals, and entitled "Wieczne dzieci" ("Eternal Children"). Lauded the bardess of the revolution, Lityńska makes powerful statements about contemporary political dissidence. She calls herself a "Child of the Opposition" and nostalgically recalls her parents' engagement in the anti-communist movement in Poland, only to conclude that:

> Today I'm 46 years old.
> I have no idea what "opposition" means today.
> Parties that cannot reach any agreement.
> Constant bargaining…
>
> LITYŃSKA 17

Lityńska also emphasizes her tiredness and specific impairments that negatively influence her will to live and fight. And yet, she concludes with the statement:

> Disabled people must fight for their own development and the harmony of their private lives.
>
> Politicians have no idea what a disabled person is.
>
> That's why they do not let us develop ourselves or dream about our future.
>
> Disabled people have the right to demand their rights in society.

> No one has the right to take away our freedom to voice our words and feelings.
>
> LITYŃSKA 17

Combing the private and the public, T21 creates its own, essentially political Dis(sensual)Art. They crip not only Polish disability arts, but also Polish society.

Translation and postscript by Katarzyna Ojrzyńska

Works Cited

21 myśli o teatrze [*21 Thoughts on Theatre*]. Głogowo: Fundacja Win-Win, 2016. Print.

Bendyk, Edwin. "Tisza be-Aw. Teatr 21 w świetnej formie" ["Tisha B'Av. Theatre 21 in an Excellent Form"]. *Antymatrix II. Z dziennika komiwojażera*, 14 Jul. 2015, https://antymatrix.blog.polityka.pl/2015/07/14/tisza-be-aw-teatr-21-w-swietnej-formie/. Accessed 11 Apr. 2019.

Chapoutot, Johann. *Greeks, Romans, Germans: How the Nazis Usurped Europe's Classical Past*. Trans. Richard R. Nybakken. Oakland, CA: University of California Press, 2016. Print.

Hoberman, John. "Primacy of Performance: Superman not Superathlete." *The International Journal of the History of Sport* 16:2 (2007): 69–85, https://www.tandfonline.com/doi/abs/10.1080/09523369908714071. Accessed 13 Apr. 2019.

"Kamyk Puzyny" ["KonstantyP uzyna's Stone"]. *Dialog* 4.713 (2016): 1–31. Print.

Lewy, Guenter. *Harmful and Undesirable: Book Censorship in Nazi Germany*. Oxford, Oxford University Press. 2016. Print.

Lipko-Konieczna, Justyna. "Zawieszony protest. I co dalej? Praca nad spektaklem *Rewolucja, której nie było*" ["Suspeding the Protest. And What Next? Devising the Performance *Revolution that Never Was*"]. *Nie ma wolności bez samodzielności: DziałaniaTeatru 21 w perspektywiezmiany* [*There is No Freedom without Independence: Activities of Theatre 21 in the Context of a Change*]. By Bogna Kietlińska. Ed. Justyna Lipko-Konieczna. Warszawa: Fundacja Teatr 21, 2019. 94–97, https://www.academia.edu/38415702/Nie_ma_wolno%C5%9Bci_bez_samodzielno%C5%9Bci._Dzia%C5%82anie_Teatru_21_w_perspektywie_zmiany. Accessed 11 Apr. 2019.

Lipko-Konieczna, Justyna, and Ewelina Godlewska-Byliniak. "Publiczne – prywatne: teatralna gra z niepełnosprawnością" ["The Public – the Private: a Theatrical Game with Disability"]. *21 myśli o teatrze* [*21 Thoughts on Theatre*]. Głogowo: Fundacja Win-Win, 2016. 7–29. Print.

Lityńska, Barbara. "Wieczne dzieci" ["Eternal Children"]. *Niepełnosprawność i Społeczeństwo: Performatywna siła protestu.* [*Disability and Society: The Performative Power of the Protest*]. Ed. Justyna Lipko-Konieczna and Ewelina Godlewska-Byliniak. Warszawa: Fundacja Teatr 21, Biennale Warszawa, 2018. 16–17, https://issuu.com/biennalewarszawa/docs/niepe_nosprawnos_c__i_spo_eczen_stw. Accessed 11 Apr. 2019.

McRuer, Robert. *Crip Times: Disability, Globalization, and Resistance.* New York, NY: New York University Press, 2018. Print.

Sobczyk, Justyna. Personal Interview. 14 Sept. 2015.

Theatre 21. *21 myśli o teatrze* [*21 Thoughts on Theatre*]. Głogowo: Fundacja Win-Win, 2016. Print.

Theatre 21. "O!Swój: Podręcznik." ["O!Swój: A Guidebook."] *Theatre 21.* Theatre 21, https://issuu.com/teatr21/docs/podrecznik_oswoj_2014. Accessed 11 Apr. 2019.

PART 6

From Life to Stage and Screen: Blue Teapot's Sanctuary

∵

The last section of the volume examines the history of the play and film *Sanctuary* which serve as an excellent example of what we have described as the Rancierian art of dissensus. Being given an opportunity to speak about their emotional and sexual needs, using the mediums of theatre and film, the actors of Blue Teapot, the Galway-based theatre company which consists of practitioners with intellectual disability, sparked a public debate on the discriminatory Irish law which severely penalized non-marital sexual activity of people with intellectual disability. As a result of this debate, the controversial regulations of Irish Criminal Law were changed and made much less restrictive. In the first article, the director of the film adaptation of Christian O'Reilly's original play, Len Collin describes his collaborative work with the actors. He challenges the harmful stereotypes which have been preventing people with ID from pursuing successful acting careers and reinforcing the practice of casting non-disabled actors in the roles of disabled characters, a strategy which playwright Kaite O'Reilly called "[c]ripping-up. The twenty-first century's answer to blacking up."[1] Collin's article is followed by a transcription of the talk that playwright Christian O'Reilly had delivered at the University of Łódź (Poland) a few years before the present book was published. His personal story sheds light not only on the creative process that led to the great success of the play on the Irish stage, but also on the development of disability activism in Ireland in the 1990s, which O'Reilly watched from a close distance after he received a job at Ireland's first Centre for Independent Living.

1 O'Reilly, Kaite. "peeling." *Graeae Plays 1: New Plays Redefining Disability*. Ed. Jenny Sealey. London: Aurora Metro, 2002, 331. Print. For a detailed discussion of this popular discriminatory strategy, see, for instance, the chapter entitled "Critical Embodiment and Casting" in Kirsty Johnston's book *Disability Theatre and Modern Drama: Recasting Modernism* (London: Bloomsbury Methuen Drama, 2016. 37–58. Print.).

CHAPTER 12

Shooting Actors who Have Intellectual Disabilities: A Reflexive Analysis on the Making of the Feature Film *Sanctuary*

Len Collin

> From the equality of rights springs identity of our highest interests; you cannot subvert your neighbor's rights without striking a dangerous blow at your own.
>
> SCHURZ 59

> Intelligence stands at the core of modern lives. It marks us out from the rest of nature. It is crucial to our sense of self and an instant yardstick for sizing up others.
>
> GOODEY 1

1 Imperfect and Glorious

Intellectual Disability covers a range of conditions from Autism, through Down's, to Fragile X Syndrome (FXS). It is not to be confused with mental health issues, such as bipolar disorder or schizophrenia, or other neurological developmental conditions, such as dyspraxia, dyslexia, and ADHD. Within the range of conditions, impairment to cognitive and physical functions may vary from mild, through moderate and severe, to profound (cf. American Psychiatric Association 33–39). The same is also true within the singular conditions, for example two persons with Down's are not necessarily equal in their abilities, or impairments, either physically or mentally. Intellectual disability (hereafter shortened to ID) is the preferred idiom used in Ireland and the US, in the UK learning disability, or learning difficulty are interchangeable terms that are used. In 2001 the UK Government defined learning disability as

> A significantly reduced ability to understand new or complex information, to learn new skills (impaired intelligence), with;
> A reduced ability to cope independently (impaired social functioning); which started before adulthood, with a lasting effect on development.
>
> Department of Health 14

 | DOI:10.1163/9789004424678_014

Although this definition is commonly regarded as accurate, the making of the film *Sanctuary*[1] challenges the statement that people with ID have a significantly reduced ability to comprehend new or complex information, or to learn new skills, thus questioning fixed understandings of disability whose constructedness Rosemarie Garland-Thomson and Katarzyna Ojrzyńska discuss in their chapter. The cast of *Sanctuary* consisted of five actors with Down's, three actors with autism, and one actor with severe epilepsy, which has resulted in ID. All of them exceeded expectations of what is and what is not possible for people with ID. They learned new skills and dealt with complex information on a daily basis throughout the shooting period. Is it really intelligence that 'marks us out from the rest of nature'? Or should we follow theatre director Declan Donnellan's advice that it is "[o]ur imaginations [that] make us human" and that "[o]ur capacity to imagine is both imperfect and glorious" (9). The cast of *Sanctuary* embrace their imperfections and have, I believe, produced a work of art that is indeed glorious.

2 Placing *Sanctuary* in Context

Actors with Intellectual Disabilities rarely appear on our TV or cinema screens. The late Paul K. Longmore accused television of supplying "[q]uick and simple solutions" (132) to people's areas of concern about societal issues, and in particular the representation of disability on the large and small screen. In his essay "Screening Stereotypes," which remains a seminal paper on the subject thirty years after its original publication in 1985, he points out the formulaic values dramatic entertainments place upon disabled characters, portraying them as either "victims," "monsters," or "heroes." In 1992 Colin Barnes elaborated on these stereotypical representations and identified the following stereotypes in his report for the British Council of Organisations of Disabled People:

> The disabled person as pitiable and pathetic;
> The disabled person as an object of violence;
> The disabled person as sinister and evil;
> The disabled person as atmosphere or curio;
> The disabled person as super cripple;
> The disabled person as an object of ridicule;
> The disabled person as their own worst and only enemy;

1 To see the trailer, visit: http://blueteapot.ie/our_performances/sanctuary-film/.

The disabled person as burden;
The disabled person as sexually abnormal;
The disabled person as incapable of participating fully in community life;
The disabled person as normal.

Most of these categories need no explanation. Only the last one seems like a desirable outcome. However, Barnes argues that it "represents little more than a 'normalisation' of disability, which does not really challenge or undermine its meaning to non-disabled people."

Barnes notes that the report, researched over four months in 1991, had three specific aims:

a. to provide a comprehensive insight into how the media creates and perpetuates negative representations of disabled people;
b. to formulate a set of principles which will enable all those who work in the media (to) eliminate disablist imagery and so redress the balance; and
c. to give disabled people a quick and accessible guide to current media complaints procedures so they can contribute to the eradication of disablist imagery in the media.

The fact that Barnes is "looking" for "negative representations" is indicative of the times, and necessitates some twenty-five years later that we should regard the last stereotype in particular with some caution. Primarily because this 'normalization' does not appear to have taken hold in mainstream media outputs, whilst the other stereotypes remain ubiquitous. There is perhaps one stereotype above all that is missing from the list, and that is "the disabled person as absent," occluded from the screen. Unless, of course, you count A-List Hollywood actors queuing up to play disabled roles for the chance of an acting gong. Stars to date playing intellectually disabled characters include: Leonardo DiCaprio in Lasse Hallström's *What's Eating Gilbert Grape* (1993), Dustin Hoffman in Barry Levinson's *Rain Man* (1988), Tom Hanks in Robert Zemeckis' *Forrest Gump* (1994), Billy Bob Thornton in his *Sling Blade* (1996), Cuba Gooding, JR in Mike Tollin's *Radio* (2003), Josh Hartnett and Radha Mitchell as an autistic couple in Peter Næss's *Mozart and the Whale* (2005), Sigourney Weaver in Marc Evans's *Snow Cake* (2006), and Irish actor Pat Shortt in Lenny Abrahamson's *Garage* (2007). As Charles A. Riley states, they "arrived on the disability scene with publicity fanfare" (71) but their "patronizing take on the subject adds injury to insult especially by contrast with the way the industry has been instrumental in advancing the human rights of other minorities" (69). In fact, as Dan Goodley and Marek Mackiewicz-Ziccardi argue in their chapter, "if no disabled people are part of the production machinery, then disability will only ever be represented in simplistic and unrealistic ways" (48).

One of the guiding principles outlined by Barnes in 1992, was the employment of disabled actors: "As it is no longer acceptable for white actors to play black people or men to play women, it should also be unacceptable for non-disabled actors to play disabled characters." In 2011, Riley is still making the same point and refers to the "all-important casting of real people with disabilities" (75). Yet, according to figures extrapolated from a report by the Screen Actors Guild, "[t]he number of actors with disabilities in principal roles does not even register on the charts" (Riley 75).

This paints a rather bleak picture, which can be demonstrated by looking briefly at the history of actors with Down syndrome who have played featured parts in films. In 1996, after casting Pascal Duquenne in *Toto le héros* (1991), Belgian director Jaco van Dormael cast Pascal as Georges in *Le huitième jour* (1996). At the 1996 Cannes Film Festival, Pascal shared the Palme D'Or for best actor with his non-disabled co-star Daniel Auteuil. This remains the high point to date for any actor with Down's, and one would have hoped that the situation for actors with Down's would have improved after such an accolade. However, award winning actor Pascal Duquenne would, according to IMDB ("Pascal Duquenne"), have to wait ten years for his next film role in Giles Daoust's *The Room* (2006). In 2015 Duquenne teamed up for the fourth time with Dormael to make an appearance in *Le tout nouveau testament*, with 2009's *Mr Nobody* being their other collaboration. Aside from an appearance in an episode of *Commissaire Moulin* (TV), that is the entire CV of a critically acclaimed actor with Down's, over a twenty-year period.

2010 saw two films of note that had actors with Down's in leading roles. Evan Sneider played Evan Grey in Justin Lerner's *Girlfriend*, and Pablo Pineda was directed by Antonio Naharro and Álvaro Pastor in *Yo, Tambien*. Pineda played a dramatized version of himself, as he is the first European student with Down's to obtain a university degree, he has since become a renowned speaker and disability advocate. In 2012 Brazilian director Marcelo Galvão, gave us *Colegas*, which starred three actors with Down's: Ariel Goldenberg, Rita Pokk, and Breno Viola. 2014 saw David De Sanctis star in *Where Hope Grows*, directed by Chris Dowling. 2016 saw Steven Brandon star in *My Feral Heart* directed by the UK's Jane Gull and, of course, *Sanctuary*, which has five actors with Down's in the ensemble cast. This is not a complete list, as other films of note include Jean Marc Vallée's *Café de Flore* (2011) with Marin Gerrier and Alison Peebles's *AfterLife* (2003) with Paula Sage.

In television, actors with Down's have fared a little better, perhaps because the output of material is greater and long running series are factory floors churning out drama at an alarming rate, which must also be factored in when researching and analyzing stereotypes of disability. Crime shows will inevitably tell stories about victims of crime and criminal acts, and medical shows will navigate similar territory where the victims are under medical investigation and therefore likely to fit into Barnes's stereotypes. The first actor with Down's of note within the television industry is Chris Burke who for four years starred as Corky Thatcher in eighty three of the eighty eight episodes of the ABC series *Life Goes On* (1989–1993). In 1992 the character of Corky got married to Amanda Swanson played by another Down's actor Andrea F. Friedman who has guested in a number of other TV series, most famously in the animation series *Family Guy* where she voiced a character named Ellen in the episode "Extra Large Medium" (2010); Luke Zimmerman played Tom Bowman in ninety episodes of *The Secret Life of the American Teenager* (ABC 2008–2013); Jamie Brewer has starred in several seasons of *American Horror Story* (20th Century Fox, 2011-), and Lauren Potter played Becky Jackson in *Glee* (20th Century Fox, 2009–2015). In the UK Timmy Lang appeared in an episode of *A Touch of Frost*, called "Appropriate Adults" (Yorkshire TV, 1995). Roles in *Bad Girls, Peak Practice*, and *Strange* followed. Sarah Gordy starred in ITV's remake of *Upstairs Downstairs*. Smaller roles in *Holby City, Call the Midwife*, and *Doctors* followed, ironically all BBC productions. Paul Abbot's *No Offence* (Ch4, 2015) featured a number of actors with Down's in its first season, primarily because it sought to solve the mystery of a serial killer who was preying on women with Down syndrome. Also worthy of note is a series from the Netherlands called *Downistie* (2011) which appeared as a segment on the TV talk show *De Wereld Draait Door*. Each episode of *Downistie* is three minutes long and takes place in a world where everyone has Down's. It is a comedy played for laughs.

3 *Sanctuary*

Blue Teapot Theatre Company, based in Galway and founded in 1996, is Ireland's first theatre company dedicated to actors with ID.[2] Many of the actors at Blue Teapot have been with the company for a decade or more. This engendered a very strong sense of community within the theatre company, in turn encouraging the actors to push their creative abilities; all that was needed was an artistic director with enough energy, vision and commitment to match the ensemble's ambitions. That person was the inspirational Petal Pilley who in 2012 commissioned Christian O'Reilly to write a play based around the difficult

2 To learn more about the company and their other productions, visit: http://blueteapot.ie/.

subject matter which, as Goodley and Mackiewicz-Ziccardi note in their chapter, "the mainstream society" perceives as essentially "uncanny" (46), especially when it relates to people with ID, who carry a particularly strong social stigma. In a highly dissensual fashion, the play advocates the right for intellectually disabled adults to sexual intimacy, a right until recently denied by law in the Irish Republic. Pilley explains:

> My hope in commissioning this play was to present a living tragedy that demands discussion, awareness and a more enlightened response from our society towards the sexuality and relationships of adults with ID.

Following the main tenets of what the editors of this volume describe in their opening chapter as the Rancierian art of dissensus, which disturbs and destabilizes a stagnated status quo "by the inscription of a part of those who have no part" (Rancière 123), the play and its later film adaptation advocated greater subjectification of people with ID and paved the way for a change in the Irish Criminal Law.

Christian O'Reilly, best known as the writer of the film *Inside I'm Dancing* (2004, dir. Damien O'Donnell), began the process of researching the characters, the world, and the socio-political arena for the play. In an interview by Caomhan Keane for *entertainment.ie*, Christian outlined that part of his approach was engaging the actors in Q and A sessions, asking questions such as: Have you ever been in a relationship? "Do you want to be in a relationship? What are the obstacles to that?" The answers were, of course, forthcoming from the actors who are a garrulous bunch and very vocal when it came to the obstacles they faced. As Christian stated, their concerns involved "being dependent on other people. Living with parents and in care homes, they didn't have the opportunity to just meet someone and bring them home." The theme of privacy suggested itself early on in the process. Christian wanted the story to come from the actors, for them to feel invested in the work of art that they were going to create together. For example, the actors chose their own character names. Kieran Coppinger wanted his character to be named Larry after Larry Lamb, who was starring in the BBC soap *EastEnders*, and Charlene Kelly chose Sophie after the character Sophie Webster from *Coronation Street* (Granada TV). Yet at the centre of the story was the very serious and very real issue relating to Section 5 of the Criminal Law (Sexual Offences) Act of 1993, which made it a criminal offence for a person if he or she "has or attempts to have sexual intercourse or … commits or attempts to commit an act of buggery with a person who is mentally impaired" (unless they are married).

The play premiered later that year at the Galway Theatre Festival. It was well received by critics and each performance was a sell-out. I was lucky enough to attend a preview. As I watched the play, I knew it would make an excellent film and floated this suggestion past Petal Pilley after the performance. Christian and I had worked together on a TV show called *Deception* for the Irish channel TV3, so we knew each other's work. Therefore, if Christian liked the idea, all we needed was to develop the script, find a producer, and raise enough money to make the film.

4 Development of the Film Script

The plot of the film (fig. 12.1) is relatively simple: Larry has Down's and Sophie has severe epilepsy. The two are attracted to each other and they both attend St Jarlath's training centre, though Larry also holds down a job at a local burger restaurant. St Jarlath's are organizing a trip to the cinema for Christmas (fig. 12.2). Larry sees this as an opportunity and arranges the rental of a hotel room through a hapless care worker, Tom, so that he and Sophie can sneak away for some "alone time" during the supervised trip to the cinema. It is not until Larry asks Tom for "the loan of a condom" that the true intentions behind Larry's

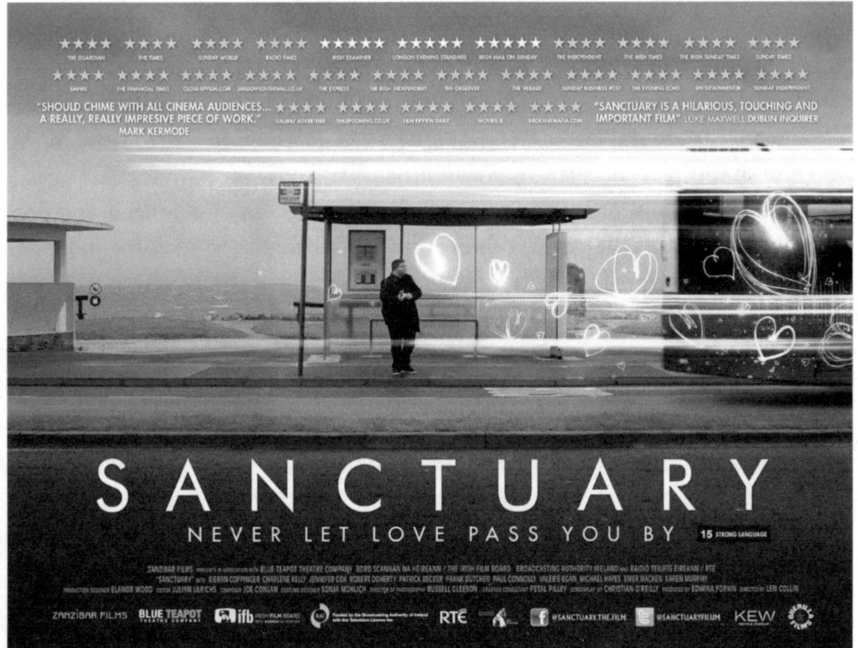

FIGURE 12.1 *Sanctuary* – the film poster showing Larry (Kieran Coppinger) waiting for the bus
COURTESY OF SARA AT FINKFILM

FIGURE 12.2 Larry (Kieran Coppinger) and Tom (Robert Doherty) on their way to the cinema
COURTESY OF LEN COLLIN

plan come to light. Larry uses Tom's discomfort to get what he wants, knowing that the situation has already gone beyond the point of no return. "No one needs to know I'm having sex with Sophie," he says. The trouble is that it is illegal for Larry and Sophie to have sex under Irish law.

Meanwhile, the other cinema attendees from St Jarlath's are beginning to get suspicious. They soon realize that they are without supervision and each sets out to explore the freedoms that are so often denied to them. Trips to the pub, the shopping centre (fig. 12.5), and the Christmas Fair follow.

In the hotel room Larry woos Sophie, but both are inexperienced and nervous about what may happen. When Sophie discovers Larry's hiding place for the condom, it angers her. She wants to be in control of the situation. It has to be her decision if and when sex happens (fig. 12.4).

Left 'on their own' in the cinema, Peter and Sandy also explore their feelings for each other. Sandy wants to look like the actress on the cinema screen, as perhaps then Peter will like her. However, Peter likes her as she is, because she exists and is real. He says: "You're sitting beside me, there's no way she could sit beside me." The characters connect on a deep level, and this opens up the opportunity for them to share a first kiss, which in its innocence is just as important as the passion on display in the hotel bedroom.

Tom returns to the cinema to find out that most of his charges are gone. It not only risks exposing his incompetence, but if Larry and Sophie are found to be alone in a hotel room together, the consequences could be truly tragic.

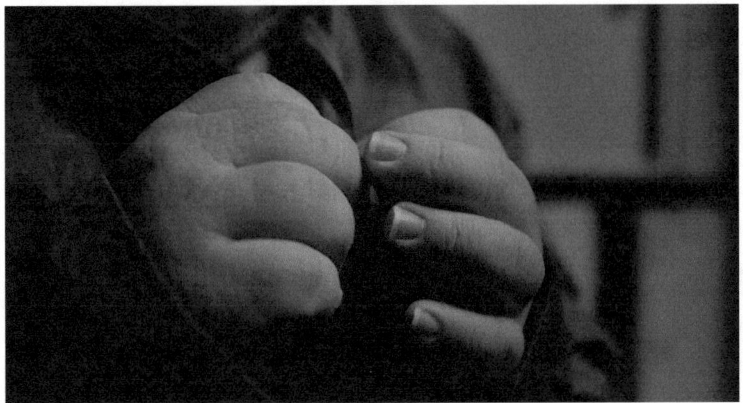

FIGURE 12.3 Larry (Kieran Coppinger) trying to unbutton his shirt
COURTESY OF LEN COLLIN

FIGURE 12.4 Sophie (Charlene Kelly) and Larry (Kieran Coppinger) in the hotel room
COURTESY OF LEN COLLIN

Christian and I worked on the script to bring out the visual elements and themes that resonated with us and the theatre audience, to expand the stories of each character, and to place them in a realistic environment. We wanted to stay true to the principles laid out by Barnes, in particular his recommendation that:

FIGURE 12.5 The characters enjoying their time at the shopping centre. From left to right: Joseph (Stephen Marcus), Alice (Valerie Egan), Andrew (Patrick Becker), and Iseult (Amy Joyce-Hastings)
COURTESY OF LEN COLLIN

> When portraying disabled people in the media it is important to remember that the general public have little insight into the environmental and social barriers that prevent them from living full and active lives. Living with disability means being confronted with environmental and social barriers daily; any portrayal of disabled people, in whatever context, which does not reflect this experience is both grossly inaccurate and a major cause of their continued existence.

Thus, we made a conscious decision to avoid fantasy in the film, a device that had been used in *Le huitième jour* and *Colegas* to add interest and depth to the characters, but also allowed the audience 'off the hook' as they were given 'quick and simple' solutions. We also wanted to avoid situations that lacked credibility. In *Colegas,* the three main characters, who all have Down's, become Brazil's number one criminals after robbing a gas station, which works well for that particular film, as it suits the genre of comedy crime caper. *Colegas* is replete with hapless police officers, car chases, and shootouts. However, we realized that cinematic audiences have never seen an accurate portrayal of the world of intellectually disabled adults in a fiction feature film before. *Le huitième jour* comes close, but really is about the character of Georges entering our world, not us entering his. Of course, all three films *Sanctuary, Le huitième jour*, and *Colegas* involve characters escaping their social limitations. In *Le huitième jour* and *Colegas*, the characters all escape from institutions. In *Sanctuary* the escape is more contained and believable, because the characters themselves have varying degrees of autonomy. The socially restricted Peter stays in the cinema as he is conditioned to do. Others are more adventurous and rebellious by turns. Again, turning to Barnes, we wanted to "portray disabled people as having individual and complex personalities with a full range of emotions and activities."

5 Pre-production

> Authors, scriptwriters, journalists, reporters and advertisers have a responsibility to check the accuracy of their work before it is made public. In order to avoid inaccuracies they should seek advice from organisations controlled and run by disabled people.
>
> BARNES

Movies do not just happen, they have to be meticulously planned: producers raise money and allocate budgets, scripts are written and re-written, actors are cast, locations are sought, accountants account, production managers hire cast and crew, contracts are drawn up, music is supervised, music is composed, and transport, equipment, and catering are arranged for each days shoot. Logistically, making a movie is a little like going to war. As no one had made a movie quite like *Sanctuary*, no one was really sure what to expect. The examples given of *Le huitième jour* and *Colegas* involved a number of actors with ID in smaller roles. *Colegas* had three main actors with Down's, though writer/director Marcelo Galvão Marcelo kept action and dialogue relatively simple, relying on his non-disabled cast to drive the narrative; but nobody had worked with an ensemble cast of actors with ID where all the actors had significant roles with reams of dialogue.

In preparing to direct *Sanctuary*, I contacted Simon Meyers, the producer of Paul Abbott's *No Offence* (2015) for Channel 4 in the UK. I asked Simon how the production had dealt with the cast members who had Down's in the series: What issues did they face? What problems were there and how did they overcome them? Simon informed me that there were literally no issues other than one small incident when a radio mic was accidentally flushed down the toilet by one of the actors. There were no special requirements with regard to on-set health care, and meals were provided that were nutritional and tasty … but were in fact rejected for McDonald's take-outs. They had Richard Hayhow as an advisor on set and this worked well.

This was in light of the fact that in pre-production for *Sanctuary* our producer Edwina Forkin had been negotiating with the Board of Blue Teapot Theatre Company the conditions of work for our cast. At first it was mooted that the actors could not work any more than four hours a day as this was what they were used to, and routine was very important. Whilst this was noted, it would be impossible to finish the film if this were adhered to. We were on a tight schedule, as we had thirty days to complete the movie. This was over a five-week working period with six-day weeks and a hiatus of two weeks over the Christmas period. We endeavoured to commit to certain rules: no actor would work more than five days in any given week. Wherever possible, we would break up the days to give actors as much rest as possible. There would always be two members of Blue Teapot staff on hand to ensure the safety of the actors, one on set and one in the 'green room' which is industry speak for any area where the actors 'chill' when not required on set.

The other area of concern was a lack of rehearsal time. The actors were used to rehearsing for their parts, and ideally this is something that most directors would appreciate. However, it was my belief that for many of the actors it would be detrimental to have rehearsals. This is because I had shot sample scenes two years earlier in late 2013, and from that experience I gained the insight that some of the actors learned their lines like lyrics to a song. If the lyrics are learned to a certain rhythm and melody, then it is almost impossible to break that rhythm and melody down. In terms of learning lines for the film this could result in an unnatural sounding delivery, so I wanted the actors raw on set. For the most part this approach was successful. On the 26 November 2015 we had the cast and crew table read for *Sanctuary*. This was the first time most of the crew had met the cast, and no one quite knew what to expect next.

6 Shooting Actors with Intellectual Disabilities

The first shot on the first day of principle photography was Larry changing his clothes in the locker room of the fast food restaurant where he works. The tension was palpable as Kieran struggled with a shirt button that refused to submit to his will. Try as he might with his fingers working at both button and shirt, the two refused to separate (fig. 12.3). It seemed like an eternity, as fingers twisted, the camera rolled and the boom operator strained with fish pole and mic. Here was a simple example of 'environmental and social barriers' faced by a person with Down's. The button eventually gave in to Kieran's fingers and popped free of the eyelet in his shirt. There was a hush as the crew waited for the next button to be attacked or for me to call "Cut" – but then something brilliant happened, Kieran simply lifted the shirt over his head, problem solved. It was the perfect introduction to the issues we may face as the shoot continued, and a reminder to myself that patience would be required at all times in order to engender confidence in my abilities as the master of ceremonies in this particular circus.

The first week we eased ourselves into the production process to help establish a working methodology with our actors. The worries over the long days seemed to be unfounded. On a typical film set shooting starts as early as possible due to available light, shooting in the winter meant we had less available light. Working with our actors we also had certain restrictions because some had further to travel and some were reliant on their carers getting them up and dressed. It is worth noting that only one of our actors from Blue Teapot lives independently, the rest either live with relatives or in group homes. So the usual call was 8.00 am for hair and make-up, with breakfast at 7.00 am and wrap at 7.00 pm. Our late shoots may start with breakfast at 11.00 am with wrap at 11.00 pm. Realistically this meant on some days an actor could be on the go for fourteen hours including transport to and from the set. Kieran Coppinger playing Larry had the lion's share of scenes and lines. He coped very well and always kept his sense of humour. Kieran is a consummate professional and always listened to direction and tried to deliver the performance required. A few times the heat and lack of air on the set of the hotel room made Kieran tired. He was not the only one, and this caused delays as we would boost the air-con between takes. Keeping energy up was often a task that I had to undertake, whether in the hotel room or outside in the bitter cold. Overall, however, energy levels were good.

Acting for the screen is more precise than acting for the stage, in so far as you must remember to repeat the same actions over and over again at precisely the same point in time in order to preserve the continuity of image and sound. Take for example the act of making a cup of tea whilst saying lines: "I met your sister Eve, I don't think she likes me. She said you were going away for Christmas." See if you can remember what to do by the end of the next paragraph, without referencing back. In the first take you picked up the milk jug with your left hand on the word 'like.' You must now remember to pick up that milk jug for every single take on the word 'like,' yet the director has given you the note to also move your right shoulder back at the same time in order to open up the angle, and she also wants you to smile at the end of the line. Meanwhile, the gaffer has come in to adjust the Kino which the DP says needs to be more Tungsten ... and asks you to feel the light. Sound asks you to be careful when moving so that your shirt does not make a rustling sound on the radio mic and Continuity tells you that you missed out the word 'Eve' in the middle of the line. The First asks you to wait a beat after he calls action and then calls out "Stand By." The Camera Op says "Rolling"; Sound says "Speed"; Camera Op says "Mark," and the Loader comes in with the clapper board and declares the shot number, scene number and take ... then claps the sticks ... you are all set to go, waiting for action and a gel falls from a light. It then takes another two minutes while the gel is reattached and the lighting is reset. Then the First will declare "First positions," and may shout: "Quiet on set!" or "Stand by," and the process is repeated for that take after a false start. At this point the actor has to remember all the requests that were asked of them. This is only the master wide; it takes on average five takes. You then will most likely have to repeat for the mid-shot and close another five times each, and then the reverses on the actor you are having the conversation with. So thirty times you may have to repeat those words and actions. Did you remember everything? Our actors did and yet they are supposed to have "a significantly reduced ability to understand new or complex information, to learn new skills (impaired intelligence)" (Department of Health 14).

Of course, not every actor was perfect all of the time, and some did have difficulty. It was after all long days, and the work of the Blue Teapot staff was invaluable, keeping energy levels up, dealing with toilet breaks, food and drink requests, running lines, etc. The most difficult actor was probably Frank Butcher. Frank is in his sixties and quite understandably does not like to be kept waiting. When he is kept waiting (which, as any actor will tell you, happens a lot on a film set), he gets moody, and when he gets moody, he cannot concentrate, and when he cannot concentrate, he forgets his lines. This has the effect of making Frank nervous, which then escalates the problem, so you have to calm him down, and allow him to settle. Different tactics were sometimes used, such as telling Frank that the camera was not on him, when it clearly was. Pretending that it was just a rehearsal, and for close-ups I would often sit in place of the other actor in the scene and coax Frank with line reminders and cues. When the pressure was off, Frank would deliver his lines with aplomb and elan.

Sometimes I had to perform this way for other actors too and perhaps use an 'endowment' to get the reaction I wanted from the performer. To get an endearing smile from Sophie, I may have to pretend to be Larry and tell Charlene, the actress playing Sophie, to imagine that my face was made of strawberries and cream and she wanted to lick the cream from the end of my nose. This would make her laugh spontaneously and the moment was captured on camera. Wherever possible, however, I wanted to catch their natural performances. For me it 'must come from the actor.' That way there is honesty and truth in the performance. When talking about difficult subjects, Charlene tends to not look at the person she is talking to. Therefore, this is what she does in the film ... this is a true, natural performance. It is not what actors are trained to do. In the edit suite, Julian, our editor, would often look for an expected reaction, which often was not there. I would explain to him: "That is their reaction, that acceptance, that look, that flick of the eye." It may not be the reaction that he was expecting, but it is there. This was perhaps the most difficult thing to deal with as the director, deciding if these muted reactions were enough at times. To demonstrate: there is a short speech that Sophie has in the hotel room. It is a very private moment for her character when she reveals to Larry a secret about her past. It is the only scene I had to reshoot.

My error was initially to try and 'stage' the scene. I presented it too theatrically, and I knew at the time it was not working. Charlene was not forgetting her lines as such, as I knew that she knew them very well indeed. She was obstructing those words from her mind. It was a similar issue to one day working with Frank, who was also obstructing. In Frank's case, he always collected his disability allowance at a certain time on a certain day, and we happened to be shooting with him that day. Monies earned from acting are looked after by Blue Teapot, who organize their tax and benefits around payments the actors receive, but any deductions are made in arrears. Frank did not have to collect his money that day, but it was clear that because this was his routine, this was the obstruction that day to his performance. So we changed the schedule slightly to allow Frank to go and collect his disability allowance, and return an hour later. When Frank returned, it was as if a great weight had lifted for him and he was able to remember every line and delivered a great performance take after take that day. The problem for Charlene was not so easy to resolve. Looking at the rushes that night, I realized my error and scheduled the scene again for a few days' time. When we came to reshoot I asked everyone to leave the set so I could talk alone with Charlene. We talked through the scene and worked out where the blockage was.

The fact was that she was getting so into the scene that she was losing her way as the thoughts occurred to her. She was in a sense 'living the scene' and the solution was to actually provide one word prompts so that she could 'be in the moment' without worrying about the lines. This is now the most powerful scene in the film. It alternates in emotion, but not necessarily in the way we would expect an Oscar winning actress to 'perform.' It is her truth, her performance, and it is honest and powerful. I had to create a place of safety for Charlene, I had to support her with patience and understanding and in the end it must come from the actor.

7 Post-production

This is where the whole film comes together. As expressed earlier, there was a huge learning curve for many of us when it came to the edit. Walter Murch lists the six priorities for an editor when making a cut, these include continuity of action, advancing the story, rhythm, the grammar of the shot, and number one is emotional truth. He states that an ideal cut should follow the six criteria, adding a caveat:

> Emotion, at the top of the list, is the thing that you should try to preserve at all costs. If you find you have to sacrifice certain of those six things to make a cut, sacrifice your way up, item by item, from the bottom.
>
> MURCH 18–19

Most editors work this way, and Murch along with Thelma Schoonmaker are gods of the cutting room. Julian, our excellent editor, also works this way – emotion first. Therefore, a big performance from the likes of Frank or Patrick was easy to edit, and a more nuanced, almost flat performance from Michael, Emer, and Charlene was a little more difficult for him to deal with. However, through time, patience, and getting to know the characters and the actors, we worked together to find the right balance, to get at the truth of the piece and the performances. Sophie for example, came across quite harsh in places. By judicial editing we were able to soften Charlene's performance, in the same way that any hesitancy in Frank's performance was left on the 'cutting room floor.' There are awards for editing in the industry and they tend to go to editors working on big flashy blockbusters. However, I would give the Oscar to Julian tomorrow for the work he completed on this feature. Between us we squeezed every ounce of emotion out of the film, whilst maintaining the rhythms of the writing and the pace of the narrative. The real challenge for Julian, however, was my commitment to the principles laid out by Barnes. Most important for me were two scenes that Julian initially wanted to cut right down to their bones: Larry getting ready for his 'date' and Sophie making a rasher sandwich. These scenes were crucial to the understanding of the characters and the issues they face on a daily basis: Larry trying to undo a shirt button, something non-disabled people take for granted … which for Larry is not difficult but takes longer to do, and Sophie assembling and cutting a sandwich. Again the non-disabled person would not give it a second thought, and neither does Sophie … but it does take longer to do … Now imagine these two in bed together, at the height of passion, trying to work out how to put a condom on. We do not have to see this, because we know and understand how difficult that must have been.

8 Conclusion

When even low budget movies cost millions, it is no wonder that corners are cut and 'shorthand' is used. 'Shorthand' in the film industry is the art of hiring people who are proven and proficient at the task required. This may seem like sensible logic. However, it can also lead to stagnation and is most evident when 'typecasting' where actors are hired primarily for who they are or appear to be, rather than their consummate skill level at pretending to be other people. Hence, a Tom Cruise movie will always be a Tom Cruise movie. Whether he is an international spy, a samurai, or a futuristic soldier, we know what to expect. The same is true of most stars, even Daniel Day Lewis who is lauded as an actor who can 'transform' himself. We know what to expect: an intense performance of an exaggerated nature. So it is no wonder that most actors leap at the chance to break out of the mould hollowed out for them, by taking on roles that demonstrate their ability to be other than themselves. It is no different for the cast of *Sanctuary*. Acting is an escape from their routine lives, a chance to inhabit another body, another mind, to escape into a new world where anything is possible. Of course, the difference for Mr Cruise and Mr Day Lewis is that they can pick any role they want, whereas Kieran Coppinger is restricted in the roles that may be on offer. Cruise has never won an Oscar but he was nominated for his role as Ron Kovic in Oliver Stone's *Born On The 4th July* (1989). Day-Lewis has won several Oscars, his first in 1990 for playing Christy Brown in Jim Sheridan's *My Left Foot*. In Ireland Pat Shortt, best known for his comedy roles, won an IFTA (Irish Film and Television Academy) for best actor for his role as Josie in Lenny Abrahamson's *Garage* (2007). The character he played is intellectually disabled. He is shown as a figure of pity, as an object of violence and ridicule, arguably as his own worst enemy, as a burden, as sexually abnormal, and as incapable of participating fully in community life. Josie's answer is to commit suicide, which is another disability trope. *Garage* swept the board at the IFTAS in the year of its release. Yet as we see, fifteen years after Barnes wrote his report on disability stereotypes, *Garage* was hitting almost every single one of them. Our hope is that *Sanctuary* will fulfil its dissensual potential, that, in other words, it will begin to redress this balance, by proving that disabled actors are more than capable of performing at the highest level – that actors with ID in particular have the stamina, the intelligence and the skills needed. All that is required is an even playing field where they are given a chance by the commissioners and development execs in the industry to showcase their talents.

At the time of writing, it is pleasurable to note that Ruth Madeley a disabled actress in the UK has been nominated for a BAFTA (British Academy of Film and Television Arts) for Jack Thorne's brilliant *Don't Take My Baby* (BBC 2015) directed by Ben Anthony. She is the perfect example of a disabled actress who should be cast more often and not just in roles that call for a disabled character.

9 Postscript

In February 2017 Section 5 of the Criminal Law (Sexual Offences) Act 1993 was repealed.[3] Sarah Lennon from Inclusion Ireland announced this to a packed Lighthouse Cinema in Dublin's Smithfield during the Dublin International Film Festival, crediting the film, the play, and the Blue Teapot cast for their part in raising awareness of the issues and helping to effect the law change. The cast themselves received the prestigious Michael Dwyer Award at the festival in recognition of their talent. The film has gone on to screen at festivals around the world in every continent.

Works Cited

American Psychiatric Association. *Diagnostic and Statistical Manual of Mental Disorders*. 5th ed. Arlington, VA: American Psychiatric Association, 2013. *DSM Library*, https://dsm.psychiatryonline.org/doi/book/10.1176/appi.books.9780890425596. Accessed 24 Apr. 2019.

Barnes, Colin. *Disabling Imagery and the Media: An Exploration of the Principles for Media Representations of Disabled People*. Krumlin: Ryburn, 1992. N. pag. *Centre for Disability Studies. University of Leeds*, https://disability-studies.leeds.ac.uk/wp-content/uploads/sites/40/library/Barnes-disabling-imagery.pdf. Accessed 24 Apr. 2019.

Criminal Law (Sexual Offences) Act of 1993. Sec. 5. *Irish Statute Book*. Office of the Attorney General, n. d., http://www.irishstatutebook.ie/eli/1993/act/20/enacted/en/html. Accessed 24 Apr. 2019.

Department of Health. *Valuing People: A New Strategy for Learning Disability for the 21st Century*. London: Department of Health, 2001. Print.

Donnellan, Declan. *The Actor and the Target*. 2nd rev. ed. London: Nick Hern, 2005. Print.

Goodey, Christopher F. *A History of Intelligence and "Intellectual Disability": The Shaping of Psychology in Early Modern Europe*. Farnham: Ashgate, 2011. Print.

3 The revised Act can be found at: http://revisedacts.lawreform.ie/eli/1993/act/20/revised/en/html.

Longmore, Paul K. “Screening Stereotypes.” *Why I Burned My Book and Other Essays on Disability*. Philadelphia, PA: Temple University Press, 2003. 131–46. Print.

Murch, Walter. *In the Blink of an Eye. A Perspective on Film Editing*. 2nd ed. Los Angeles, CA: Silman-James, 1992. Print.

O'Reilly, Christian. Interview by Keane Caomhan. *Entertainment.ie*, 24 Jul. 2013. https://web.archive.org/web/20130823010001/http://entertainment.ie/theatre/feature/Interview-with-Christian-OReilly-Sanctuary/210/4584.htm. Accessed 21 Jul. 2016.

“Pascal Duquenne (biographical note).” *IMDB*, https://www.imdb.com/name/nm0243608/?ref_=ttfc_fc_cl_t1. Accessed 24 Apr. 2019.

Pilley, Petal. Personal interview. 14 Nov. 2012.

Rancière, Jacques. *Disagreement: Politics and Philosophy*. Trans. Julie Rose. Minneapolis, MN: University of Minnesota Press, 1999. Print.

Riley, Charles A. *Disability and the Media: Prescriptions for Change*. Hanover, NH: University Press of New England, 2005. Print.

Sanctuary. Dir. Len Collin. Perf. Kieran Coppinger, Charlene Kelly, Michael Hayes, Emer Macken, Paul Connolly, Frank Butcher, Patrick Becker, Jennifer Cox, and Valerie Egan. Zanzibar Films, 2016. Film.

Schurz, Carl. “True Americanism.” 18 Apr. 1859. *Speeches, Correspondence and Political Papers of Carl Schurz*. Ed. Frederic Bancroft. Vol. 1. New York, NY: Knickerbocker, 1913. 48–72. *Hatchi Trust Digital Library*, https://babel.hathitrust.org/cgi/pt?id=mdp.39015012852516;view=1up;seq=25. Accessed 24 Apr. 2019.

CHAPTER 13

Christian O'Reilly Talks about His Writing on Disability for the Stage and for the Screen

Christian O'Reilly

I never set out to write about disability. I never had that as my agenda or cause. I didn't have a close personal connection to the subject, such as a relative with a disability. If anything, the subject found me in quite accidental circumstances.

It was around 1994, over twenty years ago now, and I had recently completed a diploma in Business Studies with a view to trying my hand at business journalism. I was also writing short stories in my spare time and trying to find my way as a writer. I needed a job and replied to an ad in the Dublin City University newsletter for a job with a company called the Centre for Independent Living as a ... well, it wasn't at all clear what the job was for. It mentioned a communications officer, a researcher and a personal assistant all in one. But I applied anyway.

I got a call inviting me to be interviewed and arranged to meet a man called Martin Naughton at the Royal Dublin Hotel. This heavy, bearded, smiling man in a wheelchair. I went to shake his hand. He told me to shake his thumb. He told me vaguely about the job and the world I was about to enter. I'm not sure what kind of impression I made, but he asked me to start work the following week.

I found my way to Bolton Street in central Dublin and entered an office full of what I can only describe as angry wheelchair-users. They were on the phone, barking orders, talking about things like accessible public transport, access to education, employment, housing. They were angry, militant, passionate – a complete contrast to the image of disability I had had before that, an image in which wheelchair-users sat passively and sadly in their chairs with nothing much to do or look forward to.

I soon learnt that the Centre for Independent Living or CIL was there to change the world. They were sick of non-disabled people telling them what they needed.

Just to tell you a bit about CIL...

What is Independent Living? As Adolf Ratzka explains,

> Independent Living is the right of all persons regardless of age, type, or extent of disability to live in the community; to have the same range of

 | DOI:10.1163/9789004424678_015

> choices as everybody else in housing, transportation, education and employment; to participate in the social, economic, and political life of their own communities; to have a family; to live as responsible, respected members of their communities with all the duties and privileges that this entails, and to unfold their potential.
>
> qtd. in "About IL"

The above for many people with significant disabilities can best be achieved by the employment of Personal Assistants. The Dublin CIL website also briefly outlines the history of the movement,

> The Independent Living movement has its origins in the civil rights movement of 1960s America. The first Center for Independent Living was established in Berkeley, California in 1972. Underpinning its establishment were attempts by people to leave residential care and live independently in the community.
>
> SHARKEY qtd. in "About IL"

The first Irish Center for Independent Living (CIL) was established in Carmichael House in Dublin in 1992.

Since 1992, Center for Independent Living (CIL) Carmichael House has supported the development of twenty-two Centers for Independent Living which have benefited the lives of many thousands of people with disabilities around Ireland. Their slogan is 'Nothing about us without us!.'

It was Martin Naughton who brought the Independent Living movement to Ireland. He wanted to challenge the rehab culture which prevailed in Ireland at the time and which told people with disabilities that they were the ones who needed to change in order to fit into society. The Independent Living philosophy is all about accepting who you are and getting society to change. Martin used to refer to CIL as "the IRA of disability." He saw his job as creating change, spreading chaos. He always said that "growth comes from chaos."

I was employed for two years as a public affairs coordinator. Effectively I was a lobbyist who had no idea how to lobby. I learnt fast. I worked closely with a man called Dermot Walsh, who had cerebral palsy. Dermot and I became great friends. Like me, he was a Manchester United fan.

As an example of the type of work we used to do…

Martin decided he wanted me to do something about the lack of accessible public transport in Dublin. We wanted to show our politicians how much of a problem this was. Most of the double-decker buses at the time had two or three steps as you entered, which meant that many wheelchair-users had to literally crawl up the steps.

We got the idea to hire a double-decker bus to bring us on a trip around Dublin. Except that we arranged for the bus to collect our group outside Dáil Éireann, the Irish Parliament. When the bus pulled up, a long line of wheelchair-users queued to get on. Except they couldn't get on because the bus was inaccessible. As the politicians arrived to begin their day's work, we didn't need to point out all that was wrong with public transport. They could see it with their own eyes.

After two years of working at CIL, I left to pursue writing. It was tough and then six months after leaving CIL, I sat up in bed with a eureka moment, realizing that this world would make a great subject for a feature film.

At this stage, I had again run out of money and had found another job, this time working as an office assistant with a company called Metropolitan Films, which has since renamed itself Octagon and has gone on to become one of the leading independent film and TV producers in Ireland.

I was having a drink with my boss James Flynn one evening and he asked me what I was working on. I told him I had this amazing idea about a man called Martin Naughton, a wheelchair-user who returns to Ireland from America and revolutionizes the Irish disability movement by introducing the Independent Living philosophy. Martin had secured EU funding under the Horizon scheme for a two-year pilot programme called Incare, in which people with significant physical disabilities were given access to personal assistance for the first time in their lives. From 1992 to 1994, twenty-nine people with disabilities participated in this programme, leaving behind dependence on family and institutions and embracing freedom, choice, and independence. When the funding ended, they faced the prospect of going back to the lives of dependence they had left behind. They refused. They campaigned. They ended up outside Dáil Éireann threatening to chain themselves to the gates and go on hunger strike. They were successful. It was against that backdrop that I wanted to tell my story. I saw it as a key moment in Irish disability history, but one that few people outside that world knew about.

I told James that I wanted to tell a story about two young wheelchair-users who lived in an institution and who had been brought up believing that independence meant tying your own shoe-lace, even if it took you four hours. I wanted to show how these two guys were transformed by a new way of thinking and how their friendship is upset when one of them hires a pretty girl as a personal assistant and falls for her. I wanted to show how they were politicized and became central to the struggle to keep personal assistance funding. I raved about the idea to James Flynn. To this day, James says it's the best pitch he has ever heard. But I wasn't trying to pitch it. After all, it wasn't my story. I had simply recognized its potential for cinema.

We agreed to develop it together. But first of all I felt I had to get permission from CIL to tell it. After all, it was their story, their philosophy was 'Nothing about us without us,' and I had to ask myself, "what right do I, as a non-disabled man, have to tell this story?" I approached Martin Naughton, the leader of this community. He gave me his blessing to write the story on the basis that I wanted to.

I set about researching the story by interviewing all the key people who had been involved in the fight for statutory personal assistance funding. They already knew and trusted me from my time working at CIL. And I had Martin Naughton's blessing, so I had full access.

I wrote a first draft of the screenplay, which was as faithful as possible to the true story. I called it *No Magic Pill.* The producers loved it. There was just one problem. They felt I couldn't tell the real story for legal reasons, without risk of being sued. To do so, they said, would have required getting permission from every single person who had been involved – not just the wheelchair-users, but any politicians involved in the true story. The bad guys, in other words. If anyone didn't like the way they had been represented, or if it was inaccurate in any way, we could be in trouble. So could we tell a fictional story that was based on or inspired by the actual story?

My next draft, which attempted to fictionalize the story, was a major departure from the true story and from the story I set out to tell – a sort of *One Flew Over the Cuckoo's Nest* meets *My Left Foot,* i.e. a prison movie about a wheelchair-user who wants to break out of an institution. The producers loved it and felt it was eighty percent there. But this new draft posed numerous questions about the film we wanted to make. Did we want to tell a political story? Or could we tell a more personal story that was universal? After all, we had to think about our audience. We couldn't just cater for people with disabilities. We wanted a film that would appeal to a non-disabled audience too.

The producers had just made a low-budget film called *H3* about the hunger strikes in Northern Ireland. It was well received critically, but didn't do well at the box office. They didn't want to make that type of film again. They wanted commercial success. They wanted a hit. I kept arguing that we should return to the original story and trust the material. They worried the original story was just too political and would exclude a non-disabled audience.

Things went downhill with each draft after that. Finally, the producers attempted their own draft, but that didn't work either. In the end they hired another writer, Jeffrey Caine, to write the screenplay from my material. The film was produced. As well as the distress of being taken off my own project, I felt I had failed the community that had entrusted me to tell its story.

And yet when I saw the film at the Edinburgh Film Festival, I loved it and felt very proud of it. It wasn't the story I had set out to tell, but it was nevertheless a mainstream film that was set in the world of disability. And in James McAvoy it had a genuine movie star, which meant the film had a shot at reaching a wide audience. But although a lot of wheelchair-users featured in the cast, the two leads were both non-disabled actors. And the film was criticized for this when it went on general release in the UK.

I think the merits of the film are as follows:

- it was a mainstream, commercial film about two wheelchair-users;
- the main characters were ordinary guys who just wanted what non-disabled guys their own age want, i.e. freedom, alcohol, and sex;
- the film opened many people's eyes to the needs of people with significant physical disabilities, showing them that people with disabilities are no different to them;
- thanks to its: (a) casting, (b) comic tone and (c) audience-friendly content as a buddy-movie, the film reached a wide audience in Ireland, particularly through DVD;
- it may not be the story I set out to tell, but it's still a film about people with disabilities – and to get a film made at all is a small miracle.

The downsides:

- it wasn't the story I set out to tell: a story with genuine historical value that remains untold;
- I felt I had let down a community that had entrusted me with its story;
- some people in the disability community were unhappy that non-disabled actors were cast as the two leads;
- could it have reached a wider audience if we had stayed true to the material?
- the film was a commercial failure outside Ireland.

And now I'll tell you about *Sanctuary*.

In 2011, I applied for a commission to write a short film for Blue Teapot, a multi-award winning theatre company, performing arts school, and outreach project for people with intellectual disabilities, based in Galway in the West of Ireland, where I live. I didn't get the commission – in fact, Len Collin, who is here today, got it – but I must have made a good impression because the following year, 2012, Blue Teapot's artistic director Petal Pilley called me up to ask to meet for a coffee.

Petal wanted to commission a play that explored sexual relationships among people with ID. She explained that most people with ID don't have an outlet for sexual expression. And I was shocked to discover that in Irish law, sex before marriage is illegal for people with ID. Petal's aim was to start a conversation.

I was wary of accepting the commission. I had graduated from the BBC Writers' Academy the year before and was in the middle of an incredibly busy year, trying to write episodes of *Casualty*, *Holby City*, and *EastEnders* for the BBC. But I was also wary because experience had shown me that theatre commissions can be tricky. I felt a sense of responsibility to the world I was being asked to write about, but what if I let them down? What if I wrote a bad play?

On the other hand, I am always attracted to worlds I know nothing about and I knew nothing about the world of intellectual disability, but had long been curious about it. In terms of getting to know the world, Petal felt that getting to know the actors (or Teapots, as they are known) as people and as professionals would enable me to write characters inspired by each of them.

So she opened the door to me in two ways:

1. By inviting me in to workshops to see the actors doing improvisations. Watching the Blue Teapot actors improvise showed me just how talented and skilled they are as an ensemble. It also showed me that they are natural performers who carry out their work with confidence and joy. Seeing their abilities as actors gave me confidence that they could perform anything I might write. It helped me raise my ambition for the play.
2. The second way Petal opened the door to me was by arranging for the group to talk with me about their feelings about relationships and the challenges they faced in having relationships.

Writing *Sanctuary* felt like a collaborative process. We had a series of conversations over a number of weeks, in which the actors talked openly, touchingly, and often hilariously about sex, relationships and the challenge of meeting someone you might fall in love with in a world that makes this extremely difficult. I would go off, generate fresh ideas, questions and characters and come back in and run all my ideas by the group and Petal. Their feedback helped me discover and shape the play into something that felt authentic to their experiences. For example, I soon knew it had to be a play about two people with ID who want to be alone together, but aren't allowed to be. So I got an idea about a man with Down's and a woman with epilepsy who, with the help of a sympathetic care worker, disappear from a group trip to the cinema and go across the road to a hotel room. I pitched it to the actors and got their feedback. Was my scenario credible? How many care workers would such a group have? Was it believable that a care worker might help a couple abscond like this?

By necessity, each character in the play was based on an actor who would be playing that character, so their personal investment was huge. This allowed for an authenticity of character which I would never have achieved otherwise. They each picked their character names and this increased their sense of ownership of the play.

This process – and indeed, this access – (a) showed me what the actors were capable of and (b) helped me discover what play I needed to write. I realized I could be as ambitious as I wanted.

When the play went into rehearsal, the main challenge, given that they are actors with ID, was the level of memorizing required. It made me wonder if a dialogue-heavy, naturalistic play was the right form for actors with ID. But in the production itself Petal dealt with this issue by announcing to the audience at the beginning of each show that the actors would be prompted if necessary. In practice, we found that the audience accepted the prompting as a convention as easily as they might accept subtitles during a film.

Sanctuary was very well received when it ran in Galway Theatre Festival in 2012. This is from a review in *Irish Theatre Magazine*:

> *Sanctuary* is a brilliant insightful piece of work that enlightens and entertains. It also brings to the fore the amazing talents of Pilley's first rate cast, who are all people with ID.... In *Sanctuary* we are reminded that no subject is off limits to achieve brilliance in theatre when the ensemble is talented.... In this production Blue Teapot have set the bar (and it's very high) for professional theatre productions with roles for and about people with intellectual disabilities.
>
> SHANNON

Steve Daunt of Newstalk FM Radio, wrote as follows:

> *Sanctuary* addresses this issue in a heart-warming yet unflinching way. O'Reilly's writing helps but the lead actors – Kieran Coppinger and Charlene Kelly – deliver groundbreaking performances as Larry and Sophie. They are adults attracted to each other. They know the law will come down hard on them. Larry knows his elderly parents would never understand while Sophie has the stifling rules of her care home to escape from but they have the determination of lovers. Sophie hauntingly tells Larry of past male care workers taking advantage of her, while Larry faces up to his own Down's syndrome. There are false starts. There is tea drinking and finally there is a kiss.
>
> That kiss blew me away. It was a first kiss between lovers. It was also a first kiss between Ireland and a group of citizens long ignored. It was

> stunning.... I was privileged to see it and humbled by it. Without doubt it was and is the most important stage kiss in Irish theatrical history.... *Sanctuary* made my weekend. If it comes back to Dublin or does another mini-tour of Ireland make sure you see it. It will change your life.

And Gary Hynes, artistic director of Druid and Tony Award winner, had this to say: "Fan-fucking-tastic. The most important piece of Irish theatre in ten years."

The production also ran at Galway International Arts Festival the following year, 2013, and at the Dublin Fringe Festival that year. It sold out every show. There were invitations to bring it elsewhere. The problem, however, is that because there is such a large cast – nine people – and because eight of those nine have ID, it means the cost of touring it and the support and resources required is just prohibitive. Which is why we're hoping to make it as a film.

For me, the merits of *Sanctuary* are as follows:

- a truly collaborative experience;
- clarity and agreement between the director, the actors and I about the issues we wanted to highlight and the story we wanted to tell;
- the full participation of actors with ID in the creative process, both as collaborators in the play itself and performers in the production;
- actors with ID playing characters with ID. This had a tremendous impact on the audience, who were seeing something they had never seen before, performed by actors who occupied a world they knew nothing about;
- I love talking about *Sanctuary*. It was one of the unexpected and most joyful experiences I've ever had as a writer.

The drawbacks were:

- was dialogue-driven, naturalistic theatre the right form, given that actors with ID can struggle with memorizing lines?
- limited exposure to audiences, given the cost and challenges of touring it.

I'll finish by showing you a clip from a documentary called *Somebody to Love*,[1] which explores the challenges, both practical and emotional, faced by people with disabilities in having relationships. The documentary followed Blue Teapot as they rehearsed and then staged *Sanctuary* at the Dublin Fringe Festival. We'll pick it up as the actors are in their dressing rooms preparing to go on stage, watching a feature about their production on national TV. The film is available on demand via Vimeo and Amazon Prime.

1 A trailer of Anna Rogers's documentary *Somebody to Love* (2014) can be watched at: https://vimeo.com/ondemand/somebodytolove.

Works Cited

"About IL." *Centre for Independent Living: Carmichael House*. The DG Group, https://web.archive.org/web/20171027145438/http://www.dublincil.org/what-is-independent-living.asp. Accessed 9 May 2019.

"Blue Teapot Theatre Company's *Sanctuary* at the Galway Theatre Festival." *Arts and Disability Ireland*, 4 Oct. 2012, https://web.archive.org/web/20160324144253/http://www.adiarts.ie/whats-on/blue-teapot-theatre-company-s-sanctuary-at-the-galway-theatre-festival. Accessed 9 May 2019.

Daunt, Steve. "Undaunted: A Kiss is Just a Kiss?" *Newstalk*, 18 Sept. 2013, https://web.archive.org/web20150812080254/http://www.newstalk.com/UNDAUNTED:-A-kiss-is-just-a-kiss. Accessed 9 May 2019.

Shannon, Breda. Rev. of *Sanctuary*, by Blue Teapot Theatre Company. *Irish Theatre Magazine* 13 Oct. 2012, http://itmarchive.ie/web/Reviews/Current/Sanctuary.aspx.html. Accessed 9 May 2019.

Somebody to Love. Dir. Anna Rodgers. Wildfire Films. 2014. Film.

Disability, Dis(sensual)Art, and the Politics of Participation

Maciej Wieczorek and Katarzyna Ojrzyńska

On 18 April 2018 a group of people with disabilities and their carers started their first sit-in protest in the Polish parliament. Their major demand was a monthly benefit of PLN 500 (an equivalent of the recently introduced 500+ child benefit) in addition to the modest state benefits that they received. The protest was suspended after forty days. Although the main demand of the protesters was not fulfilled, they received a lot of support from society and raised social awareness of a number of problems that people with disabilities encounter in Poland on a daily basis. Thus, earlier considered a social taboo and relegated to the private sphere, these problems finally received considerable attention and became a topic of public debate. The protest also stimulated the growth of a community of people who identify themselves as disabled and started the process of their subjectification.

In the media the event was initially presented as a protest of parents of disabled children. In time, however, as Justyna Lipko-Konieczna and Ewelina Godlewska-Byliniak argue, the language of the reports underwent a transformation and many journalists started using the same discourse as the protesters. Thus, "children" first turned into "people with disabilities," and then "adult people with disabilities," while "parents" became "carers." This illustrates the slow but steady change in thinking about and within the flourishing Polish disability rights movement and the gradual subjectification of Polish people with disabilities in line with the dictum 'nothing about us without us.' The transformation started with the acknowledgement of the fact that the protesters are adult citizens who consciously and wilfully exercise civil disobedience, rather than puppets in the hands of greedy parents. The broader term "carers" partly replaced the earlier-used "parents" which infantilized the disabled protesters and reinforced the fixed assumption that disability is a private problem of the family. Yet, it needs to be stressed that parents have been playing a crucial role in contemporary Polish disability activism. They created an informal group RON (Rodzice Osób Niepełnosprawnych, Parents of Disabled People). As they explain on their Facebook profile, their children are low-functioning individuals who often cannot effectively communicate or fully interact with their environment. They state: "speaking on their [our children's] behalf, we

 | DOI:10.1163/9789004424678_016

speak with their voice,"[1] and thus present themselves as supporters and facilitators of their children's self-advocacy. This idea is also strongly present in the group's logo which features the dynamic accessibility symbol and the hashtag #ZaNiezależnymŻyciem (#ForIndependentLiving).

A year later, on 23 May 2019 Polish people with disabilities and their carers again took to the streets. This time it was only a one-day protest, which served to remind state authorities about the unfulfilled demands. The streets of Warsaw became a space where Polish crip killjoys unabashedly exercised their willfulness. One of the slogans that they carried on their banners was "Będziemy przeszkadzać, panie Jarku" ("We will cause trouble, Jarek"). This was an allusion to a conversation between a wheelchair user and Jarosław Kaczyński, a fragment of which was widely distributed in the social media. In the conversation, the chairperson of the ruling Law and Justice party promises that the situation of people with disabilities will improve and quickly finishes with a request related to the upcoming election to the European Parliament: "Please support us and don't cause any trouble" ("Kaczyński").

Despite the organizers' claims to the contrary, it is clear that the protests in Warsaw were deeply rooted in politics. While their political dimension could, to some extent, be explained in relation to the somewhat clichéd argument that the personal is political, it would be far more productive to look at them through the prism of the ideas expressed by Murray Edelman in *Constructing the Political Spectacle*. For Edelman, the public sphere largely revolves around the creation of what he labels as "political spectacles." To put it simply, he argues that all possible issues problematized in such spectacles have no inherent qualities that make them important within the public sphere – they are, by their very nature, arbitrary. Any meaning that they have is ascribed to them when they are introduced into the public discourse and are turned into "political spectacles" that usually function as "reinforcements of ideologies" (Edelman 12). To explain this, Edelman cites the examples of the massacre of indigenous populations and racial segregation in North America, which were initially seen as a 'natural' course of events and have only become problematized after centuries of exploitation. The main reason why such extreme forms of discrimination remained unchallenged for a long time is quite simply that parts of the population benefited from their existence. A genuine attempt to address the problem of poverty, for instance, would entail an arduous re-examination of the status quo on many levels, bringing to light the need for a sweeping change of economic, social, or

---

1 RON's Facebook profile (in Polish) can be found at: https://www.facebook.com/pg/RodziceON/about/?ref=page_internal.

educational policies. This, in turn, would pose a grave threat to the hegemonic interests of those in power.

The creation of political spectacles is largely the domain of various media outlets, and their selection of content also depends on their individual agendas, which often serve to "reinforce established power structures and value hierarchies" (Edelman 34). This is further exacerbated by the fact that the news stories are increasingly detached from everyday life, instead focusing on statements made by officials or on events in remote parts of the globe. Thus, Edelman argues that rather than seeking to empower their audiences by providing them with information that has direct relevance for their lives, they thwart any real efforts to effect change by justifying the status quo and mustering political support through focusing on largely exaggerated problems (cf. 66–90).[2] Of course, one may mention a number of other strategies that serve a similar purpose. In the case of the earlier-mentioned Polish protest that took place in Warsaw in May 2019, Poland's national public broadcaster TVP issued a news report with a telling title "To nie jest protest polityczny?" ("This is not a political protest?") which frames the event as an instance of anti-government propaganda whose aim is not so much to improve the situation of people with disabilities in Poland, but to influence the results of the upcoming European Parliament election, an idea that the protesters attempted to refute by rejecting the label of 'politicality.' It opens with a close-up of the parents of people with disabilities, most notably, Iwona Hartwich, who was one of the organizers of the protests, and a statement: "They demand [a monthly assistance of] PLN 500 for a disabled child. These are the parents who protested in the Polish parliament last year right before the elections, just like this year," and a public announcement in which Hartwich and another mother, Anna Glinka, say out loud: "This is not a political protest." This is juxtaposed with the information that "a moment later Kuba[3] and Adrian Hartwich [sic!][4] ran for election as European Coalition candidates and one of them was elected municipal councilor"[5] (Cierpioł and Pawelec). This suggests that the protest is part of individual political campaigns behind which stand power-thirsty and money-hungry non-disabled women.

2 Consider, for instance, the media responses to the European migrant crisis and how useful they proved to be for the far-right.

3 A diminutive form of the name Jakub, which suggests a patronizing and infantilizing attitude to one of the leaders of the protest.

4 Domink Cierpioł confused the names of the leaders of the protest (Jakub Hartwich and Adrian Glinka).

5 Jakub Hartwich was elected councilor of the city of Toruń.

In this way, the news release recycles the 'moral objections' voiced by the opponents of the earlier sit-in, who reduced the disabled people who occupied the parliament to naïve puppets who had easily been manipulated by their mothers and who are not able to make their own informed, independent decisions. A year earlier, for instance, MP Bernadeta Krynicka, who is also a mother of a child with intellectual disability, stated that the disabled "children" "are held hostage by their parents" and added:

> If one has an adult disabled child, either intellectually or physically, the child is to some, or even large, extent dependent on his or her parents and under their great influence. If you tell them to come, they will come. And it's not fair.
>
> qtd. in MIERZEJEWSKA

In a similar fashion, MP Jacek Żalek compared the protest to "a reality show" in which "children are held hostage" and argued that the parents "treat their children as human shields" in order to achieve their own goals and thus should not be trusted or given any pecuniary benefits but only specific material support, such as diapers or wheelchairs, or easier access to rehabilitation. Although Żalek's words met with strong criticism from both sides of the Polish political divide, and the MP soon decided to apologize to the protesters, the basic ideas underlying his and Krynicka's statements echo distinctly in the TVP news report which was released a year later. Generally, despite the fact that some change has taken place in the representation of the disabled protesters in the media, many of the mainstream political spectacles still deprive them of agency and subjectivity. At the same time, by vilifying the organizers and portraying the protesters as an indistinguishable mass of people rather than a group of individuals with differing views, who are merely united by the same goal, such representations also divert public attention from the real problem of inequality.

All of this effectively means that the production of political spectacles is largely complicit with the working of what Jacques Rancière calls the "police" logic which, as has already been argued in the preface to the present volume, prevents real political subjectification and acts in the name of the post-democratic notion of consensus. Even in the times of communicative abundance and the proliferation of different social media, one's voice often remains unheard. As Marisol Sandoval and Christian Fuchs argue, "a statement that does not reach the masses is not a significant statement at all, only an individual outcry that remains unheard and hence ineffective" (143). It is thus still difficult for an average person, or a "part of those who have no part," to acquire a voice and create their own political spectacles as they have to go to extraordinary measures to stand up for their interests and defend them within the public sphere.[6] In fact, this requires embarking on a truly dissensual course of action, and protests are perhaps the most obvious example of how the idea of dissensus works in practice. They allow groups of people that were theretofore deprived of voice and relegated to the very margins of the social order a chance to claim the place that they have been denied within the public sphere and make their voices heard. By doing so, they disrupt the consensus, lay bare the inegalitarian distribution of the sensible, and stress the need for change, thus becoming a perfect illustration of the dissensual notion of politics as understood by Rancière.

Many countries, such as Poland and Greece, have recently been witnessing the rise of crip collectivities whose members, in many ways following the strategies developed by the disability rights movements in the UK and the USA, work towards the subjectification of people with disabilities, not only in the streets but also in the field of cultural production and in the academia. In both Poland and Greece, what preceded and stimulated the rise of disability rights movements was the development of disability culture. As Dariusz Kosiński posits,

> The thing that has recently happened on the [Polish] stage thanks to the years-long functioning of such theatre companies as Theatre 21 or Przebudzeni [The Awakened],[7] and the growing number of theatre pedagogues and artists may also take place on the public stage thanks to the protest. It is a simple but not an easy thing: it necessitates acknowledging the subjectivity of people with disabilities, and especially intellectual disability, and accepting their presence and uniqueness.
>
> KOSIŃSKI 75

Fostering the growth of disability culture and collectivity is a crucial precondition for a change to take place. Again, to illustrate this with another example from the Polish context, let us mention the case of the wheelchair-user Bogumiła (also known as "Balbina") who lives in Szczecin and who became an object of anger and ridicule after she kept blocking the buses whose drivers would not let her in on the grounds that her mobility device is not a wheelchair

6 Admittedly, technological developments (e.g. the rise of social networking) open up many new possibilities for challenging the status quo and producing counter-spectacles. See, for instance, Mason *passim*.

7 To learn more about the company, visit their Facebook profile: https://www.facebook.com/teatr.przebudzeni/ (in Polish).

but a scooter. As Lipko-Konieczna and Godlewska-Byliniak note in their lecture, the woman used exactly the same tactics as Western disability activists in the 1970s and yet her individual protest did not bring any positive outcome or meet with much understanding. The citizens of Szczecin even issued a petition to the city authorities in which they state that Bogumiła should not be allowed to use her scooter as she poses threat to fellow passengers and other "normal" citizens.[8]

The case was presented in the Polish mainstream media in an episode of the intervention show *Uwaga!* (*Attention!*) commissioned by the Polish commercial broadcaster TVN. Bogumiła is presented as a crip killjoy – a person who, as Tsakiri puts it, "refuse[s] to fake satisfaction and happiness to justify social norms that are actually oppressive for disabled people." Always vocal and loud about her needs and the discrimination she has been experiencing, Bogumiła is called by fellow citizens "a terrorist with excessive demands," "abnormal," and "stupid." Her radical tactics never meet with understanding and are the reason why she has repeatedly been labelled as "insane" and in need of psychiatric help. As we learn from the episode, she was even forced by the Municipal Centre for Social Assistance to undergo psychiatric assessment to determine whether she should be committed to a mental institution. In general, most citizens perceive her as not deserving the rights that she has been fighting for. As Lipko-Konieczna and Godlewska-Byliniak argue, if protesters act in a group, the problem they accentuate tends to be perceived as a common issue that is linked to their shared experience or identity. Single protesters tend to be easily marginalized and neutralized. In other words, a crip killjoy, such as Bogumiła, is usually instantly rendered powerless and harmless.

Therefore, in order to bring about change in social attitudes to disability, it is not enough to reach the masses. It is equally important to build a collectivity that will together help conceptualize and build what Nancy Mairs calls a habitable world that will be open to different forms of human variety. As she puts it,

> Maps render foreign territory, however dark and wide, fathomable. I mean to make a map. My infinitely harder task is to conceptualize not merely a habitable body but a habitable world: a world that wants me in it.
>
> MAIRS 63

In a sense, this corresponds to the idea of "an alternative ethical map of living interdependently with each other" postulated by David T. Mitchell and Sharon L. Snyder (69). This aim can hardly ever be achieved without expanding the

8 The petition is available at: https://www.petycjeonline.com/uwolni_szczecinian_od_terroru_w_komunikacji_miejskiej.

existing social imaginary so as to allow for the emergence of a new, more egalitarian and emancipatory mode of communal co-existence. At the same time, for the dissensual potential of disability culture and disability studies to be truly unlocked, it is crucial that the dissensus occurs at many levels. Naturally, this requires collective action and a sense of collectivity that can be found in disability rights movements whose members have been protesting in the streets, on stages and screens, and in other places where disability culture has been flourishing, as well as in the academia, among scholars who have helped reconceptualize disability and reveal the constructedness of its representations.

One of the things that connects these different modes of resistance is the fact that they embrace a radically open, critical perspective on disability, one that shares many similarities with Edward Soja's critical strategy of "thirding-as-Othering" which opens up our imaginaries to "ways of thinking and acting politically that respond to all binarisms, to any attempt to confine thought and political action to only two alternatives, by interjecting an-Other set of choices" (Soja 5). Although Soja's line of argument mainly pertains to space, it needs to be stressed that it can be effectively applied elsewhere, and he himself points to the productive intersections between his theory and, for instance, bell hooks' explorations of race, class, and gender. In his *Thirdspace: Journeys to Los Angeles and Other Real-and-Imagined Places*, he distinguishes between three distinct perspectives. The first one, Firstspace, focuses mainly on the material and formal aspects that can be studied empirically. The second one, Secondspace, is primarily the domain of ideas – it focuses on conceptualizations and representations. Finally, there is also Thirdspace, which draws upon the dualism between the material and conceptual aspects, but "extends well beyond them in scope, substance, and meaning" (Soja 11). In a sense, these categories could also be applied to disability studies. The Firstspace would largely correspond to the medical approach to disability, which looks at the disabled body through the prism of deficit and anomaly that needs to be 'cured,' while the Secondspace would be connected to the social model, which postulates the constructedness of disability. As a mixture of the two, the Thirdspace of disability would go beyond the conventional assumptions associated with the other two categories, focusing on its material aspects, but refusing to medicalize and view them as deficits, instead offering a realistic approach to the body that Siebers calls for (180), while at the same time recognizing the social constructedness of disability. In other words, Thirdspace largely corresponds to the interactional model of disability postulated by Tom Shakespeare (59).[9]

9 To learn more about different models of disability, see Garland-Thomson and Ojrzyńska's chapter.

When discussing bell hooks' seminal *Yearning: Race, Gender, and Cultural Politics*, Soja argues that she moves the process of identity formation into "a space of radical openness" in which the "key question of *who we can be and still be black* can be politically re-imagined and practiced" (97). As hooks herself puts it,

> Fundamental to the process of decentering the oppressive other and claiming our right to subjectivity is the insistence that we must determine how we will be and not rely on colonizing responses to determine our legitimacy.
>
> qtd. in SOJA 22

This, perhaps, is also one of the greatest challenges facing Critical Disability Studies as the intersections of disability, identity, and society still need to be further explored and re-imagined in a more egalitarian way that allows for full subjectification of people with disabilities. This initiative has to come from the margins, from the Rancierian "count of the uncounted" (78), and it needs to be essentially counter-hegemonic and/or dissensual. This can be done by opening up Thirdspaces through academic work, artistic practices, as well as political and social activism. Within the academia, many scholars have gone against the grain and strived to challenge the dominant ableist ways of looking at disability, thus paving the way for a major shift towards a more emancipatory and egalitarian mode of perception. Numerous examples of the work that has so far been done are discussed in the first two chapters of Part 1.

All of the texts collected in this volume describe and examine the cultural Thirdspace of disability from a number of different, yet complementary, critical perspectives. The chapters offer both general reflection on CDS's foundational concepts, such as the norm (Małgorzata Sugiera) and the crip (Dan Goodley and Marek Mackiewicz-Ziccardi), models of disability (Garland-Thomson and Ojrzyńska), and its specific representations (concrete cultural texts and events: festivals, films, plays, novels), accentuating their historicity (locating these texts and events in different temporal contexts and placing the greatest focus on the recent change; see, e.g., Agnieszka Izdebska, Christian O'Reilly, Dorota Krzemińska and Jolanta Rzeźnicka-Krupa, Wiktoria Siedlecka-Dorosz) and sociality, i.e. showing how these texts influence and help (re-)conceptualize the existing social relations that have been strongly founded on the disabled/non-disabled divide. With this volume, we hope to contribute to the ongoing 'thirding' in and of the academia, which we understand as restructuring the binary opposition between the disabled and the non-disabled.

As evidenced by a number of cultural texts discussed in this volume, equally important attempts at 'thirding' have come from within the domain of the arts. The transition towards the Rancierian aesthetic regime of the arts, which, as we have argued earlier, liberates the process of artistic creation from the constraints imposed by conventions and expectations, has paved the way for more realistic representations of disability that are not rooted in the outdated models that stigmatize impairment. By the same token, the works created by people with disabilities have come to be recognized as a genuine form of artistic expression, rather than supposedly 'inferior' endeavours of 'artisans' or by-products of therapy. As a result, films, plays, performances, and literary works have all become potent platforms for the Rancierian dissensus. They give people with disabilities the chance to speak and create their own counterhistories that present their problems in a different light, thus potentially challenging the patronizing colonial/hegemonic political spectacles associated with disability. In short, they offer a chance to create a Thirdspace that allows for the subjectification and legitimization of people with disabilities as "speaking beings" (Rancière 41), and may serve as a testing ground for new forms of social participation and inclusion or help reconfigure the existing, inegalitarian distribution of the sensible.

Importantly, these artistic Thirdspaces also conform to Soja's theory in that they offer a mixture of "subjectivity and objectivity, the abstract and the concrete, the real and the imagined, … consciousness and the unconscious, … everyday life and unending history" (Soja 56–57). As many of the chapters included in the present volume have demonstrated, Dis(sensual)Art, i.e. the art of dissensus, does not shy away from addressing harmful stereotypes and preconceptions about disability, but effectively re-imagines them. The majority of such works do not offer an escape into an imaginary, perfect world where the binary opposition between the disabled and non-disabled does not exist, instead taking reality head on. Consider, for instance, the representation of Stelios in Mondelos' *MasterPiece – Part 1*, discussed in the chapter by Maria Tsakiri. As she rightly observes, the film unsettles the audience's expectations and conventional assumptions by presenting Stelios, who has spastic quadriplegia, as James Bond. Right after delivering an appropriated version of the Bond introduction, the man addresses the viewers, asks them if they can understand what he says, and invites them to make an effort. By foregrounding Stelios' disability and clashing it with the idealized (hyper)masculinity embodied by James Bond, the film invites the audience to ponder about the societal restrictions forced on people with disabilities and foregrounds the fact that, like the ideal of masculinity, disability is a fluid category that is comprised by both its material aspects and the conceptual/interpretive framework that society imposes on it. By mixing the two spaces – the material and the conceptual one, it opens up a Thirdspace which unsettles the fixed ideas. In short, it forces the audience to grapple with the question of 'who we can be and still be disabled,' to appropriate hooks's turn of phrase. Similar tensions between the materiality of impairment and the social and cultural constructions of disability as well as those of beauty, gender, sexuality, etc. are one of the key aspects of the analyses and explorations presented in each and every section of this book, playing a particularly prominent role in Edyta Lorek-Jezińska's reading of Susan Nussbaum's *No One as Nasty*, James Casey's interpretation of Jessica Hausner's *Lourdes*, and Murray K. Simpson's analysis of Russ Meyer's films.

As the story of Christian O'Reilly's and Len Collin's *Sanctuary* shows, by creating Thirdspaces, Dis(sensual)Art can facilitate the shift towards a more egalitarian society. While the play, as O'Reilly complains had a "limited exposure to audiences" (243), its film adaptation reached many more viewers and sparked a debate that ultimately led to the de-penalization of non-marital sexual activity of people with ID. This example suggests that if Dis(sensual)Art is not widely received by the non-disabled part of society, the prospects of it actually reconfiguring the existing distribution of the sensible are limited. While such a claim would, to some extent, be accurate, it needs to be stressed that the cultural texts in question can facilitate the political subjectification of people with disabilities and help muster support for a common cause. By fostering a sense of collectivity, they plant a seed that may, eventually, grow into political activism, as was the case with the festival discussed by Maria Tsakiri in her chapter. Dis(sensual)Art thus promotes and leads to inclusion in that it offers an opportunity to re-imagine the status quo, devise a new politics of participation, and test it within the constraints of the fictional world, drawing attention to various problems and offering alternative solutions. Such demonstration of how these solutions may work in practice may, in turn, provide a fertile breeding ground for dissensual activism.

Last but not least, the Thirdspace of disability can also be found in contemporary disability activism which focuses both on concrete material issues, such as physical access and economic deprivation, and the ways of perceiving, conceptualizing, and representing disability. To use the example of the earlier-mentioned protests, it is worth noting that the participants use the real material Firstspace (streets, the buildings of parliaments, etc.) in order to bring to the fore not only accessibility-related issues, but also venture into Soja's conceptual Secondspace in the way they attempt to change the social perception of people with disabilities as rightful and worthy citizens who have the right to actively resist and oppose discriminatory rules and regulations. In this way, activism contributes to creating the Thirdspace of disability in which the traditional binary oppositions no longer hold.

What is still needed for Thirdspaces of disability to flourish is far-reaching intervention in various areas of interest. Broadly defined accessibility is one of them. When in 2015 we organized an international cultural disability studies conference at the University of Łódź, we realized that the new building of the Faculty of Philology, despite its minor drawbacks, is an accessible island floating on the vast sea of inaccessible cityscape. Yet, even this space proved not to be ready to accommodate the needs of some visitors with mobility impairments. As it, for instance, turned out, the high podium in the largest lecture hall was inaccessible for wheelchair users. This fact seems to be symbolically indicative of the limited access of people with disabilities to certain professions. As discussed by Len Collin in his chapter, acting is a prominent example of a profession which can be considered a bastion of able-bodiedness. Yet, the same concerns many other occupations. According to the recent statistics, in Poland in 2018 only 28.2 percent of people with disabilities were professionally active (Biuro Pełnomocnika Rządu).

Evidently, there is still plenty work to be done in the field of inclusion and subjectification and, most importantly, in changing contemporary perceptions and understandings of disability. Thus, we hope that by combining a variety of perspectives, those more detached and those more personal, the voices of scholars and practitioners, as well as the ideas coming from well-established and young academics who work in different fields yet share a critical perspective on disability, and from those who have had their share in disability activism, this volume will contribute to the growing dissensual ferment of thought in the academia, arts, and activism.

Works Cited

Biuro Pełnomocnika Rządu ds. Osób Niepełnosprawnych. "Rynek pracy" ["Job Market."]. *Biuro Pełnomocnika Rządu ds. Osób Niepełnosprawnych* 12 Apr. 2019, http://www.niepelnosprawni.gov.pl/index.php?c=page&id=80&print=1. Accessed: 10 Jul. 2019.

Cierpioł, Dominik, and Anna Pawelec. "To nie jest protest polityczny?" ["This is not a political protest?"]. *TVP*, https://www.tvp.info/42764470/to-nie-jest-protest-polityczny. Accessed: 10 Jun. 2019.

Edelman, Murray. *Constructing the Political Spectacle*. Chicago, IL: The University of Chicago Press, 1988. Print.

hooks, bell. *Yearning: Race, Gender, and Cultural Politics*. Boston, MA: South End Press, 1990. Print.

"Kaczyński do niepełnosprawnej: prośba, żeby nas popierać, a nie przeszkadzać" ["Kaczyński to a disabled person: Please support us and don't cause any trouble"]. *Radio Zet*, 1 May 2019, https://wiadomosci.radiozet.pl/Polska/Polityka/Kaczynski-do-niepelnosprawnej-prosba-zeby-nas-popierac-a-nie-przeszkadzac. Accessed 10 Jun. 2019.

Kosiński, Dariusz. "Odzyskiwanie obecności." *Niepełnosprawność i społeczeństwo. Performatywna siła protestu*. Ed. Ewelina Godlewska-Byliniak and Justyna Lipko-Konieczna. Warszawa: Fundacja Teatr 21, Biennale Warszawa, 2018. 73–75. Accessed 10 Jun. 2019, https://biennalewarszawa.pl/wp-content/uploads/2019/01/niepelnosprawnosxxcxx-i-spoleczenxxstw.-performatywna-sila-protestu-1.pdf.

Lipko-Konieczna, Justyna, and Ewelina Godlewska-Byliniak. "Polityczność niepełnosprawności" ["The Political Dimension of Disability"]. *Youtube*, 6 Mar. 2019. https://www.youtube.com/watch?v=7loTsT7kDeE. Accessed 10 Jun. 2019.

Mason, Paul. *Why It's Still Kicking Off Everywhere*. 2nd ed. London: Verso, 2013. Print.

Mierzejewska, Katarzyna. "Krynicka: Znalazłabym paragraf na rodziców, którzy przetrzymują dzieci w Sejmie" ["Krynicka: I could find some grounds to indict the parents who held their children hostage in the parliment"]. *Radio Zet*, 8 May 2018, https://wiadomosci.radiozet.pl/Polska/Bernadeta-Krynicka-protest-niepelnosprawych-znalazlabym-paragraf-na-rodzicow. Accessed 10 Jun. 2019.

Nancy, Mairs. *Waist-High in the World: A Life Among the Nondisabled*. Boston, MA: Beacon, 1997. Print.

Rancière, Jacques. *Dissensus: On Politics and Aesthetics*. Ed. and trans. Steven Corcoran. London: Continuum, 2010. Print.

Sandoval, Marisol, and Christian Fuchs. "Towards a Critical Theory of Alternative Media." *Telematics and Informatics* 27 (2010): 141–50, http://citeseerx.ist.psu.edu/viewdoc/download?doi=10.1.1.532.1037&rep=rep1&type=pdf. Accessed 10 Jun. 2019.

Shakespeare, Tom. *Disability Rights and Wrongs*. London: Routledge, 2006. Print.

Siebers, Tobin. "Disability in Theory: From Social Constructionism to the New Realism of the Body." *The Disability Studies Reader*. Ed. Lennard J. Davis. 2nd ed. New York, NY: Routledge, 2006. 173–83. Print.

Soja, Edward W. *Thirdspace: Journeys to Los Angeles and Other Real-and-Imagined Places*. Cambridge: Blackwell, 1996. Print.

Żalek, Jacek. "Poseł Jacek Żalek zarzuca manipulację. Cała rozmowa przeprowadzona przez tokfm.pl" ["The MP Jacek Żalek Accuses of Manipulation. The Whole Interview for tokfm.pl"]. *Youtube*, 11 May 2018, https://www.youtube.com/watch?v=cxhG64U9zqU. Accessed 10 Jun. 2019.

Index

Printed in the United States
by Baker & Taylor Publisher Services